THE ARENA

The Arena

Guidelines for Spiritual and Monastic Life

by Bishop Ignatius (Brianchaninov)

Translated from the Russian by
Archimandrite Lazarus

With a foreword by
Archimandrite Kallistos (Ware)

Holy Trinity Publications
The Printshop of St Job of Pochaev
Holy Trinity Monastery
Jordanville, New York

Printed with the blessing of His Eminence,
Metropolitan Hilarion First Hierarch
of the Russian Orthodox Church Outside of Russia

The Arena, Guidelines for Spiritual and Monastic Life [Second Edition]
© 2012 Holy Trinity Monastery

PRINTSHOP OF
SAINT JOB OF POCHAEV

An imprint of

HOLY TRINITY PUBLICATIONS
Holy Trinity Monastery
Jordanville, New York 13361-0036
www.holytrinitypublications.com

First printing: Madras, India, 1970
Second printing: Holy Trinity Monastery, 1982
Third printing: Holy Trinity Monastery, 1991
Fourth printing: Holy Trinity Monastery, 1997
Second printing of the 2nd Edition: Holy Trinity Monastery, 2017
Third printing of the 2nd Edition: Holy Trinity Monastery, 2019

Second Edition ISBN: 978-0-88465-287-8 (paperback)
ISBN: 978-0-88465-288-5 (ePub)
ISBN: 978-0-88465-289-2 (Mobipocket)

Library of Congress Control Number 2012936902

Cover Design: Aubrey Harper—behance.net/aubreyharper

Scripture passages taken from the New King James Version.
Copyright © 1982 by Thomas Nelson, Inc. Used by permission.
Psalms taken from *A Psalter for Prayer*, trans. David James
(Jordanville, N.Y.: Holy Trinity Publications, 2011).
Deuterocanonical passages taken from the Orthodox Study Bible.
Copyright © 2008 by Thomas Nelson, Inc. Used by permission.

CONTENTS

FOREWORD TO THE ORIGINAL ENGLISH-LANGUAGE EDITION

The work that follows first appeared almost exactly a century ago. Published at St Petersburg in the year 1867, it was originally named *An Offering to Contemporary Monasticism*—a beautiful title that aptly describes the character of the contents. The book is the offering of Bishop Ignatius (Brianchaninov) to his "beloved brethren," as he so often calls them in the course of its pages—his contribution to the monastic life of his day. At the same time it is the offering of his whole life's work to Christ. Writing at the end of his time on earth—he died in the same year that the book was first published—he sought to embody in a single volume the fruit of some forty years' experience in the monastic life, more than half of them spent as superior of an important community on the borders of the Russian capital. As a traveler "who has endured terrible hardships on a long and difficult journey," to use Bishop Ignatius' own words,[1] he offers to those who are undertaking the same journey his own "notes" on the path that he has followed.

Bishop Ignatius composed his *Offering* at a moment of notable revival in the monastic life of the Russian Orthodox Church. The religious communities of nineteenth century Russia were distinguished by a number of remarkable figures—saints, spiritual directors, and writers: men such as St Seraphim of Sarov, the *startsy*[2] Leonid, Macarius, and Ambrose of the Optina Hermitage, Bishop Theophan the Recluse, and not least Bishop Ignatius Brianchaninov himself. Like the other leaders of this Russian monastic revival, Ignatius was deeply rooted in the ascetic and mystical doctrine of the Greek Fathers, yet there was nothing antiquarian or academic about his devotion to the teaching of the past: for this ancient tradition was something that he had experienced directly, as a creative and dynamic reality in his personal life. In the present work—his "mystical confession" and "spiritual legacy," as he describes it in his Foreword—he attempts to present in a balanced synthesis all that he sees to be most important in the writings of the Fathers concerning the monastic life, adapting what they say to the particular needs and conditions of his own day. As such, it is a book that will be of great value to anyone who wishes to understand Orthodox monasticism in general, and in particular the Russian monastic revival of the nineteenth century.

But Ignatius' *Offering* is very far from being a work exclusively for monks. As the author himself says, "We hope that even lay people . . . may also find our book helpful."[3] As a brief glance at the table of contents will show, most of the chapters discuss matters of universal concern. Ignatius speaks of the place of the Bible in our inner life, the need for spiritual direction and the relationship between the director or *staretz* and his disciple, the meaning of prayer and the practice of the Jesus Prayer, the role of suffering, the nature of temptation and of our warfare against demonic forces; all of which are themes of vital interest not only to monks but also to those living in the world. Nor is it surprising that a book originally written with monks in view should apply equally to other Christians, for monks and lay people are both following the same "narrow way" and are engaged in the same ascetic battle. "True Christianity and true monasticism," writes Ignatius, "consist in the practice of the commandments of the Gospel."[4] The definition of the Christian and of the monk is thus one and the same. "Monasticism," he writes, "is simply the duty of fulfilling with exactitude the commandments of the Gospel. The monastic life is simply a life lived in accordance with the commandments of the Gospel."[5] But obviously the same evangelical rules that the monk seeks to carry out are also binding upon all other members of the Church. Ignatius' *An Offering to Contemporary Monasticism* is therefore at the same time an offering to every Christian.

In view of the widely ranging scope of the book, the translator of this English version has chosen another title to indicate its more general character: *The Arena*. It is a title that recalls the last hours of the Christian martyrs who met their death in such places as the Coliseum at Rome—men such as Ignatius' own namesake, St Ignatius of Antioch, who prayed that he might be ground as wheat by the teeth of the wild beasts, and whose prayer was answered. For later Christians, living in more peaceful times, there has usually been no such outward and visible arena; but they, too, are called to fight spiritually in the arena against wild beasts. As St Clement of Rome expresses it, we are all in the same arena and involved in the same struggle.[6] St Paul talks of having "fought with beasts at Ephesus,"[7] and while he may mean a literal fight against animals in an outward arena, or a fight against bestial human beings,[8] his words have also a symbolical meaning: the real struggle is always an inner one, and the arena where the struggle with the beast takes place is the unseen realm of the interior life.

Such, then, is Bishop Ignatius' basic theme: he tells us of the struggle to be undertaken by every Christian in the spiritual arena. He speaks to us all, whether monks or not, explaining how we may tame, control, and transform the beast within—the lions and howling wolves of our inner jungle—and so build in our hearts Jerusalem, the city of peace and unity.

Bishop Ignatius is one of the most able and attractive personalities in the Russian Church of his time. By family background, Dimitry Alexandrovich Brianchaninov, as he was at first known, was a member of the aristocracy, the son of a wealthy provincial landowner. In the Russian society of his time, it was distinctly unusual for a young man or woman of noble birth to enter a monastery. In fact, Dimitry's father envisaged no such future for his son, but intended him to follow the way of life normal for one of his class. Born in 1807, in due course Dimitry was sent to the Pioneer Military School of St Petersburg. Here he made excellent progress, winning the praise of his teachers, and during an inspection he was especially noticed by Grand Duke Nicholas Pavlovich, the future Emperor Nicholas I.

But Dimitry's heart was not in his military studies. From an early age he had felt a vivid and insistent call toward an entirely different path—that of the monk. In later life he recounted how, during his time at the Pioneer Military School, he used to walk by himself in deep depression, with tears in his eyes, because it seemed that there was no course open to him except the worldly career of an army officer. Even at the Pioneer Military School, however, he found time to practice inner prayer, and among his fellow pupils he discovered others with the same spiritual longings. They used to meet at night to pray together and to discuss religious questions.

The year 1827 was one of crisis in Dimitry's life. He graduated from military school, successfully taking his commission, but soon afterwards he fell critically ill. At his own request he was granted a discharge from the army. His health restored, he at once became a novice, staying at various monasteries during the next four years, and establishing contact in particular with *Staretz* Leonid of the celebrated Optina Hermitage.[9] In 1831 he took vows as a monk in a small community in his native district of Vologda, receiving the name Ignatius, and shortly afterwards he was ordained priest.

But the newly professed Father Ignatius was not allowed to remain for long in seclusion. About this time Emperor Nicholas visited the Pioneer Military School, and—unaware of Brianchaninov's discharge from the army— he asked what had become of the gifted cadet whom he still recalled clearly. The director of the school replied that Ignatius was now a monk, but he did not know where. After further inquiries Nicholas learned of Ignatius' retreat near Vologda, and ordered him to return instantly to the capital. Ignatius found himself suddenly raised to the rank of archimandrite and appointed— at the early age of twenty-six—superior of the important St Sergius Monastery at St Petersburg. This stood not far from the Palace, and so enjoyed close imperial patronage. Nicholas instructed Ignatius to transform it into a model community, where visitors to the imperial court could go in order to learn what a true monastery should be. Thus, besides his other duties as head of a large religious community, Archimandrite Ignatius also received frequent visitors from the outside world, foreigners as well as Russians. An English traveler—a fellow of Magdalen College, Oxford, named William Palmer— has left an interesting description of a meeting with Ignatius in his book, *Notes of a Visit to the Russian Church in the Years 1840, 1841.*[10]

Doubtless this was not the kind of life that Ignatius had foreseen for himself when he made his monastic profession in 1831; but he applied himself conscientiously to his new duties as abbot, giving the emperor no reason to regret his choice. After twenty-four years as superior of St Sergius, in 1857 he was raised to the episcopate, serving first as bishop of Stavropol and then of Kavkaz (Caucasus). But only four years later, at the early age of fifty-four, he resigned, to spend the remaining six years of his life in retirement at the Nicolo-Babaevsky Monastery in the Kostroma Diocese. Here he lived in seclusion, devoting his time to writing and to a wide correspondence with his spiritual children. He died in 1867 in the solitude for which he had longed from his youth.

Ignatius was a prolific author: the collected edition of his works, published after his death, runs to five substantial volumes. Most of his works are written with a monastic audience specifically in mind. But many of his books—this one among them—have at the same time a wider appeal. One of his shorter studies, an essay on the Jesus Prayer, has already been translated into English.[11]

A lover of solitude and secret prayer, Bishop Ignatius was yet by no means isolated from the life of his own time. In *The Arena* and his other works, he draws not only on his deep knowledge of the Fathers of the Church but also—although less obviously—on his varied personal experience. Brought up as a child in a wealthy home, he then passed through the full training of an army officer, and in youth he saw something of the social and political world of St Petersburg. Nor in later years did he lose contact with persons who moved in these circles, for he acted as spiritual director not merely to monks but to many lay men and women of high rank at the capital. As superior of a religious community for a quarter of a century, he acquired a far-reaching practical and administrative experience. Later he exchanged the oversight of a monastery for that of a diocese. Even in retirement he was constantly in touch, through his correspondence, with people of widely different backgrounds. His works are thus the fruit of a close familiarity with the patristic tradition, but equally they spring from a personal awareness of contemporary issues and situations.

The Arena is divided into two main sections of unequal length. The second and by far the shorter part,[12] "Rules of Outward Conduct for Novices," is fairly technical in content and, as its title indicates, is concerned predominantly with external behavior. As such, it is for the most part directly applicable only to those who are actually members of a monastery. Ignatius believed, however, that external regulations were greatly overemphasized in the Russian monasticism of his day: "With us in Russia," he complains, "bodily discipline holds the field, while the very idea of spiritual discipline has been lost."[13] In the first part, therefore, "Counsels for the Spiritual Life of Monks," constituting the bulk of the work, he is concerned with the inner life, with the basic principles that underlie all outward rules. This part of the work, so far from being restricted to a monastic milieu, is universal in its application.

What are the chief sources upon which Ignatius relies in presenting his picture of the Christian's path? First and foremost comes the Bible. Ignatius quotes frequently from Scripture, and he underlines with great clarity the part that the Gospels in particular should play in our ascetic training. "From his very entry into the monastery"—such are the opening words of *The Arena*—"a monk should occupy himself with all possible care and attention with the reading of the holy Gospel. He should make such a study of the Gospel that it may always be present in his memory, and at every moral step he takes, for every act, for every thought, he may always have ready in his memory the teaching of the Gospel."[14] "Never cease studying the Gospel till the end of your life," Ignatius adds a little later. "Do not think that you know it enough, even if you know it by heart."[15] Those who imagine that the

Orthodox Church pays insufficient attention to the Bible would do well to keep these passages from *The Arena* in mind. No "Evangelical" in Victorian England showed a greater reverence for God's Word than this nineteenth-century Russian bishop.

But for an Orthodox, the Bible does not stand in isolation. There are also the Fathers—the accumulated experience of those who, over the centuries of the Church's life, have read and reflected upon the words of Scripture. Ignatius claims that his teaching in *The Arena* is "taken entirely from the holy Fathers."[16] He appeals in particular to two Patristic authorities, St John of the Ladder (c. 579–649) and St Isaac the Syrian (died c. 700).[17] The first wrote for monks in community, the second primarily for solitaries, and so the two between them serve to provide a balanced picture of the monastic and the Christian life. Ignatius also quotes extensively from a third source—the *Answers* of Saints Barsanuphius and John the Prophet, two ascetics living in sixth-century Palestine.[18] Their "answers" are addressed sometimes to monks in community, sometimes to solitaries, and sometimes to lay people in the world; thus, in their teaching they embrace alike both the desert and the city.

Along with these main sources, Ignatius draws heavily on a more ancient monastic text: the Paterikon, or *Sayings of the Desert Fathers*, usually known in the West by the title *Apophthegmata Patrum*, and cited in this present edition as the *Skete Patrology*.[19] This is a collection of short anecdotes and sayings, usually of great simplicity and vividness, each containing a sharply defined point; the whole work forms an unrivaled "case book" of ascetic psychology. The nucleus of this Paterikon dates back to fourth- and fifth-century Egypt, and is associated in particular with the celebrated monastic center of Scetis. Ignatius, anxious as he was to return to the traditions and teaching of the earliest monks, fully appreciated the value of these *Apophthegmata*, where the spirit of primitive monasticism is to be encountered in its purest form. *The Arena* contains many stories of such Desert Fathers as Macarius, Arsenius, Poemen, Moses, John Colobos, and Sisoes, all taken from the Paterikon of Scetis. Similar stories are drawn from the Paterikon of the Monastery of the Caves, or *Petchersky Lavra*, at Kiev, the most important monastic community in ancient Russia, dating back to the middle of the eleventh century. *The Arena* also contains a number of narratives derived from the lives of the saints contained in the *Menologion* or *Synaxarion*, read daily in Orthodox monasteries.

It would be impossible to mention all the other monastic sources to which Ignatius is indebted, for in his attempt to present a synthesis of teaching on the spiritual life he has deliberately cast his net wide. He refers to figures from the earliest age of monasticism, such as St Anthony the Great (251–356), the father of the eremitic life, and St Pachomius (286–346), the founder of the first organized monastic community; to later Greek monastic leaders, for instance St Theodore of Studium (759–826) and St Symeon the New Theologian (949–1022); to writers of the hesychast tradition in the fourteenth century, among them St Gregory of Sinai, and Saints Kallistus and Ignatius Xanthopoulos;[20] to Russian spiritual authors, such as St Nil Sorsky (c. 1433–1508) and St Tikhon of Voronezh (1724–1783). The tradition to which he appeals, however, is not something restricted to the past, but a living and continuing reality. Ignatius therefore mentions on occasion his own contemporaries, among them St Seraphim of Sarov (1759–1833) and *Staretz* Leonid (1768–1841) whom he had known personally. All these varied sources, from the fourth to the nineteenth centuries, he weaves together into a unified whole, presenting a picture of the Christian way that is clear, sober, and balanced.

The profound loyalty to the Fathers does not mean that Ignatius himself is a man without originality, mechanically repeating the ideas and formulae of previous writers. He saw himself, it is true, as the guardian of a rich heritage received from the past, which he strove to impart unimpaired to a new generation. But at the same time he was aware of the need to adapt and reinterpret this inheritance. He knew that some adjustment was necessary. The essential reality of the monastic—or the Christian—life does not change, so Ignatius argues, but "circumstances have substantial influence on essential monasticism. Here I have indicated how we should use the writings of the ancients and adapt them to modern conditions, so as to avoid the sad plight of those who do not realize or notice the need for adaptation."[21] "The Fathers composed their instructions to suit the circumstances of the time and the condition of those monks for whom they were writing," he states, and so it is out of the question for someone living in the nineteenth or twentieth century "to apply to himself wholesale all that the Fathers wrote."[22] *The Arena*, then, is an attempt to understand the Patristic teaching creatively, adjusting it to the needs of a new age.

As the foundation and starting point of his spiritual teaching, Ignatius takes Christ's twofold command of love for God and for our neighbor. "The Savior of the world summarized all His particular commands in two main, general commandments: '"You shall love the Lord your God,"' He said, '"with all your heart, with all your soul, and with all your mind." This is the first and great commandment. And the second is like it: "You shall love your neighbor as yourself." On these two commandments hang all the Law and the Prophets.'"[23]

This commandment of love is binding equally upon the monk and upon the Christian in the world, but each expresses his love in a different outward form. The Christian in the world shows his love for God in and through love for his family, and by works of active and practical service to others. The monk, from love of God, has voluntarily renounced family life, and while he may certainly on occasion perform acts of direct service to his neighbor, this is not his primary task. How, then, does the monk express his love? Ignatius answers: through prayer. "Prayer should be a monk's chief task. It should be the center and heart of all his activities.... Prayer is the practical expression of a monk's love for God."[24] It is also a practical expression of the monk's love for his neighbor: the main way in which the monk serves others is by praying. As a contemporary Orthodox writer in Finland has expressed it, "Prayer is the art of artists. The artist works in clay or colors, in word or tones; according to his ability he gives them pregnancy and beauty. The working material of the praying person is living humanity. By his prayer he shapes it, gives it pregnancy and beauty: first himself and thereby many others."[25]

Starting from this basis, Ignatius goes on to discuss in more detail this activity of prayer, so fundamental to all life in Christ. He speaks in particular of one form of prayer, which for many centuries has occupied a cardinal position in Orthodox spirituality—the Jesus Prayer: "Lord Jesus Christ, Son of God, have mercy on me a sinner."[26] Through the use of this prayer, outwardly so very short and simple, a man may enter, by God's grace, into the deepest mysteries of divine contemplation. Used with discretion and regularity, the Jesus Prayer gradually acquires a rhythm of its own in the heart of him who prays: with the Name of Jesus before him he falls asleep, and on waking in the morning his first thought, his first word and action, is the invocation of the same Holy Name.[27] The Jesus Prayer accompanies him throughout the day, continuing within him even when he is engaged in other activities. So it develops into "unceasing prayer," and leads eventually to the reintegration of all his spiritual forces, to his full restoration and transfiguration according to the image and likeness of God.[28]

If possible, the Jesus Prayer should be practiced under the guidance of an experienced spiritual director. But Ignatius recognized that such directors are not easy to find. In default of a living teacher, the novice must rely on books: Ignatius therefore provides specific and practical instructions about the manner in which this prayer may best be offered. His advice here will be of special value to Christians in the world, who are likely to encounter even greater difficulty than monks in finding someone qualified to guide them. Although in his discussion of the Jesus Prayer, as elsewhere, Ignatius writes with the monk primarily in view, it should be emphasized that the Jesus Prayer is also well fitted for lay people. Its very shortness and simplicity render it eminently suitable for those who live under constant pressure, distracted by many duties, and who lack the quiet and recollection necessary for other more complicated forms of prayer. During the last thirty-five years the Jesus Prayer has in fact come to be increasingly used and appreciated by lay people, both Orthodox and non-Orthodox.

It is comparatively easy to read through and to understand—superficially at least—the directions that Bishop Ignatius gives concerning the Jesus Prayer. To carry these directions into effect, on the other hand, is the work of a lifetime. Ignatius, with his long experience as a spiritual director, understood this only too well. He knew that the contest in which the athletes of Christ are engaged is no chance or trivial matter, but one that calls for the utmost determination and humble perseverance. That is why writers from every age, Eastern and Western alike, repeatedly speak of the Christian life as a struggle, combat, or battle—why, indeed, a work such as the present has been named *The Arena*.

The beast within is not easily chained and brought into subjection. As soon as we attempt seriously to apply the commands of Christ, as soon as we try to pray in spirit and in truth, our fallen nature declares a "savage war" upon us,[29] and in this warfare it receives powerful support from the demonic forces that surround us. "For we not wrestle against flesh and blood," writes St Paul, "but against principalities, against powers, against the rulers of the darkness of this age, against spiritual hosts of wickedness in the heavenly places."[30] Such also is the conviction of Bishop Ignatius, and he has therefore included a long section in *The Arena* on the struggle against evil spirits and the forces of the devil.[31] The extreme vividness and precision with which he speaks here may surprise some Western readers. But he does no more than reflect faithfully what is a constant trait in Eastern ascetic literature from the time of St Anthony the Great onward.

Profoundly conscious as he was of the weakness of fallen human nature and of the strength of the demonic powers arrayed against us, Ignatius has deliberately introduced into *The Arena* a note of severity, of strictness and austerity, which will at first sight appear a little daunting. Echoing the words of our Lord, he insists from the outset that the way that leads to life is "narrow and sorrowful."[32] "Sorrow and sufferings are appointed by the Lord Himself for His true slaves and servants during their life on earth."[33] If this is true of Christians in general, it is true preeminently of the monk, for "the monastic life is in the fullest sense a martyrdom, though an invisible one."[34] "A monk's life is a chain of continual struggles and sufferings."[35] Ignatius lays particular emphasis on the penitential aspect of monasticism: "A monk's life is nothing less than active and continual repentance.... The whole monastic life is included in weeping and penitential prayer.... A monk's greatest success is to see and acknowledge that he is a sinner."[36] Something of what is involved in this approach to monasticism may be seen in Ignatius' strict command that a monk must not form a special friendship with any particular brother in the community, nor grow closely attached to the handwork on which he is daily employed. It is better to knit socks than paint icons, for then the dangers of attachment are less![37]

These and other passages in *The Arena* convey, as an immediate impression, a somewhat somber and forbidding picture of Christian living. At times Ignatius seems in particular to display undue severity towards non-Orthodox Christendom. Western readers may be taken aback by his remarks on St Francis of Assisi.[38] If they look carefully, however, they will see that he is not attacking Francis himself, but a sentimental and exaggerated style of hagiography which today has fortunately passed out of fashion.

There are moments when Ignatius even appears frankly pessimistic. It is his conviction that both monasticism and Christianity have seen a steady decline throughout their histories, a sad falling away from the heroic days of the early Church. "Monastic obedience in the form and character in which it was practiced by the monks of old is a lofty spiritual mystery. Its attainment and full imitation have become impossible for us.... We see at the present time a general decline of Christianity." At best we can hope to feed only "on the crumbs that fall from the spiritual table of the Fathers."[39] Ignatius laments in particular the extreme rarity of hermits during his own time, and the almost complete absence of genuine *startsy* with true spiritual insight.

Yet for all its austerity, *The Arena* is by no means a work of despair or defeatism. Bishop Ignatius was firmly convinced that the monastic and Christian way, despite its difficulties, is in the last resort one of gladness and rejoicing. If the monk or the Christian is called to repentance and suffering, this sorrow is at the same time indissolubly linked with joy. The grief that he experiences, to use a phrase of St John of the Ladder, is a "joy-making grief," *charopoion penthos*. As the same writer puts it, "That which is called mourning and grief contains joy and gladness interwoven within it like honey in the comb."[40] In the words of the Macarian Homilies (fourth to fifth century), "Christians possess the consolation of the Spirit, which is tears and mourning and lamentation, and these very tears are their delight.... Those who have tasted the gift of the Spirit feel all these things at once: joy and consolation, fear and trembling, exultation and mourning."[41]

Such is the twofold character of all Christian experience. United with Christ in His crucifixion, we are united with Him also in the triumph of His resurrection. The author of *The Arena* does not underestimate the sacrifice demanded of those who would mount the cross with our Lord. But at the same time he does not overlook—although he speaks of it less explicitly—the gladness of the risen life in which they also participate.

Bishop Ignatius chooses to close the main part of his work on a note of sober warning, quoting the text, "Everyone who exalts himself will be humbled, and he who humbles himself will be exalted."[42] This is typical of his general approach. Yet his *Offering* does not stop here. In the Conclusion to Part I, he quotes a verse from St Paul: "Oh the depth of the riches both of the wisdom and knowledge of God!"[43] *The Arena* ends in a cry of joy and gratitude.

Archimandrite Kallistos
Holy Saturday, 1966
The Monastery of St John the Theologian, Patmos

INTRODUCTION

Now that I am drawing near the end of my earthly pilgrimage, I have thought it my duty to compile a legacy of the spiritual blessings that the right hand of my God has lavished upon me. By *legacy* or *will*, I mean soul-saving instruction. Those who carry out these instructions will enter into possession of spiritual riches. I offer this legacy as a gift to my beloved fathers and brothers, the monks of today. By spiritual goods or riches (which include all other goods), I mean monasticism, to which I was called from childhood by a wonderful call and by unutterable mercy. I was not allowed to offer my life as a sacrifice to vanity and corruption. I was taken, snatched from the broad way that leads to eternal death, and I was put on the narrow and sorrowful way that leads to life. The narrow way has a most profound meaning. It rises from the earth, leads out of the darkness of vanity, leads to heaven, leads to Paradise, leads to God, and places one before His face in unending light for eternal happiness. In order to satisfy the needs of as many people as possible, it was necessary to express this legacy in a book. This book contains rules for the outward conduct of monks, and counsels for the spiritual life.

I can quite correctly call this work my mystical confession. I ask you to receive my confession with attention and Christian indulgence. You will find it worthwhile. The teaching I offer is taken entirely from the sacred teaching of the holy Fathers of the Orthodox Church who were acquainted both theoretically and experientially with the teaching of the Gospel which they had made their own. My sins of commission and omission; my insufficiently firm and unswerving following of the instructions of the Fathers; my lack of a spiritual director; my frequent, almost constant, meeting with directors suffering from blindness and self-delusion; my voluntary and involuntary dependence on them; my being surrounded on all sides by occasions of temptation and not of edification; my attention to teaching that the world hostile to God regarded as the highest wisdom and holiness but that was darkness and vileness and merited only scorn and repudiation—these were the causes for me of many upheavals.

The upheavals with which I was tested were bitter, oppressive, cruel, and were stubbornly, exhaustingly prolonged. The outward upheavals, in the judgment of my conscience, were nothing in comparison with the upheavals to which my soul was subjected. Savage are the waves of the sea of life! There gloom and darkness hold sway; there storms are constantly brewing and springing up with fierce winds—rejected spirits; ships lose their pilots; safe harbors are turned into whirlpools, into fatal abysses; "every mountain and island is moved out of its [spiritual] place";[1] shipwreck seems inevitable. And it would be inevitable if the incomprehensible providence of God and His equally incomprehensible mercy did not save His chosen.

"Long did my soul wander"[2] without finding a true harbor either outside or within myself. "I was stuck fast in the deep mire, where no ground is"—a correct and firm state of soul, unwavering in virtue. "I am come into deep waters, and a tempest hath run over me. I am weary of crying, my throat is become hoarse; my sight hath failed me, because I have been waiting so long upon my God."[3] "For the enemy hath persecuted my soul ... he hath laid me in darkness."[4] "I am poured out like water, all my bones are out of joint ... my strength is dried up like a potsherd."[5] "The pains of death surrounded me, and the overflowings of ungodliness made me afraid. The pains of hell encircled me; the snares of death overtook me."[6] "My spirit is despondent within me, and my heart within me is vexed."[7]

From this state I raise my voice to my fathers and brothers, a voice of anxious warning. That is what a traveler does who has endured terrible hardships on a long and difficult journey. His notes are a precious treasure which he passes on to those who are intending to undertake a similar journey or who have already set out without knowing the way or with only a superficial knowledge of the way from antiquated descriptions.

The modifications pointed out here are not changes in essential monasticism, but are due to altered circumstances; yet circumstances have a substantial influence on essential monasticism. Here I have indicated how we should use the writings of the ancients and adapt them to modern conditions, so as to avoid the sad plight of those who do not realize or notice the need for adaptation.

St John of the Ladder says that certain people who had passed through swampy places got stuck in the mud. But while still covered with filth they told others who passed that way of how they had sunk there, doing this for their salvation. And the Almighty delivered from the swamp or slough of despondency those who, for the salvation of their neighbors, warned them against falling into it.[8]

"Make straight paths for your feet and direct your ways aright. Do not turn aside to the right or to the left, but turn your foot from an evil way; for God knows the ways on the right hand but those on the left are perverse; and He shall make your paths straight and guide your steps in peace."[9] Amen.

Bishop Ignatius

PART I

COUNSELS FOR THE SPIRITUAL LIFE OF MONKS

CHAPTER I

On the Study of the Commandments
of the Gospel and Life According
to the Commandments of the Gospel

From his very entry into the monastery, a monk should occupy himself with all possible care and attention with the reading of the holy Gospel. He should make such a study of the Gospel that it may always be present in his memory, and at every moral step he takes, for every act, for every thought, he may always have ready in his memory the teaching of the Gospel. Such is the injunction of the Savior Himself. This injunction is linked with a promise and a threat. In sending His disciples to preach Christianity, the Lord said to them, "Go therefore and make disciples of all nations, baptizing them in the name of the Father and of the Son and of the Holy Spirit, teaching them to observe all that I have commanded you."[1]

The promise consists in the fact that the person who fulfills the commandments of the Gospel will not only be saved but will also enter into the most intimate union with God and become a divinely built temple of God. The Lord said: "He who has My commandments and keeps them, it is he who loves Me. And he who loves Me will be loved by My Father, and I will love him and manifest Myself to him."[2]

From these words of the Lord it is evident that the commandments of the Gospel must be so studied that they become the possession, the property of the mind; only then is the exact, constant fulfillment of them possible such as the Lord requires. The Lord reveals Himself spiritually to the doer of the commandments, and He is seen with the spiritual eye, with the mind. The person sees the Lord in himself, in his thoughts and feelings transfigured by the Holy Spirit. On no account must the Lord be expected to appear to the eyes of sense. This is clear from the words of the Gospel that follow those we have just quoted: "If anyone loves Me, he will keep My word; and My Father will love him, and We will come to him and make Our home with him."[3] It is evident that the Lord comes to the heart of the person who carries out the commandments and makes his heart a temple and dwelling of God. In this temple is God seen. He is seen not with the bodily eyes but with the mind. He is seen spiritually. This form of vision is incomprehensible to the beginner and cannot be explained to him in words. Accept the promise with faith. In due time you will understand it by blessed experience.

The threat to a person remiss in the fulfillment of the commandments of the Gospel is contained in the prediction for him of unfruitfulness, estrangement from God, perdition. The Lord said: "I am the vine, you are the branches. He who abides in Me, and I in him, bears much fruit for without Me you can do nothing. If anyone does not abide in Me, he is cast out as a branch and is withered; and they gather them and throw them into the fire, and they are burned. . . . Abide in My love. If you keep My commandments, you will abide in My love."[4] "Not everyone who says to Me, 'Lord, Lord,' shall enter the kingdom of heaven, but he who does the will of My Father in heaven. Many will say to Me in that day [the day of judgment], 'Lord, Lord, have we not prophesied in Your name, cast out demons in Your name, and done many wonders in Your name?' And then I will declare to them, 'I never knew you; depart from Me, you who practice lawlessness!' "[5]

The giver, teacher, and model of humility, our Lord Jesus Christ, called His all-holy, almighty, divine commandments "the least"[6] on account of the very simple form in which they are expressed and which makes them easy to understand and easy to carry out for every type of person, even the most uneducated. But at the same time the Lord added that a deliberate and constant breaker of even one commandment *will be called least in the Kingdom of Heaven*, or, according to the explanation of the holy Fathers, will be deprived of the heavenly kingdom and will be cast into the fire of gehenna.[7]

The Lord's commandments are "Spirit and life."[8] They save the doer of them. They restore a dead soul to life. They make a carnal and worldly person spiritual. On the other hand, a person who neglects the commandments ruins himself and remains in a carnal and worldly state, in a fallen condition, and develops the fall in himself. "But the natural man (i.e., the sensual man) does not receive the things of the Spirit of God, for they are foolishness to him."[9] And therefore it is indispensable for salvation to be changed from a sensual man into a spiritual, from the old man into the new.[10] "Flesh and blood cannot inherit the kingdom of God."[11] And therefore it is essential for salvation to be freed not only from the influence of the flesh or coarse passions, but also from the influence of the blood by means of which the passions act on the soul. "They that go far from Thee [not by position of body but by disposition of soul that dodges from doing the will of God] shall perish; Thou has destroyed all them that are unfaithful against Thee"[12] by following their own will and their own understanding, by refusing the commandments of the Gospel or the will of God. The latter necessarily accompanies the former. "But it is good for me," as a true monk, "to cleave unto God, to put my trust in the Lord."[13]

CHAPTER 2

People Will Be Judged at God's Judgment According to the Commandments of the Gospel

We shall be judged according to the commandments of the Gospel at that judgment that God has appointed for us Orthodox Christians and on which depends our eternal destiny. The judgment is private for every Christian immediately after his death, and it will be general for all men at our Lord Jesus Christ's second coming to earth. At both judgments God Himself is present and judges. At the private judgment He judges by means of angels of light and fallen angels; at the general judgment He judges by means of His incarnate Word.[1] The reason for this different form of judgment is obvious. Man submitted to the fallen angel voluntarily. Consequently he must first settle his account with the fallen angel according to the extent to which fellowship with the rejected spirit has been broken by the Christian with the help of redemption. At the general judgment both the fallen spirits and the people seduced by them must stand for trial as those who have sinned before the Divine Majesty. Therefore God Himself—God the Word Who took upon Himself humanity, by Whom our redemption was accomplished, and by Whom all the fallen must be saved—will judge all of us who have fallen and who have not purified ourselves by repentance. The codex or collection of laws by which we shall be tried and on the basis of which sentence will be pronounced at both judgments is the Gospel.

The Lord said: "He who rejects Me, and does not receive My words, has that which judges him—the word that I have spoken will judge him in the last day. For I have not spoken on My own authority; but the Father Who sent Me gave Me a command, what I should say and what I should speak. And I know that His command is everlasting life."[2] From these words of the Lord, it is evident that we shall be judged by the Gospel, and that negligence in carrying out the commands of the Gospel is an actual rejection of the Lord Himself.

Let us take all care, brothers, to become doers of the commandments of the Gospel. When death will come is unknown. We may be suddenly called to judgment when we are least expecting it. Blessed are those who have prepared themselves for their passage to eternity by a life in accordance with the Gospel! Woe to the easy-going, the careless, the self-willed, the self-opinionated! Woe to those who have not broken fellowship with Satan! Woe to those who have not entered into fellowship with God! Greater woe to those who have entered into fellowship with God, and then abandoned it!

CHAPTER 3

The Monastic Life Is Life According to the
Commandments of the Gospel

The holy monks of old called the monastic life a life according to the commandments of the Gospel. St John of the Ladder defines a monk thus:
"A monk is one who is guided only by the commandments of God and the
word of God in every time and place and matter."[1] The monks subject to St
Pachomius the Great had to learn the Gospel by heart so as to have the laws
of the God-Man like a continually open book in the memory, in order to have
them constantly before the eyes of the mind and have them printed on the
soul for their easier and more unfailing fulfillment. The blessed elder Seraphim of Sarov says, "We should so train ourselves that the mind, as it were,
swims in the law of the Lord by which we must guide and rule our life."

By studying the Gospel and trying to put its precepts into practice in
thought, word, and deed, you will be following the Lord's direction and the
moral tradition of the Orthodox Church. In a short time, the Gospel will lead
you from childhood to spiritual maturity in Christ, and you will become that
blessed man of whom the inspired Prophet sang,

hath not walked in the counsel of the ungoldly,
nor stood in the way of sinners,
and hath not sat in the seat of the scornful.
But his delight is in the Law of the Lord,
and in His Law will he exercise himself day and night.
And he shall be like a tree planted by the water-side,
that will bring forth his fruit in due season;
his leaf also shall not fall,
and all whatsoever he doeth, it shall prosper.[2]

The Holy Spirit teaches and guides true servants of God, men who have
become God's own: "Heed my Law, O my people; incline your ears unto the
words of my mouth."[3]

8

On the Precariousness of the Monastic Life When It Is Not Based on the Commandments of the Gospel

He who has based his life on the study of the Gospel and the practice of the commandments of the Gospel has based it on solid rock. In whatever predicament he is placed by the circumstances of life, his task is always with him.[1] He is constantly active, constantly struggling, constantly progressing, although his activity, his struggle, and his progress are unnoticed and incomprehensible to others. Whatever troubles and trials he may encounter, they can never defeat him.

The Lord said, "Whoever hears these sayings of Mine, and does them, I will liken to a wise man who built his house on the rock: and the rain descended, the floods came, and the winds blew and beat on that house; and it did not fall, for it was founded on the rock."[2] Here life and the set of the soul are compared to a house. This house acquires extraordinary stability from the infinite, divine power with which Christ's words are charged. It is evident that the strength that the practice of Christ's commandments wins for the soul can be won by no other means or method. Christ's power acts in His commandments.

To the words just quoted, the Lord added the following: "But everyone who hears these sayings of Mine, and does not do them, will be like a foolish man who built his house on the sand: and the rain descended, the floods came, and the winds blew and beat on that house; and it fell. And great was its fall."[3] Easily ruined is the seemingly good life of those who make their foundation an exclusively bodily struggle, or even a series of ascetic exercises, sometimes very difficult and remarkable, but who do not pay due attention to the commandments of the Gospel. Very often ascetics do not pay the least attention to the commandments of the Gospel, openly disregard them, and do not value them or realize their importance in the least. When such ascetics encounter unexpected trials and temptations or an unforeseen change in their life, not only is their faith soon shaken but they even run the risk of that complete moral collapse that is called in the Gospel the "great ruin" of the house of the soul.

Let us take as an example a hermit living in profound solitude who has put all his hope of success and salvation in that solitude. Suppose that suddenly this hermit is obliged by force of circumstances to leave his solitude and live among crowds. Being unfortified by the commandments of the Gospel, he is bound to be exposed to the violent impact of the temptations that are encountered so abundantly in human society. That is natural. He had no other power to protect him except outward solitude. Deprived of that, he is deprived of all support and must of necessity yield to the power of other outward impressions. This is not said in the least to disparage the solitary life that guards against temptations and distractions and that especially facilitates the study and practice of the commandments of the Gospel. It is said so that even a hermit in his solitude may take particular care to study and practice the Gospel commandments by means of which Christ, "the power of God and the wisdom of God,"[4] is installed in the soul.[5]

True Christianity and true monasticism consist in the practice of the commandments of the Gospel. Where this practice is absent, there is neither Christianity nor monasticism, whatever the outward appearance may be. "The righteous shall inherit the land, and dwell therein for ever."[6]

Scripture calls the righteous those who try in the most careful manner to carry out truly and solely the righteous will of God, not at all their own erroneous, apparently righteous will. Only those who fulfill God's righteousness can inherit the land, that is to say, can rule or get dominion over their own heart, their flesh, their blood.

> The mouth[7] of the righteous is exercised in wisdom,
> and his tongue will be talking of judgment;
> the Law of his God is in his heart,
> and his foot-steps shall not slide.[8]

CHAPTER 5

On Guarding Oneself from Occasions of Sin or Temptation

While basing our life on the commandments of the Gospel, at the same time we should choose for our place of residence a monastery as far removed from occasions of sin as possible. We are weak and corrupted by sin. An occasion of sin that is before our eyes or near us will inevitably find sympathy in our sinful corruption and will produce an impression on us. This impression may at first pass unnoticed, but when it develops and grows strong in a person, then it rules him and may lead him to the verge of perdition. And sometimes an impression of this kind acts with extreme rapidity, and does not give the tempted person time to reflect or think, so to speak. Suddenly the mind is darkened, the disposition of the heart changes, and the monk is cast down and keeps falling time after time.

St Poemen the Great has said, "It is good to avoid causes of sin. A man who is near an occasion of sin is like a person standing on the edge of a precipice, and the enemy can easily cast him down headlong whenever he likes. But if we are physically far from occasions of sin, we are like a person who is standing far away from a precipice. Even if the enemy were to drag us to the edge of the precipice, yet while we are being dragged we can resist and God will help us."[1]

Causes or occasions of sin are the following: wine, women, wealth, health of body when excessive, authority or power, and honor or fame and name. "These," says St Isaac the Syrian, "are not sins in themselves, but on account of our weakness and as our nature is easily drawn by them to various sins, there is need of peculiar caution in regard to them."[2]

The Fathers forbid postulants to choose a monastery that is famous in the eyes of worldly people. The vainglory that the whole monastery shares must inevitably infect each individual member as well. Experience shows that all the brethren of a community can be infected with the spirit of vainglory, not only on account of the material privileges or superiority of their monastery, but also on account of the high opinion of lay people concerning the special piety of its rule. Hence arises scorn for the brethren of other communities, which implies pride, and this saps the possibility of progress or success in the monastic life which is based on love for our neighbors and humility toward them.

As an example of how an occasion of sin, acting little by little on a monk, unnoticed and unfelt, can eventually get the better of him and cause a terrible fall, we quote the following story.

In the Egyptian Scetis[3] there was an elder who had fallen seriously ill and was accepting the services of the brethren. Seeing the brethren working for him, he thought of moving nearer to civilization so as not to trouble the brethren. Abba Moses (probably the one whom St John Cassian calls the most discerning of the Fathers of the Scetis who in general were distinguished for an abundance of spiritual gifts) said to him, "Do not move into the vicinity of civilization, lest you fall into fornication." The elder was surprised and offended by these words, and replied, "I have a body that is dead, and is that what you are talking about?" He did not listen to Abba Moses and moved into the neighborhood of worldly settlements. When the local inhabitants heard about him, they started coming to him in crowds. And a certain young woman came to serve him for God's sake. He healed her. Evidently the girl had some illness, and the elder had the gift of working miracles. Then some time later he fell with her, and she became pregnant. The local inhabitants asked her by whom she was pregnant. She replied, "By the elder." They did not believe her. The elder said, "I did it. But save the child that is due to be born." The child was born, and was fed at the breast. Then, on one of the feasts of the scetis, the elder went back with the child on his shoulders and entered the church when all the brethren were gathered there. When the brethren saw him, they wept. He said to them, "You see this child? It is the son of disobedience." After that, the elder returned to his former cell and began to offer repentance to God.[4]

Such is the power of temptation, when a monk is brought face to face with an occasion of sin. The gift of healing did not prevent him from failing into fornication. His body that had become dead to sin through old age, sickness, and prolonged monastic discipline, again revived through being subjected to the constant or frequent action of temptation.

As an example of how an occasion of sin can instantly affect a monk, darken his mind, pervert his heart, and cast him headlong into sin, we again cite a church story.

The bishop of a certain town fell ill, and all despaired of his life. There was a convent of nuns there. When the abbess learned that the bishop was desperately ill, she visited him, taking two sisters with her. While she was talking to the bishop, one of her sisters who was standing at the bishop's feet, touched his foot with her hand. From this touch a fierce conflict of lust flared up in the sick man. The passions are cunning. He asked the abbess to leave the sister with him to serve him, offering as a pretext for his request that his own servant was unsatisfactory. Quite unsuspecting, the abbess left the sister. Through the action of the devil, the bishop experienced a return of his strength, and fell into sin with the nun, who became pregnant. The bishop left his diocese and went to a monastery where he ended his life in repentance. And God gave evidence of His acceptance of his repentance by granting the penitent the gift of working miracles.[5]

Such is our weakness! Such is our infirmity! Such is the influence that occasions of sin have on us! They have caused the fall even of holy prophets,[6] and holy bishops, and holy martyrs, and holy hermits or solitaries. All the more ought we who are weak and passionate to take all precautionary measures, and guard ourselves from the influence of all such occasions. The passions in monks are hungry. If left unwatched they will bring on the objects of their desire with the fury of ravenous beasts loosed from their chains.

CHAPTER 6

God-Pleasing Life in Human Society Must Precede God-Pleasing Life in Silence and Solitude

For those who are beginning the monastic life, cenobitic monasteries are more suitable since they provide wide scope for the practice of the commandments of the Gospel. But even if you have entered a state-supported monastery,[1] do not be despondent and do not leave it without good reason. In a state-supported monastery, also make every effort to cultivate, refine, and educate yourself by the commandments of the Gospel.

There is a general rule that says that a monk must first train himself by the practice of the commandments in human society where spiritual activity is combined with bodily activity. Afterwards, when he has made sufficient progress, he may occupy himself exclusively with spiritual activity in solitude and silence, if he proves apt for it. Souls fit for solitude and silence are rare. A beginner cannot possibly bear purely spiritual activity. By means of spiritual activity we enter the world of spirits, and that is just why experienced monks retire into solitude. In the world of spirits, it is fallen spirits that first meet a Christian, since he belongs to their company spiritually on account of the fall. And he must prove the good direction of his free will and the set of his soul by the rejection of fellowship with the fallen spirits and by the acceptance of fellowship with God, which is granted *as a free gift* by the Redeemer.

Spirits easily discourage and defeat a soul who has entered into conflict with them without sufficient experience and without due preparation.[2] The fulfillment of the commandments in human society provides the person who fulfills them with the clearest and most exact experiential knowledge of fallen human nature and the nature of fallen spirits. It was by means of the fall that mankind entered into fellowship with the fallen spirits and into the same category of beings as rejected creatures, hostile to God, doomed to burial in the prisons of hell.

The holy Fathers declare that "anyone who truly wants to be saved should first live with people and endure annoyances, slights, privations, and humiliations, and be freed from the influence of his feelings and senses, and only then go into complete solitude or silence. This our Lord Jesus Christ demonstrated even in His own case. For it was only after enduring all this that He finally mounted the Holy Cross, which means the mortification of the flesh and passions and holy and perfect peace."[3]

You can be certain that you will succeed everywhere, both in a cenobitic monastery and in a state-endowed foundation, if you occupy yourself with the study and practice of the commandments of the Gospel. On the other hand, wherever you go you will always remain without success and without spiritual understanding, you will always come to a state of self-deception and spiritual confusion and disorder, if you neglect the study and practice of the evangelical commandments.

Never cease studying the Gospel till the end of your life. Do not think you know it enough, even if you know it by heart. The Lord's commandments are "exceedingly broad,"[4] even though they are expressed in few words. The Lord's commandment is infinite, just as the Lord Who uttered it is infinite. The practice of the commandments and progress in them is unlimited. The most perfect Christians, brought to a state of perfection by divine grace, remain imperfect in regard to the commandments of the Gospel.

CHAPTER 7

On Guarding Oneself from the Good That
Belongs to Fallen Human Nature

Has some good thought come to you? Stop! Whatever you do, do not rush to implement it or carry it out overhastily, without thinking. Have you felt some good impulse or inclination in your heart? Stop! Do not dare to be drawn by it. Check it with the Gospel. See whether your good thought and your heart's good impulse tally with the Lord's holy teaching.

You will soon see that there is no agreement whatever between the good of the Gospel and the good of fallen human nature. The good of our fallen nature is mixed with evil, and therefore this good has itself become evil, just as delicious and wholesome food becomes poison when it is mixed with poison.

Guard yourself from doing the good of fallen nature. By doing this good, you develop your own fall, you develop within you self-opinion and pride, and you will attain the closest conformity with demons. On the other hand, by doing the good of the Gospel as a true and faithful disciple of the God-Man, you will become like the God-Man. "He who loves his life will lose it, but he who hates his life in this world will keep it for eternal life."[1] "Whoever desires to come after Me, let him deny himself, and take up his cross, and follow Me. For whoever desires to save his life will lose it, but whoever loses his life for My sake and for the gospel's will save it."[2]

The Lord orders the complete renunciation of fallen nature, and hatred for its motives and impulses, not only for those that are obviously evil, but for all without exception, even the apparently good. It is a great disaster to follow the righteousness of fallen nature. This implies and involves rejection of the Gospel, rejection of the Redeemer, rejection of salvation. "Whoever does not hate . . . his own life also, he cannot be My disciple," said the Lord.[3]

Explaining the above words of our Lord, Barsanuphius the Great says,

How does a man renounce himself? Simply by forsaking his natural desires and following the Lord. That is why the Lord speaks here strictly of what is natural, and not of what is unnatural. For if anyone forsakes only what is unnatural, he has not yet forsaken anything of his own for God's sake, because what is unnatural does not properly belong to him. But whoever has forsaken what is natural, always says with the Apostle Peter, "We have left all and followed You. Therefore what shall we have?"[4] And he hears the blessed voice of the Lord, and by His promise is assured of the inheritance and possession of eternal life.[5] Since Peter was not rich, what did he renounce and what was his claim? Surely he renounced his own natural desires? For unless a man dies to the flesh and lives in the spirit, his soul cannot rise. Just as in a corpse there are no natural desires whatever, so too there are none in a person who is spiritually dead to the flesh. If you have died to the flesh, how can natural desires live in you? But if you have not attained this measure of spirituality, and are mentally still in your infancy, humble yourself before a teacher, that he may "chasten [you] with mercy,"[6] and "do nothing without counsel"[7] even though it may seem to you apparently good. For the light of demons eventually turns to darkness.[8]

Exactly the same must be said also about the light of fallen human nature. Following this light and its development within oneself produces a total inner darkness and completely estranges the soul from Christ. A stranger to Christ is a stranger to God. "Whoever denies the Son does not have the Father"[9]—he is godless. In our time the majority of people, proud of their progress and claiming to be Christians who do a lot of good, have been striving for the perfection of the righteousness of fallen nature and have turned their backs with scorn on the righteousness of the Gospel. Let this majority listen to what the Lord says:

> "These people draw near to Me with their mouth,
> And honor Me with their lips,
> But their heart is far from Me.
> And in vain they worship Me,
> Teaching as doctrines the commandments of men."[10]

The man who practices human righteousness is full of self-opinion, arrogance, self-deception. He preaches and blows his own trumpet about his good deeds without paying the least attention to what our Lord forbids.[11] He repays with hatred and revenge those who dare to open their mouths for the most reasonable and well-meaning contradiction of his righteousness. He considers himself deserving and more than deserving of both earthly and heavenly rewards.

On the other hand, one who practices the commandments of the Gospel is always immersed in humility. Comparing the loftiness and purity of the holy commandments with his own fulfillment of them, he constantly admits that his efforts are extremely unsatisfactory and unworthy of God. He sees himself meriting temporal and eternal punishments for his sins, for his unbroken fellowship with Satan, for the fall that is common to all men, for his own continuance in a fallen state, and finally for his insufficient and frequently fickle fulfillment of the commandments. Whenever trouble or suffering comes his way by the ordering of divine providence, he submissively bows his head, knowing that by means of suffering God trains and educates His servants during their earthly pilgrimage. He is kind and merciful to his enemies and prays for them as brothers who have been lured away by demons, as members of one body who are spiritually sick, as his benefactors, and as instruments of the providence of God.

CHAPTER 8

Concerning the Enmity and Conflict Between Fallen Nature and the Commandments of the Gospel

If you deny yourself and constantly renounce your own opinions, your own will, your own righteousness—or what amounts to the same thing: the knowledge, understanding, will, and righteousness of fallen nature—in order to plant within you the knowledge of God, the will of God, and the righteousness of God taught us in the holy Gospel by God Himself, then fallen nature will open fire within you and declare a savage war against the Gospel and against God. Fallen spirits will come to the help of fallen nature.

Do not fall into despondency on this account. By your firmness in the struggle, show the tenacity of your purpose and the stability of your free will. When thrown down, get up. When duped and disarmed, rearm yourself afresh. When defeated, again rush to the fight. It is extremely good for you to see within yourself both your own fall and the fall of the whole of mankind. It is essential for you to recognize and study this fall in your own experience, in your heart and mind. It is essential for you to see the infirmity of your knowledge and intellect, and the weakness of your will.

The vision of one's fall is a spiritual vision. The vision of one's infirmity and weakness is a spiritual vision.[1] In this matter the spectator is the mind. The vision is obtained by grace, which is planted in us by baptism. By the action of grace, the blindness of the mind is dispelled, and it begins to see clearly in the arena of its struggle what hitherto it has not seen through being outside this arena. It discovers the existence of what it did not even suspect.

Another spiritual vision is associated with the vision of the fall of man; the vision of fallen spirits. Again this vision is a spiritual vision, a gift of grace.[2] In this case, too, the spectator is the mind. From the practice of the commandments and by striving to fulfill them in the most exact manner, the mind gradually begins to discern fallen spirits in the thoughts and feelings that they bring, begins to discern the distressing intercourse of human beings with fallen spirits, the subjection of men to fallen spirits, the activities and wiles of spirits for the destruction of men.

In spiritual visions there is nothing sensory. They are acquired by care and diligence in the practice of the commandments of the Gospel and by struggling with sinful thoughts and feelings. A person who has not known these visions by experience can have no conception of them whatever, cannot even know that they exist.[3]

The Holy Spirit has superbly described in the Psalter the war and struggle of an athlete of Christ with his own fall and with fallen spirits. The monks of early times learned the Psalter by heart, and they expressed in the words of the Spirit their prayers for their rescue from the pit of the passions, for deliverance from the jaws of the enemy, the devil.[4]

CHAPTER 9

On Reading the Gospel and the Writings of the Fathers

From what has already been said, it becomes increasingly clear that the chief occupation of a novice in his cell should be the reading and study of the Gospel and of the whole New Testament. The whole New Testament can be called the Gospel, since it contains nothing but the Gospel teaching. But a novice should first of all study the Lord's commandments in the Gospels of Matthew and Luke. From the study of the commandments in these Evangelists combined with the actual practice of the commandments, the other Scriptures that constitute the New Testament also become more easily understandable.

While reading the Evangelists, the novice should also read *The Herald;* that is, the explanation of the Gospel by Blessed Theophylact, Archbishop of Bulgaria. The reading of *The Herald* is indispensable. It is an aid to the right understanding of the Gospel and consequently to the most exact practice of it. Moreover, the rules of the Church require that Scripture should be understood as the holy Fathers explain it, and not at all arbitrarily. By being guided in our understanding of the Gospel by the explanation of the holy Fathers, by the explanation received and used by the Church, we keep the tradition of the Holy Church.[1]

Very useful for our time are the works of St Tikhon of Voronezh. They have no exclusive aim. They serve as excellent direction for athletes of Christ living in the world, and for cenobitic monks, and for monks living in state-subsidized monasteries, and for solitaries living the contemplative life. The grace of God inspired the Saint to produce writings especially suitable for our contemporary needs. In these writings, the teaching of the Gospel is explained.

There is nothing to prevent a person from living according to the commandments of the Gospel in any monastery, whatever may be the rule of that monastery, however far that monastery may be even from being well ordered. This is said to encourage and set at rest those who are not satisfied with the running of their monastery, whether rightly or wrongly. For every monk it is surer and better to seek the cause of his dissatisfaction in himself, rather than in his surroundings and circumstances. Self-condemnation always brings peace and rest to the heart. It does not therefore by any means follow that a well-ordered monastery should not be preferred to a lax or disorderly monastery, when the choice depends on us. But that is not always the case.

Having set oneself as a rule of life the learning and carrying out of the commandments of the Gospel, without allowing oneself to be diverted or distracted by the directions given by the different writings of the holy Fathers,[2] one can begin to read them in order to obtain as intimate and exact a knowledge as possible of the laborious, painful, but not joyless monastic struggle. In reading the writings of the Fathers, it is essential to observe their gradational character: they are written for differing stages and degrees of the spiritual life. On no account should they be read hurriedly.

First of all, books written for cenobitic monks should be read, such as: *Instructions* by St Dorotheus, the *Catechetical Sermons* of St Theodore the Studite, the *Directions for the Spiritual Life* by St Barsanuphius and St John the Prophet, beginning with "Answer 216" (the preceding answers are given primarily for hermits and so are less suitable for novices), *The Ladder of Divine Ascent* by St John of the Ladder, the *Works* of St Ephrem the Syrian, and the *Cenobitic Institutes and Conferences* by St John Cassian.

Later, after some considerable time, books written by the Fathers for solitaries may also be read, as for example, *The Philokalia*, the *Skete Patrology*, the chapters of St Isaiah the Solitary, the *Mystic Treatises* of St Isaac the Syrian, the writings of St Mark the Ascetic, the words and homilies of St Macarius the Great, the prose and verse works of St Symeon the New Theologian, and other similar writings of the Fathers on the active life.

All the books enumerated here belong to the category of active or ascetic writings, since they deal with and explain the active monastic life. Says St John of the Ladder, "As you are leading an active (ascetic) life, read active (ascetical) books."[3] Active books stir a monk to monastic activities or struggles, especially to prayer. The reading of the other writings of the holy Fathers leads to meditations and contemplations that, for an ascetic insufficiently purified of the passions, is premature.[4]

CHAPTER 10

On Discretion in Reading the Patristic Books on the Monastic Life

The books of the holy Fathers on the monastic life must be read with great caution. It has been noticed that novices can never adapt books to their condition, but are invariably drawn by the tendency of the book. If a book gives counsels on silence and shows the abundance of spiritual fruits that are gathered in profound silence, the beginner invariably has the strongest desire to go off into solitude, to an uninhabited desert. If a book speaks of unconditional obedience under the direction of a spirit-bearing father, the beginner will inevitably develop a desire for the strictest life in complete submission to an elder.

God has not given to our time either of these two ways of life. But the books of the holy Fathers describing these states can influence a beginner so strongly that out of inexperience and ignorance he can easily decide to leave the place where he is living and where he has every convenience to work out his salvation and make spiritual progress by putting into practice the evangelical commandments, for an impossible dream of a perfect life pictured vividly and alluringly in his imagination.

St John of the Ladder says in his chapter on Silence, "In the refectory of a good brotherhood there is always some dog watching to snatch from the table a piece of bread, that is, a soul; and taking it in its mouth, it then runs off and devours it in a lonely spot."[1]

In the chapter on Obedience this guide of monks says, "The devil suggests to those living in obedience a desire for impossible virtues. Similarly to those living in solitude he suggests unsuitable ideas. Scan the mind of inexperienced novices, and there you will find distracted thought: a desire for solitude, for the strictest fast, for uninterrupted prayer, for absolute freedom from vanity, for unbroken remembrance of death, for continual compunction, for perfect absence of anger, for profound silence, for surpassing purity. And if by divine providence they lack these in the beginning, they rush in vain to another life and are deceived. For the enemy urges them to seek these perfections before the time, so that they may not persevere and in due time attain them. But to those living in solitude the fraud extols hospitality, service, brotherly love, community life, visiting the sick. And the deceiver's aim is to make the latter as impatient as the former."[2]

The fallen angel tries to deceive monks and drag them to perdition by suggesting to them not only sin in its various forms but also the most exalted virtues unsuited to their condition. Do not trust your thoughts, opinions, dreams, impulses, or inclinations, even though they offer you or put before you in an attractive guise the most holy monastic life. If the monastery in which you are residing gives you the possibility of living a life according to the commandments of the Gospel and unless you are exposed to temptations to mortal sin, do not leave your monastery. Endure courageously its defects, both spiritual and material. Do not think you can find a sphere of activity not given by God to our time.

God desires and seeks the salvation of all. And He is always saving all who wish to be saved from drowning in the sea of life and sin. But He does not always save in a boat or in a convenient, well-equipped harbor. He promised to save the holy Apostle Paul and all his fellow travelers, and He did save them. But the Apostle Paul and his fellow passengers were not saved in the ship, which was wrecked; they were saved with great difficulty, some by swimming and others on boards and various bits of the ship's wreckage.[3]

CHAPTER 11

On the Solitary Life

Let it not be hidden from beloved brethren that the highest kinds of monastic life—that is to say, solitude in a remote desert or silence in reclusion, or living with a Spirit-bearing elder in unconditional obedience to him—were not established by chance, or by the will and intelligence of man, but by the special providence, design, vocation, and revelation of God.

Anthony the Great, the head of monasticism, the founder of the hermit life, did not retire into the desert until he had been clothed with power from on high, and then only because he was called by God. Although this is not stated clearly in his biography, subsequent events in the life of the Saint prove it conclusively. That he was guided by the divine voice and commanded to go into the remote (inner) desert for the strictest silence is actually stated in his "Life."[1]

To St Macarius the Great, a contemporary of St Anthony though slightly younger, an angel appeared who showed him a wild and barren plain—which later became the famous Egyptian Scetis—and told him to settle there, promising that the arid plain would be peopled with a multitude of anchorites.[2]

St Arsenius the Great, while living in the imperial palace, prayed to God that he might be shown the way of salvation, and he heard a voice: "Arsenius! Flee from men and you will be saved." Arsenius went off to the scetis mentioned above, and there again he prayed that God would guide him to salvation, and again he heard a voice: "Arsenius! Flee (from men). Be silent. These are the roots of sinlessness."[3]

St Mary of Egypt was called to solitude in the Transjordan desert by the command of God.[4] God, Who called to silence and solitude His chosen (that is, those whom He foresaw to be fit for solitude and silence), provided them with such aids and means for that way of life as man himself cannot obtain. And even in those times when monasticism flourished and when there were many Spirit-bearing directors, those regarded as fit for silence, especially for solitude, were rare.

"True, intelligent silence," says St John of the Ladder, "few can practice; in fact, only those who have obtained divine consolation to encourage them in their labors and help them in their struggles."[5] "Solitude ruins the inexperienced."[6] Recluses and solitaries were often subjected to the greatest spiritual disasters. It was precisely those who had gone into reclusion of their own free will, without being called by God, who suffered such spiritual shipwreck.

In *The Prologue* we read the following narrative. There was a monastery in Palestine at the foot of a high and steep cliff, and in the cliff there was a cave above the monastery. The monks of that monastery related how some time previously one of their brotherhood expressed the desire to live in the cave and asked the abbot for permission. The abbot had the gift of discernment. He said to the brother, "Son! How is it that you want to live alone in the cave when you have got no victory whatever over the passionate thoughts of the soul and flesh? A person who wants to live in silence should be under the guidance of a director, and should not rule himself. You, who are far from having attained due proficiency, ask me to allow you to live alone in a cave, but I think you do not realize the manifold snares of the demons. It would be far better for you to serve the fathers, to receive from God help through their prayers, and to praise and glorify the Lord of all with them at the appointed hours, than for you to struggle alone with your impure and crafty thoughts. Have you not heard what the divinely oracular Father John, author of the Ladder says: 'Woe to the man who is living alone! If he falls into despondency or sloth, there is no one to raise him up. But when two or three are gathered in My name, there am I in the midst of them, said the Lord.'"

So spoke the abbot, but he could not divert him from his soul-destroying thoughts. Seeing the brother's insuperable desire and his constant request, the abbot at last allowed him to live in the cave. Blessed on his way with the abbot's prayer, he climbed up into the cave. At the hours for taking food, one of the brethren of the monastery brought it to the cave, and the recluse had a basket on a rope which he let down to receive the food.

When he had spent some time in the cave, the devil who always opposes and struggles with those who wish to live in a manner pleasing to God, began to trouble him with evil thoughts day and night. After some days, having transformed himself into an angel of light, he appeared to him and said: "Be it known to you that for the sake of your purity and moral life, the Lord sent me to serve you."

"What good have I done," the monk replied, "that an angel should serve me?"

"All that you have done is great and eminent," retorted the devil. "You have left all the beauties of the world and have become a monk. You labor in fasting, prayer, and vigil. And now you have left your monastery and have settled for life here. How can angels not serve your holiness?"

In this way the soul-destroying snake led him to arrogance and pride, and began to appear to him continually. Once, a man who had been robbed by thieves came to the monk. The unclean demon who, to deceive him, kept appearing to him in the form of an angel, said to him:

"This man has been robbed by thieves. What they stole is hidden in such and such a place. Tell him to go there and take it."

The man who had come to the cave bowed, but the monk said to him from above:

"All right, brother, I know why you have come. You are in distress because thieves came to you and stole so and so. Do not be sad! They put what they stole in such and such a place. Go there and you will find it all, and pray for me."

The man was amazed. He obeyed and found what had been stolen. He glorified the monk throughout that country, saying that the monk who lived in the cave was a prophet. Crowds of people began to flock to the monk. As they listened to him, they were astonished at the teaching that he gave by the inspiration of the devil. He foretold to each one what would happen to him, and his predictions came true. The unfortunate man spent a considerable time in this delusion. On the second day of the second week after the ascension of our Lord Jesus Christ, the vile demon appeared to the monk, and said to him:

"Know, father, that for the sake of your irreproachable and angelic life other angels will come and take you, in the body, to heaven. There, with all the angels, you will enjoy the vision of the unutterable beauty of God."

So saying, the devil vanished. But the most merciful God Whose love for us is so great and Who does not desire the destruction of men, put into the monk's heart the idea to tell the abbot what had happened. When the brother who usually brought food to the recluse came, the hermit looked out of the cave and said to him:

"Brother, go and tell the abbot to come here." The brother delivered the message to the abbot. The abbot went at once. He climbed the ladder into the cave and said to the hermit:

"Why have you ordered me to come here, son?'

He replied, "What can I give you, holy father, in return for all that you have done for my unworthiness?"

"What good have I done for you?" asked the abbot.

"Truly, father," said the monk, "it is through you that I have been granted many and great blessings. It was by you that I was clothed in the angelic likeness.[7] Through you I see angels and am granted to converse with them. Through you I have received the gift of spiritual insight and prophecy."

On hearing this, the abbot was astonished and said:

"Wretched man! You see angels? You have been granted the gift of spiritual insight? Alas for you, wretched man! Didn't I tell you not to go to the cave lest devils deceive you?"

When the abbot said this, the brother replied:

"Do not say that, venerable father! For the sake of your holy prayers I see angels. Tomorrow I shall be carried to heaven by them with my body. Be it known to your holiness that I want to ask the Lord our God to allow angels to take you, too, so that you may be with me in the glory of heaven."

On hearing this, the abbot struck him on the face and said:

"Wretched man! You are being driven mad. But now that I have come here, I will not go away but will stay here and see what happens to you. The vile demons, which you call angels, I shall not see; but when you see them coming, tell me."

The abbot ordered the ladder to be taken away, and he stayed in the cave with the deluded man, continuing in unceasing psalm-singing and fasting. When the hour came in which the dupe hoped to ascend to heaven, he saw demons come and say, "We have come, father."

Then the abbot threw his arms round him and cried, "Lord Jesus Christ, Son of God, help Thy deluded servant and do not let the impure demons get possession of him again."

When the abbot said this, the demons seized the dupe and began to pull him, trying with all their might to wrench him from the abbot's embrace. The abbot adjured the demons. They tore the dupe's mantle off him and vanished. The mantle was seen ascending through the air on high, and was finally lost to sight. After some time the mantle again appeared fluttering down, and fell on the earth. Then the abbot said to the deluded monk:

"Foolish and wretched man! You see what the demons have done with your mantle. That is what they intended to do with you, too. They intended to raise you in the air like Simon Magus[8] and then let you drop, so as to crush you and fatally cast out your wretched soul."

The abbot called the monks, told them to bring the ladder, brought down the deluded man from the cave into the monastery, and set him to work in the bake-house, in the kitchen, and in other monastic obediences so as to humble his thoughts. In this way he saved the brother.[9]

Our compatriots Saints Isaac[10] and Nikita[11] of Petchersk were subjected to grievous temptation through prematurely going into reclusion. We see in the life of St Isaac, a contemporary of Saints Anthony and Theodosius, that he went into reclusion of his own will. He undertook the most rigorous physical discipline. Desiring a still more rigorous life, he shut himself in one of the narrowest caves of the Kiev-Petchersk Monastery. His food was a prosphoron,[12] his drink was water; even this scanty fare he took only every other day. With such rigorous bodily discipline and with insufficient experience and knowledge of the spiritual life and combat, it is impossible not to ascribe a certain value both to one's discipline and to oneself.

The temptations brought to him by demons are usually based on the ascetic's inner state. Devils appeared to Isaac in the form of angels of light. One of them shone more than the others, and the demons called him Christ and demanded that the ascetic should worship him. By giving the worship due to the one God to a devil, the ascetic subjected himself to demons who tortured him with violent dancing till he was half dead. St Anthony, who served the recluse, came to him with the usual food. But noticing that he made no reply and realizing that something unusual had happened to him, with the help of other monks he broke open the door, hermetically closed, into Isaac's cave.

They carried him out like a corpse and placed him in front of the cave. Noticing that he was still alive, they carried him down to a bed in a cell. Saints Anthony and Theodosius took turns looking after him. From this temptation, Isaac became feeble in mind and body. He could not stand or sit, and when he was lying down he could not turn from one side to the other. He lay for two years motionless, deaf and dumb.

In the third year, he began to talk and asked to be lifted and set on his feet. Then he began to walk like a child. But he did not express the least desire to visit the church. At first he could scarcely be forced to go, but little by little he began to attend the services. Then he started to go even to the refectory, and gradually learned to take food. During the two years that he lay motionless, he never touched either bread or water. Finally he was completely delivered from the strange and terrible impression produced on him by the appearance and action of demons. Subsequently St Isaac attained to a high degree of holiness.

St Nikita was younger than St Isaac, but was a contemporary. Drawn by zeal, he asked the abbot to bless him to live in reclusion. The abbot (who was then St Nikon) forbade him, saying:

"My son! It is not good for you who are young to be idle. Better for you to live with the brethren. By serving them you will not lose your reward. You know yourself how Isaac was deluded by demons in reclusion. He would have perished if the special grace of God, through the prayers of our holy fathers Anthony and Theodosius, had not saved him."

"Father," Nikita replied, "I will never be deceived by anything of that kind, but I want to stand firmly against the wiles of the demons and to ask God to give me the gift of miracle-working, like Isaac the Recluse, who even till now performs many miracles."

"Your desire," said the abbot again, "is beyond your power. Be on your guard lest, having been exalted, you fall. I, on the contrary, order you to serve the brethren, and you will receive a crown from God for your obedience."

Nikita, drawn by the strongest zeal for the life of reclusion, had not the least desire to attend to what the abbot said to him. He carried out what he had set his mind on. He shut himself up in reclusion and continued praying without ever going out. After some time, on one occasion when he was praying he heard a voice praying with him, and he smelled an extraordinary fragrance. Deceived by this, he said to himself, "If this were not an angel, he would not have prayed with me and there would not have been the fragrance of the Holy Spirit." Nikita began to pray earnestly, saying: "Lord, manifest Thyself to me intelligibly, that I may see Thee."

Then there was a voice which said to him, "I will not appear to thee because thou art young lest, having been lifted up, thou fall down."

The recluse replied with tears, "Lord, I will never be deluded, because the abbot taught me not to attend to diabolic delusion, but I will do all that You order me."

Then, having obtained power over him, the soul-destroying snake said, "It is impossible for a man while still in the flesh to see me. But look, I am sending my angel to stay with thee. Carry out his will."

With these words a demon in the form of an angel appeared to the recluse. Nikita fell at his feet and worshipped him as an angel. The demon said:

"Henceforth do not pray, but read books. In this way thou wilt enter into constant converse with God and wilt receive the power to give salutary teaching to those who come to thee, and I will unceasingly pray to the Creator of all for thy salvation."

The recluse believed these words and was still further deceived. He stopped praying and occupied himself with reading. He saw the demon constantly praying and rejoiced, supposing that an angel was praying for him. Then he began to talk much from Scripture to those who came to him, and to prophesy like the Palestine recluse.[12]

His fame spread among worldly people and reached the grand prince's court. Actually he did not prophesy but he told those who came to him where stolen goods had been put or where something had happened in a distant place, obtaining his information from the demon who attended him.[13] Thus he told the Grand Prince Izyaslav about the murder of Prince Gleb of Novgorod, and advised him to send his son to Novgorod to take over the princedom and rule in his stead. This was sufficient for worldly people to hail the recluse as a prophet. It is observable that worldly people and even monks without spiritual discernment are nearly always attracted by humbugs, imposters, hypocrites, and those who are in demonic delusion, and they take them for saints and genuine servants of God.

No one could compare with Nikita for knowledge of the Old Testament. But he could not bear the New Testament, never took his talks from the Gospels or the apostolic Epistles, and would not allow any of his visitors to mention anything from the New Testament. From this strange bias in his teaching, the fathers of the Kiev-Petchersk Monastery realized that he was deceived by a demon. At that time there were many holy monks endowed with spiritual gifts and graces in the monastery. They drove the devil from Nikita by their prayer. Nikita stopped seeing him. The fathers brought Nikita out of reclusion and asked him to tell them something out of the Old Testament. But he affirmed with an oath that he never read those books which he previously knew by heart. It turned out that he had even forgotten how to read, so great was the influence of the Satanic delusion; and it was only with great difficulty that he learned to read again. Through the prayers of the holy fathers, he was brought to himself, he acknowledged and confessed his sin, he bewailed it with bitter tears, and he obtained a high degree of sanctity and the gift of miracle-working by a humble life among the brethren. Subsequently St Nikita was consecrated as Bishop of Novgorod.

More recent experiences confirm what those of past times have proved unmistakably. Even now, delusion—called in monastic parlance self-deception combined with diabolic deception—is the unfailing consequence of premature withdrawal into remote solitude or of singular asceticism in the solitude of one's cell.

The author of these ascetic counsels as a young man in 1824–1825 visited the Monastery of St Alexander Nevsky for consultation regarding his thoughts with the monk Joannikius, the chandler of the monastery, a disciple of the elders Theodore and Leonid, who had kept in touch with Leonid even after the death of Theodore who was a relative of his. At that time, many of the laity who lived an ascetic life used to go to Joannikius for spiritual counsel. A soldier of the Pavlovsky regiment called Paul also went to him. He had recently been converted from schism, having previously been an instructor of the schismatics, for he was literate. Paul's face shone with joy. But when the most ardent zeal had flared up within him, he had given himself up to immoderate bodily asceticism not in keeping with his state and while he had insufficient understanding of spiritual discipline. Once, at night, Paul was standing at prayer. Suddenly a light appeared near the icons like sunshine and in the midst of the light shone a white dove. A voice came from the dove:

"Receive me. I am the Holy Spirit. I have come to make you my dwelling."

Paul expressed glad consent. The dove went into him through his mouth and Paul, macerated by fasting and vigil, suddenly felt within him the most violent passion of lust. He abandoned prayer, and ran to a brothel. His hungry passion became the satisfaction of insatiable lusts. All the houses of ill fame and every available harlot became his constant haunt. At last he came to himself again. His deception and seduction by a diabolic apparition and his defilement as a result of delusion he explained in a letter to Hieroschemamonk Leonid, then living in the Alexandro-Svirsky Monastery. In the letter there were signs of the fallen man's former high spiritual state. The young man mentioned above was then cell servant of Hieroschemamonk Leonid (1827–1828), and with the elder's blessing he read Paul's letter.

Hieroschemamonk Leonid left the Svirsky Monastery in the spring of 1828 and went first to the Ploschansky Hermitage and then to Optina. His cell servant went with him and took the opportunity to visit certain monasteries of the dioceses of Kaloozh and Orlov. When he was at the famous White Birch Hermitage, a report was being spread of the ascetic life of the monk Serapion who, while reading his private rule of prayer in his cell, had seen an angel. Not only lay people but even monks—since with us in Russia bodily discipline holds the field, while the very idea of spiritual discipline has been lost—were praising Serapion and holding him up as a model of the monastic life.

In 1829 Serapion was transferred to the Optina Hermitage to be under the spiritual direction of Hieroschemamonk Leonid on account of the disorder of his soul. In one of his consultations with the elder, he pulled out a considerable piece of Father Leonid's beard. Out of respect for his ascetic fame, Serapion had been placed in the Scetis of Optina Hermitage. One night he went to the superior of the scetis, Hieromonk Anthony, and told him that John the Baptist had just appeared to him and had ordered him to cut the throats of this Anthony, Hieroschemamonk Leonid, Hieromonk Gabriel, and the landowner Zhelyabovsk who was then staying as a guest in the scetis.

"But where is your knife?" asked the astute and fearless Anthony.

"I've no knife," replied the dupe.

"Then why have you come to cut my throat without a knife?" retorted Anthony, and he sent him back to his cell. Later Serapion had to be put into a home for the mentally deranged, where he died. Before his death, it was reported that he came to his senses, and passed away with the hope of salvation.

It should be noted that when the fallen spirit wants to get dominion over Christ's ascetics, he does not act imperiously or domineeringly, but tries to draw a man to consent to the proposed delusion, and after getting his consent he takes possession of the person who has given his consent. Holy David, in describing how the fallen angel attacks man, has very rightly said: "He lurketh in secret as a lion in his den, that he may ravish the poor; to ravish the poor, when he getteth him into his net."[14]

The Holy Spirit acts autocratically as God. He comes when a person has humbled and abased himself and does not in the least expect His coming. He suddenly changes the mind, changes the heart. By His direct action He embraces the person's whole will and all his faculties without giving him time to think about what is taking place in him.

"While the grace of the Holy Spirit descends upon anyone, it does not show him anything ordinary or sensory, but it secretly teaches him what he has never before seen or imagined. Then the mind is secretly instructed by the Holy Spirit in sublime and hidden mysteries which, according to the divine Paul, the human eye cannot see nor can the mind grasp by itself.... The human mind left to itself and not united to God judges according to its power. But when it is united with the fire of the God-head and the Holy Spirit, then it becomes totally possessed by the Divine Light, and becomes all light, and is set on fire in the flame of the Holy Spirit, and is filled with Divine understanding, and in the Divine fire it is quite unable to think of its own concerns and of its likes and dislikes."[15] So spoke St Maximus Kapsokaiivitis to St Gregory of Sinai.

On the other hand, in the case of apparitions due to demons, man always retains his freedom to judge the apparition, to accept it or reject it. This is clear from the demon's attempts to deceive God's saints. Once, when St Pachomius the Great was living in solitude out of earshot of the monastery, the devil appeared to him in a great light and said:

"Rejoice, Pachomius! I am Christ, and I have come to you as to my friend."

Reflecting on the matter to himself, the Saint thought, "The coming of Christ to a person is always linked with joy, free from fear. Then all human thoughts vanish; then the mind is fixed on the object of its vision. But on seeing what has appeared to me, I am filled with disturbance and fear. This is not Christ but Satan."

After this reflection, the Saint boldly said to the apparition, "Devil, leave me! Cursed are you and your vision, and the cunning of your evil designs." The devil immediately vanished, filling the cell with a vile stench.[16]

It is impossible for a person who is still in the realm of carnal sophistry and who has not received the spiritual realization of fallen human nature not to give some value to his actions and not to consider himself of some worth, however humbly he may speak and however humble he may appear outwardly. True humility is incompatible with carnal sophistry and impossible for it; humility is a property of spiritual understanding. Says St Mark the Ascetic, "Those who have not come to consider themselves debtors to every commandment of Christ honor the Law of God in a bodily manner, without understanding either what it says or on what it is based. Therefore, they think it can be fulfilled by actions."[17]

From the words of the holy Fathers, it is clear that a person who thinks he has some good work to his credit is in a state of self-deception. This state of self-delusion serves as a basis for delusion by demons. In a Christian's wrong conception the fallen angel gets a foothold, and to this false idea he easily adds his own deception, and by means of his deception he subjects the person to his power, and casts him into so-called *diabolic delusion*. From the experiences cited above it is evident that not one of those who were deluded considered himself unworthy of a vision of angels; consequently he considered himself of some worth. The carnal and natural man cannot judge otherwise concerning himself. Therefore, the holy Fathers said generally of all ascetics insufficiently trained in the spiritual life and not guided by grace that solitude ruins them.

Very instructive is the conduct of St Barsanuphius the Great and his fellow ascetic St John the Prophet (who were themselves recluses in the Community of Abbot Seridas) in connection with hermits and silence. All the brethren of that monastery or at least the majority of them were guided by the instructions of these great saints who were filled to overflowing with the Spirit of God. Even the Abbot Seridas himself, whom Barsanuphius the Great called his son, was guided by their instructions. Seridas even served the holy elder who lived in a cell without coming out and received only Seridas and through him gave written answers to the rest of the brethren. Guided by the directions of the inspired men, the brethren of the monastery made rapid and abundant spiritual progress. Some of them became capable of the life of reclusion to which they were called by God Who foresaw their aptitude.

Thus the Great Barsanuphius predicted to John Mirosavsk that God intended him for silence. And having prepared this monk by a life according to the commandments of the Gospel in the monastic community in the forge of obedience, at the time indicated by God he led him into reclusion. From the correspondence of Barsanuphius the Great with John Mirosavsk, it is evident that John, even after entering reclusion, was stormed by passionate thoughts. Other monks who were allowed to become recluses were troubled by passions even more; yet they were not forbidden reclusion.

On the other hand, holy Abba Dorotheus, who was distinguished for both worldly and spiritual wisdom and for skill in directing other monks and who demonstrated this spiritual gift in actual practice, was forbidden by Spirit-bearing elders from becoming a recluse despite his great desire to do so.

"Silence," they told him, "gives occasion to a person for presumption, before he has found himself, that is, before he is pure. Only when a person has already taken up the cross can genuine silence take place. And so, if you have compassion for your neighbors, you will receive help; but if you refrain from compassion, wishing to mount to what is above your means, you will lose even what you have. And so, do not turn aside either inwards or out-wards, but keep to the middle way, and 'because the days are evil. Therefore do not be unwise, but understand what the will of the Lord is.'[18] My words mean do not presume to undertake silence, and do not despair of yourself when you are in the midst of cares; the middle way is safe from falling. In silence you must have humility, and in the midst of cares you need to keep watch over yourself and to control your thoughts. All this is not confined to any particular time. Everyone must bear with gratitude what comes to him in the course of events. The more a person descends into humility, the more progress he makes and the more he succeeds. Staying in your cell does not make you experienced, just because you remain in it without trouble (evi-dently, inexperience in warfare with devils leads a person shut up in a cell to such grievous conflict and suffering as is quite unknown to a cenobitic monk).[19] But through abandoning all cares before the proper time, the enemy will prepare for you not rest or peace, but more disturbance, so that he will force you at last to say, 'It would be better if I had never been born.' "[20]

St Dorotheus, who is recognized as a saint by the universal Church, is one of the most outstanding ascetical writers. He lived in a community among the brethren, and after the death of his holy directors, he founded his own monastery and was its superior.

St John of the Ladder remarks that those who are prone to conceit and self-confidence and to other passions of the soul should on no account choose the life of a solitary for themselves, but should remain among brethren and save themselves by the practice of the commandments;[21] because every kind of life, whether in the desert or in a community, when it is in accordance with the will of God and when its aim is to please God, is rich in blessing.[22]

From premature reclusion stems diabolic delusion, not only obvious delusion, but also that which is invisible outwardly. Mental and moral delusion is incomparably more dangerous than the former as it is extremely difficult to cure, and is often insusceptible to treatment. This kind of delusion, which is based on pride or self-confidence, is called by the holy Fathers *opinion*.[23] It consists in this: an ascetic receives false ideas about spiritual objects or about himself, but he takes them for true ones. False ideas and visions, through the natural sympathy and cooperation of the mind with the heart and of the heart with the mind, are invariably accompanied by deceptive pleasurable sensations of the heart. These are no other than the action of refined sensuality and vainglory. Those who are infected by this delusion become preachers of false ascetical teaching, and sometimes become heresiarchs for the eternal destruction of themselves and their neighbors.

St Isaac the Syrian in his 55th Word says that a certain Malpas lived a strict ascetic life in solitude with the object of attaining a high spiritual state. But he fell into pride and obvious delusion by demons and became the inventor and leader of the heresy of the Euchites.

As an example of a book written in the state of delusion called *opinion*, we cite the following: "When Francis was caught up to heaven," says a writer of his life, "God the Father, on seeing him, was for a moment in doubt to as to whom to give the preference, to His Son by nature or to His son by grace— Francis."[24] What can be more frightful or madder than this blasphemy, what can be sadder than this delusion!

At the present time in our country solitude in an uninhabited desert or wilderness may be regarded as quite impossible. Even reclusion is very difficult, and is more dangerous and impracticable than ever before. In this we must see the will of God and submit to it. If you want to be a hermit pleasing to God, love silence and train yourself for it with all the strength you can muster. Do not allow yourself to utter an idle word either in church, or in the refectory, or in your cell. Do not allow yourself to go out of the monastery except in the case of extreme need and for the shortest time. Do not allow yourself any acquaintanceship, especially any close acquaintanceship, either outside or inside the monastery. Do not allow yourself to be familiar with anyone and avoid all pernicious distractions. Behave like a pilgrim and stranger both in the monastery and in your life on earth in general. In this way you will become a hesychast, a recluse, a hermit, an anchorite, a solitary. If God sees that you are capable of living in a desert or in reclusion, then He Himself by His unutterable judgments will provide you with a desert and a silent life as He provided Blessed Seraphim of Sarov, or He will make provision for reclusion as He did in the case of Blessed George, recluse of the Zadonsky Monastery.

NOTE

In our times, in a mental home in Moscow there lived a would-be prophet to whom crowds of inquisitive people flocked. The prophet's name was Ivan Yakovlevitch. Inhabitants of Moscow visited a certain monk living in solitude and began to praise their prophet in his presence. They said that they were convinced that he had the gift of spiritual insight by their own experience when they asked him about their relative who was serving a term of hard labor in Nerchin. For an hour Ivan Yakovlevitch gave no answer. When his questioners pressed him for an answer, he asked them, "Is it far to Nerchin?" They replied, "More than 6,000 versts." "You can't run there so quickly then!" retorted the prophet. Eventually he told them that the convict had rubbed his legs raw. Some time later the questioners received from the relative in Nerchin a letter in which he described the hardships of his life and mentioned that his legs were rubbed raw by the chains or shackles. "Just imagine what spiritual insight Ivan Yakovlevitch has!" concluded the Moscow inhabitants. The monk replied, "There is no spiritual insight here, but clear contact with fallen spirits. The Holy Spirit does not need time. He immediately reveals both earthly and heavenly secrets. Ivan Yakovlevitch sent the devil that lives with him from Moscow to Nerchin, and he brought back empty, material information which satisfied the prophet's vainglory and the curiosity of carnal people, his questioners. The Holy Spirit always tells something spiritual, soul-saving, really necessary, while the fallen spirit always tells something carnal or earthly as one who by his fall crawls in sinful passions and materiality."

As an example of the action and character of true and holy spiritual insight which is the gift of God, we give a remarkable incident from Church history. St Athanasius the Great, Archbishop of Alexandria, in telling Bishop Ammon about his flight from the Emperor Julian the Apostate, had this to say:

> In those times, I saw great men of God—Theodore, superior of the monks of Tabenna, and Pammon, abba of the monks living in the vicinity of Antinoes. Intending to hide at Theodore's place, I went up in his boat which was covered on all sides. Pammon accompanied us from a sense of respect. The wind was unfavorable. I prayed with a straitened heart. Theodore's monks got out on the shore and towed the boat. Abba Pammon, seeing my sorrow, comforted me. I replied to him:
>
> "Believe me, my heart does not have so much courage in time of peace as it does in time of persecution, because by suffering for Christ and being strengthened by His grace, I hope to receive so much the more mercy from Him, even though I were killed." I had not even finished speaking when Theodore glanced at Abba Pammon and smiled. Pammon looked at him and smiled back.
>
> "Why are you laughing at what I say?" I said to them. "Are you accusing me of cowardice?"
>
> Turning to Pammon, Theodore said, "Tell the Patriarch the cause of our amusement."
>
> Pammon answered, "That is for you to do."
>
> Then Theodore said, "This very hour Julian has been killed in Persia, as God foretold of him: 'He is like death, and cannot be satisfied.'[25]
>
> "A Christian emperor will arise, an outstanding man, but his life will be short. So do not bury yourself in the Thebaid, do not be troubled, but secretly go to meet the new emperor. You will meet him on the way, you will be received very graciously by him, and you will return to your church, but God will soon take him from this life." Everything happened just as he said.[26]

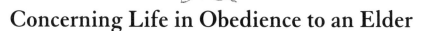

CHAPTER 12

Concerning Life in Obedience to an Elder

What has been said of solitude and reclusion must also be said of obedience to elders in the form in which it was practiced in ancient monasticism—such obedience is not given to our time.

St John Cassian says that the Egyptian Fathers, among whom monasticism especially flourished and produced astonishing fruits, "affirm that it is good to give spiritual direction and to be directed by those who are really wise, and they state that this is a very great gift and grace of the Holy Spirit."[1]

An indispensable condition of such submission is a Spirit-bearing guide who by the will of the Spirit can mortify the fallen will of the person subject to him in the Lord, and can mortify all the passions as well. Man's fall and corrupt will implies a tendency to all the passions. It is obvious that the mortification of a fallen will, which is effected so sublimely and victoriously by the will of the Spirit of God, cannot be accomplished by a director's fallen will when the director himself is still enslaved to the passions.

"If you wish to renounce the world and learn the life of the Gospel," says St Symeon the New Theologian to the monks of his time, "do not surrender (entrust) yourself to an inexperienced or passionate master, lest instead of the life of the Gospel you learn a diabolic life. For the teaching of good teachers is good, while the teaching of bad teachers is bad. Bad seeds invariably produce bad fruits. Every blind man who undertakes to guide others is a deceiver or quack, and those who follow him are cast into the pit of destruction according to the word of the Lord, 'If the blind leads the blind, both will fall into a ditch.'"[2]

Elders who take upon themselves the rôle—we use this unpleasant word which properly belongs to the language of the world in order to explain more exactly a matter that is essentially nothing less than soul-destroying acting and the most deplorable comedy!—elders who take upon themselves the rôle of the ancient holy elders without having their spiritual gifts should know that their very intention, their very thoughts and ideas concerning the great monastic activity of obedience, are false; let them know that their very outlook or way of thinking, their reason or understanding, and their knowledge are self-deception and diabolic delusion which cannot fail to give birth to a corresponding fruit in the person guided by them. Their wrong and defective attitude can only for a time remain unnoticed by the inexperienced beginner under their direction, if this beginner has but a little understanding and occupies himself with holy reading with the pure intention of finding salvation. In due time it is bound to be discovered, and this unpleasant discovery will lead to a most unpleasant separation, to most unpleasant relations between the elder and his disciple, and to the spiritual derangement and confusion of both.

It is a terrible business, out of self-opinion and on one's own authority, to take upon oneself duties that can be carried out only by order of the Holy Spirit and by the action of the Spirit. It is a terrible thing to pretend to be a vessel of the Holy Spirit when all the while relations with Satan have not been broken and the vessel is still being defiled by the action of Satan! It is disastrous both for oneself and one's neighbor; it is criminal in God's sight, blasphemous.

It will be useless to point out that St Zachariah who was living in obedience to an inexperienced elder, his natural father Karion, attained to monastic perfection,[3] or that St Acacius found salvation while living with a cruel elder who drove his disciple with inhuman floggings to an untimely grave.[4] Both were in obedience to incompetent elders, but they were guided by the counsels of Spirit-bearing fathers and the most edifying examples which were in abundance before their eyes. Therefore, they could only have remained in outward obedience to their elders. These cases are outside the general rule and order. "The mode of action of Divine Providence," says St Isaac the Syrian, "is completely different from the common human order. You should keep the common order."[5]

Perhaps you retort: A novice's faith can take the place of an incompetent elder.

It is untrue. Faith in the truth saves. Faith in a lie and in diabolic delusion is ruinous, according to the teaching of the Apostle Paul. "They did not receive the love of the truth, that they might be saved," he says of those who are voluntarily perishing. "And for this reason God will send them [will permit them to suffer] strong delusion, that they should believe the lie, that they all may be condemned who did not believe the truth but had pleasure in unrighteousness."[6]

"According to your faith let it be to you,"[7] said the Lord, the Truth itself, to two blind men, and He healed them of their blindness. Falsehood and hypocrisy has not the right to repeat the words of Truth itself for the justification of criminal conduct whereby liars and hypocrites subvert their neighbors.

There have been instances (they are very, very rare) when faith, by the special providence of God, has operated through sinners and achieved the salvation of these sinners. In Egypt, the robber chief Flavian, intending to rob a certain women's convent, put on the monastic habit and went to the convent. The nuns took him for one of the holy fathers, conducted him to the church and asked him to offer prayers for them to God, which Flavian did against his will and to his own amazement. Then food was set before him. After finishing his meal, the nuns washed his feet. In the convent one of the sisters was blind and deaf. The nuns brought her and gave her some of the water to drink with which the stranger's feet had been washed. The patient was immediately healed. The nuns glorified God and the holy life of the strange monk, and they spread the news of the miracle that had taken place. The grace of God descended upon the robber chief. He offered repentance, and was changed from a chief of robbers into a renowned father.[8]

In the life of St Theodore, Bishop of Edessa, we read that a harlot, forced by her desperate partner Ader, offered a prayer to God for her dead son, and that the child arose at the harlot's prayer. Terrified at what had happened, the harlot at once left her sinful life, entered a monastery, and by an ascetic life attained to holiness.[9]

Instances of this kind are exceptions. As we contemplate them, we shall act correctly if we wonder at the ways of providence and the inscrutable judgments of God, and are strengthened in faith and hope. We shall act very wrongly if we take these instances as models for imitation. As our guide to conduct, we have been given by God himself the Law of God, that is to say Holy Scripture and the writings of the Fathers. The Apostle Paul says decisively, "We command you, brethren, in the name of our Lord Jesus Christ, that you withdraw from every brother who walks disorderly and not according to the tradition which he received from us."[10] By *tradition* here is meant the moral tradition of the Church. It is expounded in Sacred Scripture and in the writings of the holy Fathers.

St Poemen the Great ordered that a penitent should immediately break with an elder if living with him proved to be harmful to the soul.[11] Evidently this meant that the elder in question was breaking the moral tradition of the Church. It is another matter when no harm is done to the soul, and one is only disturbed by thoughts. Disturbing thoughts, however, are obviously diabolic. We must not yield to them. They operate just where we receive spiritual profit, which is what the demons want to snatch from us.

Monastic obedience in the form and character in which it was practiced by the monks of old is a lofty spiritual mystery. Its attainment and full imitation has become impossible for us. We can only examine it reverently and intelligently, and appropriate its spirit. We show right judgment and evince salutary intelligence when, in reading about the rules and experiences of the ancient Fathers and of their obedience—equally amazing both in the directors and in those who were being directed—we see at the present time a general decline of Christianity and recognize that we are unfit to inherit the legacy of the Fathers in its fullness and in all its abundance. And it is a great mystery of God, a great blessing for us, that it is left to us to feed on the crumbs that fall from the spiritual table of the Fathers. These crumbs are not the most satisfying food, but they can prevent spiritual death, though not without a feeling of need and hunger and nostalgia.

CHAPTER 13

Concerning Life under Spiritual Direction

B y *crumbs* in the previous chapter we meant the spiritual life reserved for our time by the providence of God. It is based on the guidance in the work of salvation provided by Holy Scripture and the writings of the holy Fathers, with such advice and instruction as can be borrowed from contemporary fathers and brethren.

In a very real sense, this obedience of the ancient monks, in another form, is well suited to our weakness which is preeminently spiritual. Novices in ancient times were told the will of God immediately and directly by their Spirit-filled directors. Now aspirants and monks must seek out the will of God in Scripture for themselves, and so are exposed to frequent and prolonged doubts and fallacies. Then, progress was rapid by the nature of the work. Now, it is slow, again by the nature of the work. Such is the will of God in our regard. We must submit to it, and respect it with gratitude.

Our present monastic life by the light of Scripture and the advice of fathers and brethren is hallowed and sanctioned by the example of the head of monasticism, St Anthony the Great. He was not in obedience to an elder, but in his novitiate he lived apart and borrowed directions from Scripture and from various fathers and brethren: from one he learned continence, self-control, and abstinence; from another he learned meekness, patience, and humility; from another he learned to keep a strict watch over himself and to practice silence. He tried to appropriate the virtue of each virtuous monk, obeying all as far as possible, humbling himself before all, and praying unceasingly to God.[1]

Novices, act in the same way! Give the superior and the other monastic authorities sincere obedience not to please men but God, free from all selfish motive and desire to win favor—obedience for God's sake. Obey all the fathers and brethren in matters that do not conflict with the Law of God, or with the rule and order of the monastery, or with the management of the monastic authorities. But on no account obey what is evil, even though you have to put up with a certain amount of trouble and suffering for your firmness and your refusal to please men. Ask the advice of virtuous and sensible fathers and brothers; but take their advice with extreme caution and discretion. Do not be carried away by advice on account of the first impression it makes on you. On account of your passions and blindness, some passionate and harmful counsel may appeal to you merely because of your ignorance and inexperience, or because it pleases some hidden passion deep-seated within you of which you are unaware.

With weeping and heartfelt groanings implore God not to allow you to turn aside from His all-holy will and follow a fallen human will, your own or that of your neighbor—your adviser. Both in regard to your own thoughts and your neighbor's thoughts and counsels, consult the Gospel. Conceited and self-opinionated people love to teach and give directions. They are not concerned as to the value of their advice. It does not occur to them that they can cause irreparable damage to their neighbor by their misguided advice, which is taken by an inexperienced beginner with irresponsible confidence, with excitement of the flesh and blood. They want success, whatever the nature of that success may be, whatever may be its origin! They want to make an impression on the beginner, and subject him morally to themselves. They want human praise. They want to be reputed saints, astute elders, teachers with spiritual insight. They want to nourish their insatiable vanity, their pride. The Prophet's prayer was always apt, but it is especially apt now:

Save me, O Lord, for there is not one godly man left;
for truth hath minished from among the children of men.
They have talked of vanities every one with his neighbor;
they do but flatter with their lips, and dissemble in their double heart.[2]

False and hypocritical speech cannot fail to be evil and harmful. Against such an attitude it is essential to take precautionary measures. "Study Divine Scripture," says St Symeon the New Theologian, "and the writings of the holy Fathers, especially the active or practical ones, so that by comparing their teachings with the teaching and conduct of your teacher and elder, you may see them (his teaching and conduct) as in a mirror and understand how to act. If it agrees with Holy Scripture you can make it your own and retain it in your mind; but if it is bad and false you must reject it, lest you fall into delusion. For you must know that many false teachers and impostors have appeared in our days."[3]

St Symeon lived in the tenth century after the birth of Christ, nine centuries before our time.[4] Yet even then the voice of a righteous man in Christ's holy Church was heard deploring the lack of true, Spirit-filled directors, and the many false teachers. In the course of time, satisfactory guides of monasticism dwindled more and more. Then the holy Fathers began to recommend more and more the guidance of Holy Scripture and the Patristic writings. St Nil Sorsky, referring to the Fathers who wrote before him, says:

It is no light task (they say) to find an undeluded teacher for this wonderful practice (true monastic prayer of the heart and mind). By undeluded they mean one whose theory and practice is attested by Divine Scripture, and who has acquired spiritual discernment. Even then, said the holy Fathers, it was scarcely possible to find an undeluded teacher of such subjects; but now that they have dwindled to such an extreme degree, they must be sought with all diligence. However, if such a teacher is not to be found, then the holy Fathers order us to learn from Divine Scripture and listen to our Lord Himself Who says, "Search the Scriptures," and you will find in them "eternal life."[5] "For whatever is written in the Holy Scriptures was written for our instruction."[6]

St Nil lived in the fifteenth century. He founded a scetis, or monastery, not far from White Lake, where he practiced prayer and profound solitude. It will be good for elders of modern times to listen and note with what humility and self-effacement St Nil speaks of the instructions he gave his brethren.

No one should hide the word of God by his negligence, but he should confess his weakness and at the same time not hide God's truth, lest we become guilty of transgressing the commandments of God. Let us not hide the word of God, but let us make it known. The Divine Scriptures and the words of the holy Fathers are as numerous as the sands of the sea. Diligently searching them out, we teach them to those who come to us and who are in need of them (who require them, ask for them). More correctly, it is not we who teach, because we are unworthy to do so, but it is the blessed and holy Fathers who teach from Divine Scripture.[7]

There you have a superb model for our guidance today! It is thoroughly safe and reliable both for the instructor and the instructed. It is a correct expression of moderate progress or proficiency. It is linked with the rejection of conceit, stupid insolence, and temerity, into which fall those who imitate outwardly Barsanophius the Great and other famous Fathers, without having their grace. What was in them an expression of the abundant presence of the Holy Spirit, in indiscreet and hypocritical imitators serves as an expression of profound ignorance, self-deception, pride, and temerity.

Beloved fathers! Let us expound the word of God to our brethren with all possible humility and reverence, acknowledging ourselves to be insufficient for this ministry and guarding ourselves from vainglory which violently assails passionate people when they teach their brethren. Just think—we must give an account of every idle word![8] How much more serious will be our account for the word of God, preached with vainglory and at the instigation of vainglory!

> The Lord shall destroy all lying lips,
> and the tongue that speaketh proud things;
> Which have said, Our tongue will we magnify,
> our lips are our own;
> who is lord over us?[9]

The Lord will destroy those who seek their own glory, and not God's. Let us fear the Lord's threat! Let us speak the word of edification at the demand of real necessity, not as teachers but as those in need of teaching who are anxious to be partakers of the teaching given by God in His all-holy word. "As each one has received a gift, minister to one another, as good stewards of the manifold grace of God. If anyone speaks, let him speak as the oracles of God [with the fear of God and with reverence for God's words, and not as if they were his own words]. If anyone ministers, let him do it as with the ability which God supplies [and not as if it were his own], that in all things God may be glorified through Jesus Christ."[10]

He who acts in his own strength, acts for vainglory; he offers both himself and those who listen to him as a sacrifice to Satan. He who acts in the strength of the Lord, acts for the glory of God; he achieves his own salvation and that of his neighbors through the Lord and only Savior of men. Let us beware of giving a beginner some rash teaching not based on the word of God and a spiritual understanding of the word of God. Better acknowledge one's ignorance than display knowledge harmful to souls. Let us be on our guard against a great catastrophe—turning a credulous beginner from a slave of God into a slave of men,[11] by drawing him to carry out the fallen will of man instead of the all-holy will of God.[12]

The modest relation of a counselor to a learner is entirely different from that of an elder to a novice in unconditional obedience, a slave in the Lord. Advice or counsel does not involve the condition of unfailing compliance; it can be carried out or not carried out. No responsibility rests with a counselor for his advice, if he has given it with the fear of God and with humility, and not of his own accord, but because he was asked and urged to give it. Likewise the one who receives advice is not bound by it; it is left to his freewill and discretion to carry out the advice received or not to carry it out.

It is obvious that the way of counsel and following Holy Scripture is suited to our feeble time. We will observe that the Fathers forbid us to give advice to our neighbor of our own accord, without our neighbor's asking us to do so. The voluntary giving of advice is a sign that we regard ourselves as possessed of spiritual knowledge and worth, which is a clear sign of pride and self-deception.[13] This does not refer to superiors and authorities who are obliged at all times and whenever necessary, even without being asked, to teach the brethren entrusted to their care.[14] But when visiting other monasteries, they should be guided by the advice of St Macarius of Alexandria to St Pachomius the Great. Pachomius asked Macarius about teaching and judging the brethren. Abba Macarius replied, "Teach and judge your own subjects, but judge no outsiders."[15] All superiors who wish to please God have kept and keep this rule.

The Aim of the Monastic Life Consists in Studying the Will of God, in Making It One's Own, and in Obeying It

The essence of the monastic life consists in healing our impaired will, uniting it with the will of God, and sanctifying it by this union. Our will, in its fallen state, is hostile to the will of God. On account of its blindness and its hostility to God, it is constantly endeavoring to oppose the will of God. When its efforts are unsuccessful, it leads a person to irritability, discontent, confusion, sorrow, despondency, acedia, grumbling, blasphemy, and despair. In the renunciation of one's own will to follow the will of God consists the self-renunciation commanded by the Savior, which is an indispensable condition of salvation and Christian perfection. In fact, this is so indispensable that unless this condition is satisfied, salvation is impossible, and Christian perfection even more impossible. "In His will is life," says the Prophet.[1]

In order to do the will of God, it is necessary to know it. Only with this knowledge is the renunciation of one's damaged will possible and its healing by the will of God. The will of God is a divine mystery. "No one knows the things of God," says the Apostle Paul, "except the Spirit of God."[2] Consequently, men can obtain knowledge of the will of God only through divine revelation. "Teach me to do Thy will," prayed inspired David, "for Thou art my God. Thy good Spirit shall lead me into the land of righteousness."[3]

Open Thou mine eyes,
that I may recognize the wondrous things of Thy law.
I am a pilgrim upon earth,
O hide not Thy commandments from me.[4]

The will of God is revealed to mankind in the Law of God.[5] But preeminently, with special clarity and detail, it is made known to us by the incarnate Word of God. As the highest knowledge, it is received by faith. "For I have come down from heaven," said the Savior, "not to do My own will, but the

48

will of Him who sent Me. This is the will of the Father who sent Me, that of all He has given Me I should lose nothing, but should raise it up at the last day. And this is the will of Him who sent Me, that everyone who sees the Son and believes in Him may have everlasting life; and I will raise him up at the last day."[6] "For I have not spoken on My own authority; but the Father who sent Me gave Me a command, what I should say and what I should speak. And I know that His command is everlasting life."[7]

The study of the will of God is a task filled with joy, filled with spiritual consolation. At the same time it is a task that presents great sorrows, disappointments, trials, and temptations. It is also inseparable from self-renunciation, the mortification of our fallen nature, and the saving destruction of the soul. It involves the crucifixion of the old man.[8] It requires that the carnal mind and outlook be renounced, spurned, annihilated. "Do not be conformed to this world, but be transformed by the renewing of your mind, that you may prove what is that good and acceptable and perfect will of God,"[9] says the Apostle Paul.

With such precision and authenticity has the Son of God revealed God's will to men, with such substantial consequences has He linked this revelation of the will of God, that sacred Scripture calls Him the *exegesis of God*;[10] that is to say, the One Who reveals in as full a manner as men are capable of receiving—not capable by themselves, but through the superabundant action of divine grace. Such also is the meaning of our Lord's words: "I have manifested Your name to the men whom You have given Me out of the world.... I have declared to them Your name, and will declare it, that the love with which You loved Me may be in them, and I in them."[11] The revelation of the name of Him Who is above every name is the most perfect knowledge of Him Who is above all knowledge. The supreme knowledge that is revealed as a result of the sanctification of man by the divine will leads to divine love, to the union of man with God.

Some of the commandments of the Gospel teach us how *to act* in a manner pleasing to God; others teach us how *to react* so as to please God when outside forces act upon us. It is more difficult to learn the latter than the former. But the former will be understood satisfactorily when the soul learns and accepts the latter. It is essential to convince oneself that God rules the destiny of the world and the destiny of every individual. The experiences and trials of life will not be slow to confirm and establish this teaching of the Gospel. A consequence of the acceptance by faith of this teaching is a humble submission to God, the flight of troubles and worries, peace of soul, the power of fortitude. He who thus accepts the teaching of the Gospel takes "the shield of faith with which [he] will be able to quench all the fiery darts of the wicked one."[12]

This faith is called by the holy Fathers *practical* or *active* as distinct from *dogmatic* faith.[13] It makes its appearance in a man from the practice of the commandments of the Gospel; it grows in proportion to the extent that he puts them into practice; it fades in so far as he disregards them. In due time, this faith is transformed by grace into a living faith which fills the Christian with spiritual power and by which God's saints "subdued kingdoms, worked righteousness, obtained promises, stopped the mouths of lions, quenched the violence of fire, escaped the edge of the sword, out of weakness were made strong, became valiant in battle, turned to the armies of the aliens."[14]

It is essential to maintain an attitude of reverent trust toward the inscrutable (for us) judgments of God in all the manifestations of His will and in all that He permits, both in God's special and general providences, alike in private and public or social life, equally in civil as in moral and spiritual affairs. "Humble yourselves," says the Apostle Peter, "under the mighty hand of God ... casting all your care upon Him, for He cares for you."[15] We should humble ourselves after that superb example presented to us by Holy Scripture in the prayer of the three holy children whose fidelity to God was put to a severe test in Babylon, and who acknowledged that all God's providences are the consequences of His just judgment.[16] *It is inevitable that temptations come*,[17] declared our Lord. And in foretelling the terrible calamities that would befall those who believed in Him and all mankind, He said, "See that you are not troubled; for all these things must come to pass."[18] If so, then neither have we the right, nor is it feasible, to say or think anything against the decrees or decisions pronounced by the all-good, all-wise, almighty God.

"You will be betrayed even by parents and brothers, relatives and friends," our Lord forewarned us, "and they will put some of you to death. And you will be hated by all for My name's sake."[19] "Whoever kills you will think that he offers God service ... In the world you will have tribulation; but be of good cheer, I have overcome the world."[20]

Having portrayed and foretold the position of true Christians during this earthly life, a position foreordained for them by God, the Lord added, "But not a hair of your head shall be lost."[21] This means: God will indefatigably take care of you; He will keep unsleeping watch over you; He will hold you in His almighty hand. Therefore, no sorrow or suffering will come to you except by His all-holy will, or with His permission, for your salvation.

Our Lord concluded His instruction to His disciples regarding the trials of earthly life that would befall them with a decisive and definite commandment: "By your patience possess your souls."[22] Acknowledge and confess God to be the ruler of the world. Reverently and with self-renunciation, submit and surrender yourself to His will. From this recognition and submission, holy patience will blossom in your souls. It will be known to you by the peace that it will bring to your soul. Let every word against the judgments of God die on our lips. As the Evangelist St Luke said of himself and his companions: "We ceased, 'The will of the Lord be done.'"[23]

It needs to be known that every thought in the nature of contradiction and resistance to the judgments of God comes from Satan and is his offspring. Such a thought, since it is opposed to God, must be rejected at its very inception. An example of this has been given us by our Lord. When He told the disciples about His impending sufferings and violent death, then the Apostle Peter, moved by the natural compassion of an old man, "began to rebuke Him, saying, 'Far be it from You, Lord; this shall not happen to You!' The Lord answered Peter by exposing the origin of the thought that he had expressed: 'Get behind me, Satan! You are an offense to Me; for you are not mindful of the things of God, but the things of men.'"[24]

Why is our spirit troubled by the judgments and providences of God? Because we do not honor God as God; because we do not surrender ourselves to God as God; because we do not give ourselves our proper place before God; because of our pride, our blindness, our fallen, spoilt, perverse will is not mortified and renounced by us.

> Then should I not be confounded,
> when I consider all Thy commandments.
> I will thank Thee with an unfeigned heart,
> when I shall have learned the judgments of Thy righteousness.[25]

"Thou art God my Saviour, and upon Thee have I waited all the day long"[26] by bearing generously and good-naturedly throughout my life on earth all the troubles and sufferings which it pleases Thee to allow me to have for my salvation.

St John of the Ladder defines the gift of *spiritual discernment*, which is given by God exclusively to monks who go by the way of humility and lowly-mindedness, in the following manner: "Generally speaking, discernment is, and is recognized as, a sure understanding of the divine will on all occasions, in every place and in all matters; and it is only found in those who are pure in heart, and in body, and in speech."[27]

CHAPTER 15

Love for Our Neighbor Is a Means of
Attaining to Love for God

The Savior of the world summarized all His particular commands in two main, general commandments: "'You shall love the Lord your God,'" He said, "'with all your heart, with all your soul, and with all your mind.' This is the first and great commandment. And the second is like it: 'You shall love your neighbor as yourself.' On these two commandments hang all the Law and the Prophets."[1]

Although the commandment of love for God is as far superior to the commandment of love for God's image (man) as God is superior to His image, yet the commandment of love for our neighbor serves as a foundation for the commandment of love for God. He who has not laid the foundation labors in vain to construct a building; it cannot possibly stand without the foundation. By love for our neighbor we enter into love for God. A Christian's love for God is love for Christ,[2] and love for our neighbor is love for Christ in our neighbor. By loving our neighbor—by loving him in the Lord, that is, as the Lord commands us—we acquire love for Christ, and love for Christ is love for God.

The union of love for God with love for our neighbor is superbly explained in the epistles of the holy Apostle and Evangelist John the Theologian. It is impossible to love God, according to St John's teaching, without first loving one's brother. And love for one's brother consists in carrying out the Lord's commandments in this regard.[3]

The same teaching is given by the holy directors of monasticism. St Anthony the Great says, "On our neighbor depends life and death (of the soul). By winning our brother we win God; by offending our brother we sin against Christ." St John Kolovos, one of the greatest Fathers of the Egyptian Scetis, says, "It is not possible to build a house by beginning from the top, but the structure must be begun from the foundation and built up to the roof." When asked what the foundation meant, he replied, "The foundation is our neighbor. We must win him and begin with him. On him are based all the commandments of Christ."[4] St Mark the Ascetic says, "It is impossible to be saved other than through one's neighbor."[5] This is what is held and taught by all the holy Fathers; this is the general Christian teaching, the teaching of the Church, the teaching of Christ.

Direct all your attention to the acquisition of love for your neighbor as the basis of your life and your monastic task. Love your neighbor according to the dictates of the commandments of the Gospel, not at all according to the dictates and impulses of your heart. The love planted by God in our nature was damaged by the fall and cannot act correctly. On no account allow it to act! Its actions have lost their purity; they are abominable in God's sight, like a polluted sacrifice. The fruits of its actions are soul-destroying, deadly. Love your neighbor in the following way: Do not get angry with him and do not bear resentment or a grudge against him. Do not allow yourself to say to your neighbor any reproachful, abusive, sarcastic, or caustic words. Maintain peace with him as far as possible. Humble yourself in his presence. Do not try to have your revenge on him either directly or indirectly. Whenever possible, yield to him. Get out of the habit of arguing and quarrelling, and reject it as a sign of pride and self-love. Speak well of those who speak evil of you. Pay good for evil. Pray for those who cause you various offenses, wrongs, temptations, persecutions.[6] Whatever you do, on no account condemn anyone; do not even try to judge whether a person is good or bad, but keep your eyes on that one evil person for whom you must give an account before God—yourself.[7]

Treat your neighbors as you would like them to treat you.[8] Forgive and pardon men their offenses against you from the depth of your heart, so that your heavenly Father may forgive you your countless offenses, your terrible debt of sin that can easily cast you down and confine you for all eternity in the prisons of hell.[9]

Do not acquire attachment, especially impure passion, for your neighbor; by the term neighbor is meant not only the male but the female sex as well. If, however, you are wounded by a dart of the enemy and are somehow unexpectedly poisoned by it, do not despond, knowing that we have an inherent proneness to be infected by every kind of passion and that even great saints suffered in this way. Make every effort and put all your energy into the healing of yourself.

Finally, do not harm your brother by talkativeness, gossip, close acquaintance, and familiar conduct with him. If you avoid these pitfalls in regard to your neighbor, you will show and acquire for him the love commanded by God and pleasing to God; thereby you will open the way for yourself to the love of God. St Symeon the New Theologian has said, "Do not acquire special love for any person, especially for novices, even though it may seem to you that that person's life is extremely good and above reproach. For spiritual love mostly changes into passionate love, and you will fall into unprofitable sufferings. This occurs most of all with those endeavoring to live the spiritual life. You should regard yourself as a stranger to every brother in the community, especially to those whom you knew in the world, and love all equally."

St Isaac the Syrian says, "Love for the young is fornication, which God abominates. For that wound there is no plaster. But he who loves all equally out of compassion and without distinction has attained perfection. A young person followed by a young person makes the discerning weep and wail over them. But an old man who follows a youth has acquired a passion more fetid than the passion of the young. Even though he were to converse with the young on virtue, yet his heart is wounded."[10]

CHAPTER 16

Humility in Our Dealings as a Means of
Attaining to Love for Our Neighbor

Love for our neighbor is preceded and accompanied by humility in our human relationships. Hatred toward our neighbor is preceded by condemnation and criticism of him, detraction and disparagement, slander and backbiting, scorn for him; in other words, pride.

Holy monks constantly remembered Christ's words: "Assuredly, I say to you, inasmuch as you did it to one of the least of these My brethren, you did it to Me."[1] They did not stop to consider whether their neighbor deserved their respect or not; they paid no attention to his numerous and obvious defects. Their attention was taken up with seeing that they did not somehow fail to realize that our neighbor is the image of God, and that Christ accepts what we do to our neighbor as if it were done to Him.

The proud fallen angel hates this notion and does all in his power to filch it from the Christian. This notion is foreign to the carnal and animal outlook[2] of fallen human nature, and special attention is required to retain it in the memory. It requires considerable spiritual effort and it requires the cooperation of divine grace for the heart damaged by sin to grasp this notion so as to have it constantly in mind,[3] in our relations with our brethren. But when by the mercy of God we grasp this notion, it becomes a source of the purest love for our neighbor, a love for all equally. Such love has a single cause—the Christ Who is honored and loved in every neighbor.

The realization of this truth becomes a source of the sweetest compunction, of the most fervent, undistracted, most concentrated prayer. Holy Abba Dorotheus used to say to his disciple, St Dositheus, whenever the disciple was overcome by anger, "Dositheus! You get angry, and are you not ashamed that you get angry and offend your brother? Do you not realize that he is Christ and that you offend Christ?"

The great St Apollos often used to tell his disciples regarding the reception of strange brethren who came to him that they must be given honor with a prostration to the earth. In bowing to them we bow not to them but to God. "Have you seen your brother? You have seen the Lord your God. This," he said, "we have received from Abraham.[4] And that we must welcome and show hospitality to the brethren we have learned from Lot who urged (persuaded) the angels to spend the night at his house."[5]

This way of thought and behavior was adopted by all the monks of Egypt, the very first in all the world in monastic proficiency and gifts of the Holy Spirit. These monks were deemed worthy of being foreseen and foretold by the Prophet: "Men of prayer will come from Egypt"[6]

St John Cassian, an ecclesiastical writer of the fourth century, relates the following:

> When we (St Cassian and his friend in the Lord St Germanus), wishing to learn the rules of the elders, arrived from the region of Syria in the province of Egypt, we were astonished to find that they received us there with extraordinary kindness. Moreover they never observed the rule for the use of food, for which a fixed hour is appointed, contrary to what we had learned in the Palestinian monasteries. Wherever we went the regular fast for that day was relaxed, with the exception of the canonical (Church) fast on Wednesdays and Fridays. We asked one of the elders, "Why do you all without distinction disregard the daily fasting?" He replied, "Fasting is always with me, but you I must send away eventually and I cannot always have you with me. Although fasting is beneficial and constantly necessary, yet it is a gift and a voluntary sacrifice, whereas the observance of love in a practical way is an invariable duty required by the commandment. I receive Christ in your person, and I must show Him wholehearted hospitality; but when I have seen you off after showing the love of which He is the cause, I can make up for the relaxation by increased fasting in solitude. 'Can the wedding guests fast while the bridegroom is with them? But when the bridegroom is taken away from them, then they will fast lawfully.' "[7]

While living in a monastery with brethren, regard only yourself as a sinner and all the brethren without exception as angels. Prefer all to yourself. When your neighbor is preferred to you, rejoice at it and approve it as a most just act. You will easily attain to such an attitude of soul if you avoid close acquaintanceship and familiarity. On the other hand, if you allow yourself to be free and easy and familiar with people you will never reach the outlook of the saints and will never be able to say and feel sincerely with the Apostle Paul, "Christ Jesus came into the world to save sinners, of whom I am chief."[8]

Through humility in your dealings with your neighbor, and through love for your neighbor, hardness and callousness is expelled from the heart. It is rolled away like a heavy rock from the entrance to a tomb, and the heart revives for spiritual relations with God for which it has been hitherto dead. A new vista opens to the gaze of the mind: the multitudinous wounds of sin with which the whole of fallen nature is riddled. It begins to confess its wretched state to God and implore Him for mercy. The heart assists the mind with mourning and compunction. This is the beginning of true prayer.

On the other hand, the prayer of a resentful person is compared by St Isaac the Syrian to sowing on rock.[9] The same must be said of the prayer of one who condemns and despises his neighbor. God not only does not attend to the prayer of one who is proud and angry, but He even permits a person praying in such a state of soul to undergo various, most humiliating temptations so that by being struck and oppressed by them he may resort to humility in his relations with his neighbor and to love for his neighbor.

Prayer is the practical expression of a monk's love for God.[10]

CHAPTER 17

On Prayer

Prayer is the daughter of the fulfillment of the Gospel commandments, and is at the same time the mother of all the virtues, according to the general opinion of the holy Fathers. Prayer produces virtues from the union of the human spirit with the Spirit of the Lord. The virtues that produce prayer differ from the virtues that prayer produces; the former are of the soul, the latter—of the spirit. Prayer is primarily the fulfillment of the first and chief commandment of those two commandments in which are concentrated the Law, the Prophets, and the Gospel.[1] It is impossible for a person to turn with all his thought, with all his strength, and with all his being toward God, except by the action of prayer, when it rises from the dead and, by the power of grace, comes to life as if it received a soul.[2]

Prayer is the mirror of the monk's progress.[3] By examining his prayer, a monk discerns whether he has attained salvation or is still in distress on the troubled sea of the passions outside the sacred harbor. As a guide to such discernment, he has the divinely inspired David who, talking prayerfully to God, says:

> By this I know Thou favorest me,
> that mine enemy doth not triumph against me.
> But Thou hast taken my side by reason of my innocence,
> and hast established me before Thee for ever.[4]

This means: I have learned, O Lord, that Thou hast shown me kindness, and hast taken me to Thyself, on account of my constant and victorious rejection, through the power of prayer, of all thoughts, images, and feelings that come from the enemy. This kindness and mercy of God to man appears when a person feels kindness and mercy toward all his neighbors and forgives all offenders.

Prayer should be a monk's chief task. It should be the center and heart of all his activities. By means of prayer a monk clings to the Lord in the closest manner and is united in "one spirit" with the Lord.[5] From his very entry into the monastery, it is essential to learn to pray properly, so that in prayer and by means of prayer he may work out his salvation. Regularity, progress, and proficiency[6] in prayer are opposed by our corrupt nature and by the fallen angels who strive their utmost to keep us in their slavery, in the fallen state of aversion from God which is common to men and fallen angels.

❧🌿❧

CHAPTER 18

On Preparation for Prayer

On account of the signal importance of prayer, preparation should precede its practice. Before praying, *prepare yourself; and do not become like a man who tempts the Lord.*[1] "When we are going to stand in the presence of our King and God and converse with Him," says St John of the Ladder, "let us not rush into it without preparation, lest seeing from afar that we are without the weapons and clothing required for standing in the presence of the King, He should order His servants and slaves to bind us and banish us far from His presence and tear up our petitions and fling them in our face."[2]

The first preparation consists in rejecting resentment and condemnation of our neighbors. This preparation is commanded by our Lord Himself: "'Whenever you stand praying,'" He orders, "'if you have anything against anyone, forgive him, that your Father in heaven may also forgive you your trespasses. But if you do not forgive, neither will your Father in heaven forgive your trespasses.'"[3] Further preparation consists in the rejection of cares by the power of faith in God and by the power of obedience and surrender to the will of God; also a realization of one's sinfulness and the resultant contrition and humility of spirit. The one sacrifice that God accepts from fallen human nature is a contrite spirit. "For if Thou hadst desired sacrifice, I would have given it," says His Prophet to God on behalf of everyone who has fallen and remains in his fallen state. It is not merely some partial sacrifice of body or soul, but "Thou delightest not in burnt offerings. The sacrifice unto God is a contrite spirit; a contrite and humble heart God shall not despise."[4] St Isaac the Syrian repeats the following saying of another holy father: "If anyone does not recognize himself as a sinner, his prayer is not acceptable to God."

Stand at prayer before the invisible God as if you saw Him, and with the conviction that He sees you and is looking at you attentively. Stand before the invisible God just as a guilty criminal convicted of countless crimes and condemned to death stands before a stern, impartial judge. Exactly! You are standing before your sovereign Lord and Judge; you are standing before the Judge in Whose sight no living soul will be justified,[5] Who always *wins when He is judged.*[6] He does not condemn when, in His unspeakable love for men, He forgives a man his sin and enters not into judgment with His servant.[7] Conscious of the fear of God, and feeling from its action His presence when you pray, you will see without seeing, spiritually, Him Who is invisible. You will realize that prayer is to stand by anticipation at the awful judgment of God.[8]

Stand at prayer with bowed head, with your eyes cast to the ground, on both legs equally and without moving; assist your prayer by sorrow of heart, sighs from the depth of your soul, and abundant tears. A reverent outward demeanor at prayer is most essential and most helpful for all wrestling at the work of prayer, especially for beginners in whom the disposition of the soul conforms largely to the posture of the body.

The Apostle Paul orders thanksgiving when we pray: "Continue earnestly in prayer," he says, "being vigilant in it with thanksgiving."[9] The Apostle says that thanksgiving is ordered by God Himself: "Pray without ceasing, in everything give thanks; for this is the will of God in Christ Jesus for you."[10] What is the meaning of thanksgiving? It means praising God for His countless blessings, poured out on all mankind and on everyone. By such thanksgiving the soul is filled with a wonderful peace; and she is filled with joy in spite of the fact that sorrows beset her on all sides. By thanksgiving a man acquires a living faith so that he rejects all worry about himself, tramples on fear of men and devils, and surrenders himself wholly to the will of God.

Such a disposition of the soul is an excellent preparatory disposition for prayer. "As you have therefore received Christ Jesus the Lord," says the Apostle Paul, "so walk in Him [live in Him], rooted and built up in Him and established in the faith, just as you have been taught, abounding in it with thanksgiving," that is, by means of thanksgiving obtaining an abundance of faith."[11] "Rejoice in the Lord always. Again I will say, Rejoice! ... The Lord is at hand. Be anxious for nothing, but in everything by prayer and supplication, with thanksgiving, let your requests be made known to God."[12] The importance of the spiritual effort of thanksgiving is explained with particular fullness in *Directions for the Spiritual Life* by the holy Fathers Barsanuphius and John.

CHAPTER 19

On Attention at Prayer

Prayer requires the inseparable presence and cooperation of the attention. With attention, prayer becomes the inalienable property of the person praying; in the absence of attention, it is extraneous to the person praying. With attention, it bears abundant fruit; without attention, it produces thorns and thistles.[1]

The fruit of prayer consists in illumination of mind and compunction of heart, in the quickening of the soul with the life of the Spirit. Thorns and thistles are a sign of deadness of soul and pharisaical self-esteem which springs from the hardening of a heart that is contented and elated by the quantity of the prayers and the time spent in reciting those prayers.

The rapt attention that keeps prayer completely free from distraction and from irrelevant thoughts and images is a gift of God's grace. We evince a sincere desire to receive the gift of grace—the soul-saving gift of attention—by forcing ourselves to pray with attention whenever we pray. Artificial attention, as we may call our own unaided attention unassisted by grace, consists in enclosing our mind in the words of the prayer, according to the advice of St John of the Ladder. If the mind, on account of its newness to the work of prayer, gets out of its enclosure in the words, it must be led back into them again. The mind in its fallen state is naturally unstable and inclined to wander everywhere. But God can give it stability and will do so in His own time in return for perseverance and patience in the practice of prayer.[2]

Especially helpful in holding the attention during prayer is an extremely unhurried pronunciation of the words of the prayer. Pronounce the words without hurrying so that the mind may quite easily stay enclosed in the words of the prayer, and not slip away from a single word. Say the words in an audible voice when you pray alone; this also helps to hold the attention.

It is particularly easy to practice attentive prayer when performing the rule of prayer in one's cell, and one should train oneself to do so. Beloved brother, do not refuse the yoke of a certain amount of monotony and compulsion in accustoming yourself to the exercises of your monastic cell and especially to the rule of prayer. Arm yourself in good time with the all-powerful weapon of prayer. Accustom yourself to the practice of prayer while you have the opportunity.

Prayer is all-powerful on account of the all-powerful God Who acts in it. It is "the sword of the Spirit, which is the word of God."[3] "Prayer by its nature is communion and union of man with God; by its action it is the reconciliation of man with God, the mother and daughter of tears, a bridge for crossing temptations, a wall of protection from afflictions, a crushing of conflicts, boundless activity, the spring of virtues, the source of spiritual gifts, invisible progress, food of the soul, the enlightening of the mind, an axe for despair, a demonstration of hope, release from sorrow, the wealth of monks."[4]

At first we must force ourselves to pray. Soon prayer begins to afford consolation, and this consolation lightens the coercion and encourages us to force ourselves. But we need to force ourselves to pray throughout our life,[5] and few indeed are the ascetics who, on account of the abundant consolation of grace, never need to force themselves.

Prayer acts murderously on our "old man," the unregenerate self or nature. As long as it is alive in us, it opposes prayer like death.[6] Fallen spirits, knowing the power of prayer and its beneficial effect, endeavor by all possible means to divert us from it, prompting us to use the time assigned to prayer for other occupations; or else they try to annul it and profane it with mundane distractions and sinful inattention, by producing at the time of prayer a countless swarm of earthly thoughts, sinful daydreams and reveries, imaginings and fantasies.

CHAPTER 20

On the Cell Rule

The cell rule consists in a certain number of prostrations, in a certain number of prayers and psalms, and in the practice of the Prayer of Jesus. It is fixed for each person according to his powers of body and soul. As these powers vary indefinitely in individuals, the rule is offered to ascetics[1] in the most varied of forms. The general principle for the rule of prayer consists in this, that it should on no account exceed the ascetic's strength, or sap that strength, or undermine his health and so force him to give up every kind of rule. Abandoning the rule of prayer is generally the result of a rule, adopted or imposed, which is beyond one's strength. On the other hand, a moderate and prudent rule remains a monk's property for the whole of his life, goes on developing and growing naturally till the end of his life, and gains character both in outward form and inner value according to his progress.

For a strong and healthy body, a rule requiring a greater number of prostrations and a larger quantity of prayer is indicated, and less for a weak body. Human bodies differ so much from one another in strength and capacity that some are more exhausted by thirty prostrations than others are by three hundred.

CHAPTER 21

Concerning Bows

Bows are divided into bows to the ground and bows from the waist.[1] They are generally appointed for the evening rule before going to bed. It is best to make bows before reading the evening prayers, that is, to begin the rule with bows. Bows tire and warm the body to some extent and reduce the heart to a state of contrition; in such a state, the ascetic prays with greater zeal, warmth, and attention. The prayers have quite a different taste when they are read or said after bows.

Bows must be made extremely unhurriedly, for the bodily labor must be animated by mourning of heart and prayerful cries of grief on the part of the mind. When about to make prostrations, give your body a most reverent attitude, such as a slave and creature of God should have in the presence of his Lord and God. Then collect your thoughts from wandering everywhere, and with extreme unhurriedness, just aloud to yourself, enclosing the mind in the words, and from a contrite and humble heart, say the prayer, "Lord Jesus Christ, Son of God, have mercy on me a sinner." Having said the prayer, unhurriedly make a prostration, with reverence and the fear of God, without excitement, with the feeling of a person repenting and asking for the forgiveness of his sins, as if you were at the feet of the Lord Jesus Christ Himself. Do not picture to yourself in your imagination the form or figure of the Lord, but have a conviction of His presence; have a conviction that He is looking at you, at your mind and heart, and that His reward is in His hand. The former is impermissible fancy, which leads to disastrous self-deception; but a conviction of the presence of the omnipresent God is a conviction of a most holy truth. Having made the prostration, bring the body to reverence and calm again, and again say unhurriedly the above prayer; then make a prostration again in the way described above.

Do not worry about the number of bows. Pay all your attention to the quality of your prayer performed with prostrations. Without speaking of the effect on the spirit, a small number of bows made in the way described above will have a much greater effect on the body itself than a large number made hurriedly, without attention, for quantity. Experience will soon prove this. When you get tired, pass from prostrations to bows from the waist. The extent of the bow from the waist is fixed by this: that when making it, the extended hand should touch the ground or floor.

Regarding it as one's imperative duty in making bows to ensure the soul's abundant working which consists in attentiveness, unhurriedness, reverence, and the intention to offer penitence to God, the ascetic will soon discover the quantity of bows his constitution can stand. By slightly reducing this number as a concession to his weakness, he can make a daily rule for himself; and when it has been approved and blessed by his spiritual father or his superior, or by a monk whom he trusts and whose advice he follows, he can perform the rule daily.

For the spiritual guidance of our beloved brethren we shall not be silent about the following: bows performed for number, and not animated by the right working of the mind and heart, are more harmful than profitable. Having performed them, the ascetic begins to rejoice. "There," he says to himself like the Pharisee mentioned in the Gospel, "God has granted me again today to make, say, 300 prostrations! Glory to God! Is that an easy matter? In these times, 300 prostrations! Who keeps such a rule nowadays?" And so on. We must remember that bows heat the blood, and by heating the blood excessively, they help to stimulate mental activity. Having reached such a state, the poor ascetic, just because he has no idea of the soul's true working, surrenders to mental activity harmful to the soul, surrenders to vainglorious thoughts and fancies, based on his ascetic labor, through which he thinks he is making progress. The ascetic enjoys these thoughts and fancies, cannot have enough of them, adopts them, and so plants within himself the fatal passion of conceit. Conceit soon begins to make its appearance in the secret condemnation of neighbors and in an open disposition to preach to them. Obviously such a disposition is a sign of pride and self-deception; unless a monk considered himself above his neighbor, he would never dare to teach him. Such is the fruit of all bodily labor, unless it is animated by the intention to repent and unless it has repentance as its sole aim, if the labor is given a value in itself.

True monastic progress consists in this, that the monk sees himself to be the most sinful of all men. Such was the manner of thought of the true servants of God, true monks. It was formed in them from the right working of the soul. Accompanied by the right working of the soul, even bodily labor has vast significance, being the expression of repentance and humility by acts of the body. "Look upon my humbleness and my hardship, and forgive all my sins,"[2] cries holy David prayerfully to God, combining in his pious effort bodily labor with deep penitence and profound humility.

CHAPTER 22

On Adapting the Cell Rule to the
Monastic Rule

In some Russian communities—extremely few—that follow the rule of the Sarov Monastery, the evening rule is performed in church with bows. In some cenobitic monasteries, the rule is performed without bows. In the majority of monasteries, the evening rule is left to the choice of the brethren, and is performed in the cells by those who wish to do so. In the Sarov Monastery, and in other communities that follow its rule, the labors are so considerable that, over and above the church rule, hardly any of the brethren can perform the cell rule. But some have great bodily strength, so that the physical labors even of the Sarov and Valaam Monasteries are not enough to exhaust their bodies, so vigorous are their constitutions.

For those who have a superabundance of strength, or live in communities in which the rule is not combined with bows, or where there is no common evening rule, we offer the following humble advice: the evening rule should be adapted to the rule given by the angel to St Pachomius the Great. It should be adapted because at the present time, both on account of our feebleness and on account of the generally accepted rules in our monasteries, it is impossible for us to accomplish fully and exactly the rule given by the angel to suit the monks of antiquity. What we have said should cause no offense. Our own monastic discipline is also blessed from on high; it corresponds with our weakness and our time. In conformity with what is prescribed by the rule taught by the angel, the cell rule can assume the following order of prayers: Glory to Thee, Our God, Glory to Thee; Heavenly King; Trisagion; Our Father; Lord Have Mercy (twelve); Come Let Us Worship; Psalm 50; the Creed; and then the Jesus Prayer: "Lord Jesus Christ, Son of God, have mercy on me a sinner."

With the Jesus Prayer, some make twenty prostrations and twenty bows from the waist, others make thirty prostrations and thirty bows, others forty prostrations and forty bows, and so on. It is useful to add some prostrations and bows to the prayer to the Mother of God: "My most holy Lady, Mother of God, save me a sinner." After finishing the appointed number of prostrations and bows, one must on no account remain idle and allow the mind and heart to turn indiscriminately to whatever thoughts and feelings present themselves; one should pass immediately to the set prayers or the Jesus Prayer. Having performed the bodily labor and thereby warmed the body and blood, the ascetic gets a special disposition for spiritual activity as was said above, and unless he at once gives his soul correct and saving activity, it can easily turn to wrong and fatal activity, to vain and harmful considerations and fancies. The fruit obtained by correct bodily labor must be guarded with care and used with profit. The invisible thieves and enemies never sleep! Our own fallen nature will not be slow to produce the weeds[1] that are native to it. The purity, alertness of mind, and compunction of heart obtained by prayer with prostrations must at once be used for prayer without bows, said with the lips unhurriedly and quietly, aloud to oneself, with the enclosure of the mind in the words of the prayer, and with the sympathy of the heart with the words of the prayer.

In communities where the evening rule is not performed in church but in the cells, the "Prayers Before Sleep" should be read after bows. Besides this, those who wish and who feel that they are strong enough read akathists, canons, the Psalter, and the intercession.[2] We must remember that the essence of the work of prayer consists not in the quantity of the prayers read but in reading such prayers as are read with attention and with the sympathy of the heart, so that a deep and strong impression may be left on the soul.[3]

The quantity of prayers needed for the rule is ascertained in the same way as the quantity of bows. Read with due attention and deliberation some prayers that you consider especially nourishing for your soul. Having noted the time the reading took and having figured out how much time you can give to prayer or psalm-reading, make a suitable cell rule of prayer. The reading of the akathists to sweetest Jesus and the Mother of God acts very beneficially on beginners, while for those who have made some progress and have already experienced some illumination of the mind, the reading of the Psalter is to be recommended. For the attentive reading of one kathisma, about twenty minutes is required. The holy Fathers performed the prayerful reading of the psalms and other set-prayers with such unhurriedness—which is indispensable for attention and for enclosing the mind in the words of the prayer—that they called this reading *psalmody* or *psalm-singing*. Psalmody is not singing tunes or music at all, but extremely unhurried reading, which by its slowness resembles singing.

In those communities where the evening rule is performed in church without bows, after completing the rule with bows one should engage not in psalmody but in prayer and on no account allow oneself to be distracted by vain and soul-harming thoughts and fancies. Those monks who for some reason are often forced to stay in their cell without going out, perform the rule with bows on rising from sleep before the morning prayers on account of the beneficial effect of bows on both body and soul as we have explained above.

CHAPTER 23

On the Jesus Prayer

Strictly speaking, by prayer the holy Fathers mean the Jesus Prayer, which is said thus: "Lord Jesus Christ, Son of God, have mercy on me a sinner." St John of the Ladder says of silent contemplatives[1] that "some of them sing and spend most of their time in it, while others persevere in prayer."[2] By the term *singing* we must understand here the prayerful reading of the psalms (there were not at the time of St John of the Ladder the other forms of prayer that are used now), and by the term *prayer,* the Jesus Prayer. The following words of the same Saint have an identical meaning: "Devote the greater part of the night to prayer and only what is left to reading the Psalter."[3] That is how the meaning of the words *prayer* and *psalmody* is explained in St John of the Ladder's work, *The Ladder of Divine Ascent*, and later by the great ascetics and guides of monasticism, St Symeon the New Theologian and St Gregory of Sinai.

The Jesus Prayer is divided into two forms: vocal and mental. The ascetic passes from vocal to mental prayer automatically on this condition: when vocal prayer is attentive. At first the Jesus Prayer should be practiced vocally. The Jesus Prayer is performed standing; but in the event of weakness or exhaustion it may be performed sitting, or even lying down. The essential properties of this prayer should be attention, the enclosure of the mind in the words of the prayer, extreme unhurriedness in pronouncing it, and contrition of spirit. Although these conditions are necessary for all prayer, they are more easily observed and more needed in the practice of the Jesus Prayer. In psalmody, the diversity of thought in which prayer is clothed involuntarily attracts the attention of the mind and causes it some diversion. But in the case of the Jesus Prayer, the mind is concentrated on a single thought: the thought of the sinner's forgiveness by Jesus. Outwardly this activity is the most dry, but in practice it proves to be the most fruitful of all the soul's activities. Its power and value derive from the all-powerful, all-holy name of the Lord Jesus Christ.

Prophesying about the God-Man, the Prophet Joel foretold, "Whoever calls on the name of the Lord shall be saved."[4] The holy Apostle Paul repeats this prophet's words.[5] "If you confess with your mouth," he says, "the Lord Jesus, and believe in your heart that God has raised Him from the dead, you will be saved."[6] The holy Apostle Peter, after healing a man who had been lame from his birth by the name of the Lord Jesus Christ, bore witness before the Jewish Sanhedrin in the following words: "Rulers of the people and elders of Israel: If we *[the holy Apostles Peter and John]* this day are judged for good deed done to a helpless man, by what means he has been made well, let it be known to you all, and to all the people of Israel, that in the name of Jesus Christ of Nazareth, whom you crucified, whom God raised from the dead, by Him this man stands here before you whole.... For there is no other name under heaven given among men by which we must be saved."[7]

The use of the all-holy, divine name *Jesus* in prayer, and prayer in His name, was appointed by our Lord Jesus Christ Himself. We can be convinced of this from the most sublime and profound conversation recorded in the Gospel of St John[8] which the Lord had with the holy apostles after the Mystical Supper, in that momentous hour that preceded the Lord's voluntary departure to the place of His betrayal and agony, for the salvation of mankind. The teaching given by the Lord in that hour has the character of a final, deathbed instruction in which He gathered and expounded before His disciples, and in their persons before the whole of Christendom, the most soul-saving and final commandments, sure and infallible pledges of eternal life.

Among other pledges and spiritual gifts, there is given and ratified the command and permission to pray by the name of Jesus: "Whatever you ask in My name, that I will do, that the Father may be glorified in the Son. If you ask anything in My name, I will do it."[9] "Most assuredly, I say to you, whatever you ask the Father in My name He will give you. Until now you have asked nothing in My name. Ask, and you will receive, that your joy may be full."[10]

What is it that will be given to a person who prays in the name of the Lord Jesus that can fill him to overflowing with joy? He will be given—we reply in the words of our Lord—the Holy Spirit "Whom the Father will send in My name."[11] This knowledge, based on experience, belongs to the holy Fathers, and is their tradition.[12]

CHAPTER 24

On the Practice of the Jesus Prayer

I f you live in a monastery where the evening rule is performed with bows in
church, then on returning to your cell engage at once in the Jesus Prayer.
If you live in a monastery where the evening rule is performed in church but
without bows, then on returning to your cell first perform the rule with bows
and after that get busy with the Jesus Prayer. If you belong to a monastery
where there is no common evening rule but it is left to each one individu-
ally to perform it in his cell, first perform the rule with bows, then engage in
prayer or psalmody, and finally the Jesus Prayer.

At first set yourself to say a hundred Jesus Prayers unhurriedly and with
attention. Later, if you see that you can say more, add another hundred.
In course of time, if need be, you can still further increase the number of
prayers said. To say a hundred prayers attentively and unhurriedly about
half an hour is needed; but some ascetics require even longer. Do not say the
prayers hurriedly, one immediately after another. Make a short pause after
each prayer, and so help the mind to concentrate. Saying the prayer without
pauses distracts the mind. Breathe with care, gently and slowly; this precaution prevents distraction. When you have finished praying the Jesus Prayer
do not give yourself up to different considerations and dreams, always empty,
seductive, and deceptive; but according to the guidance received in the work
of prayer, pass the time till sleep. On going to sleep, repeat the prayer; fall
asleep with it.

So train yourself that on waking from sleep your first thought, your first
word and action is the Jesus Prayer. Say it a few times, get out of bed, and
hurry to Matins. During Matins, whenever possible, engage in the Jesus
Prayer. If you have some free time between Matins and the liturgy, engage in
the Jesus Prayer. Do exactly the same after dinner as well. The Fathers advise
us after dinner to occupy ourselves with the remembrance of death. That is
perfectly correct, but actually the living Jesus Prayer is inseparable from a

living remembrance of death.[1] A living remembrance of death is linked with living prayer to the Lord Jesus Who abolished death and gave men life eternal by His temporary subjection to death.

During the church services, it is useful to practice the Jesus Prayer. It prevents distraction and helps the mind to attend to the church singing and reading. Try to train yourself to the Jesus Prayer to such an extent that it becomes your unceasing prayer, for which it is very convenient on account of its brevity and for which long prayers are unsuitable. The Fathers have said, "A monk, whether he is eating or drinking, whether he is in his cell or engaged on an obedience, whether he is traveling or doing anything else, must unceasingly cry, 'Lord Jesus Christ, Son of God, have mercy on me a sinner.'"

CHAPTER 25

On Unceasing Prayer

Unceasing prayer was enjoined by God Himself. The Savior of the world said, "Ask, and it will be given you; seek, and you will find; knock, and it will be opened to you." [1] "And shall God not avenge his own elect who cry out day and night to Him, though He bears long with them? I tell you that He will avenge them speedily." [2]

The Apostle Paul repeats the Lord's teaching and says: "Pray without ceasing" [3] "I desire therefore that the men pray everywhere, lifting up holy hands, without wrath and doubting." [4] By the term *men* the Apostle means Christians who have attained to Christian perfection. Only mature or perfect Christians can pray "without wrath and doubting," that is, in profound peace, with the purest love for one's neighbor and without the least resentment or criticism of him, without the distraction of irrelevant thoughts and imaginations (without doubting). Such people can at all times and in all places offer prayer to God, raising and lifting up to Him holy hands, the mind and heart being purified of the passions and sanctified by the Spirit.

It is obvious that unceasing prayer cannot be the possession of a novice; but in order to become eventually capable of unceasing prayer he must practice frequent prayer. Frequent prayer in due time passes automatically into unceasing prayer. Because the easiest way of practicing unceasing prayer is to pray the Jesus Prayer, a beginner should apply himself to the Jesus Prayer as often as possible. Do you happen to have a moment free? Do not waste it in idleness! Do not waste it by using it for some impracticable and fatuous castle-building, or for some vain and trivial employment! Use it for the practice of the Jesus Prayer.

If from weakness or, more correctly, on account of your fallen nature, you happen to be distracted by alluring thoughts and fancies, do not get despondent and do not grow slack. Repent before God of your levity and frivolity, confess your fallen nature and your distraction, fall down mentally before

75

His mercy, and take precautionary measures against seductive dreams and seductive thoughts.

He who does not train himself to frequent prayer will never receive unceasing prayer. Unceasing prayer is a gift of God, given by God to a slave and servant of His of proven fidelity. "It is impossible to draw near to God other than by unceasing prayer."[5] Unceasing prayer is a sign of God's mercy toward a man; it is a sign that all the powers of his soul are bent on God.

Have mercy upon me, O Lord,
for I will call upon Thee all day.
Give joy to the soul of Thy servant,
for unto Thee have I lifted up my soul.[6]

CHAPTER 26

On the Oral, Mental, and Cordial Jesus Prayer

He who wishes to avoid all error in practicing the Jesus Prayer should test himself and his exercises by frequently reading the following writings of the Fathers: (1) the article on sobriety[1] by St Hesychius of Jerusalem; (2) the chapters on sobriety[1] by St Philotheus of Sinai; (3) the discourses on secret activity in Christ by St Theoleptus, Metropolitan of Philadelphia; (4) the works of St Symeon the New Theologian and St Gregory of Sinai; (5) the articles of St Nicephorus and the writings of Saints Kallistus and Ignatius Xanthopoulos; (6) the traditions of St Nil Sorsky; (7) St Dorotheus' *Symposium*; and more.

The reader will find in *The Philokalia* in St Symeon the New Theologian's article "On the Three Ways of Prayer," in St Nicephorus' article, and in the writings of Saints Kallistus and Ignatius Xanthopoulos, instruction on the art of leading the mind into the heart with the help of natural breathing, or in other words, a mechanism or technique that assists the acquisition of mental prayer. This teaching of the Fathers has caused and continues to cause difficulty to many readers, though there is really no difficulty in it. We advise beloved brethren not to try to discover this mechanism within them if it does not reveal itself of its own accord. Many wishing to learn it by experience have damaged their lungs and gained nothing. The essence of the matter consists in the union of the mind with the heart during prayer, and this is achieved by the grace of God in its own time, determined by God. The above mechanism is fully replaced by the unhurried enunciation of the prayer, by a short rest or pause after each prayer, by gentle and unhurried breathing, and by the enclosure of the mind in the words of the prayer. By means of these aids we can easily attain to a certain degree of attention. The attention of the mind at prayer very soon begins to attract the sympathy of the heart. Sympathy of the heart and mind little by little begins to pass into a union of the mind with the heart, and then the mechanism offered by the Fathers appears

77

of its own accord. All the mechanical means having a material character are offered by the Fathers solely as aids to the attainment of attention in prayer as easily and quickly as possible, and not as something essential.

The essential, indispensable property of prayer is attention. Without attention there is no prayer. True grace-given attention comes from the mortification of our heart to the world.[2] Aids always remain merely aids. The same holy Fathers who suggest that we should lead the mind into the heart with the breathing say that when the mind has acquired the habit of uniting with the heart (or, more correctly, when it has obtained this union by the gift and action of grace), it does not need the help of a mechanism for this union, but simply of its own accord and by its own proper movement it unites with the heart. And it must be so. The separation of the mind from the heart, and their opposition to one another, have resulted from our fall into sin. It is natural for divine grace, when it stretches out its finger to heal a man, crushed and broken to pieces by his fall, to join together his severed parts and to unite the mind not only with the heart and soul but even with the body, and to give it a single, true ardor[3] for God.

With the union of the mind and heart the ascetic receives the power to resist all passionate thoughts and passionate feelings. Can this be the result of any technique? No! It is the result of grace; it is a fruit of the Holy Spirit Who overshadows the unseen labor of the Christian ascetic; and it is incomprehensible to carnal and natural men.

In reading the Fathers about the place of the heart that the mind discovers by prayer, we are to understand the spiritual power of the heart placed by the Creator in the upper part of the heart.[4] It is this power that distinguishes the human heart from the hearts of animals, who have the power of the will or desire and power of jealousy or anger equally with human beings. The power of spirituality is expressed in the conscience, or in the consciousness of our spirit (it is quite independent of knowledge),[5] in the fear of God, in spiritual love for God and our neighbor, in a feeling of penitence, humility, meekness, in contrition of spirit or deep sorrow for sin, and in other spiritual emotions unknown to animals. The power of the soul is the mind, and although it is spiritual, yet it has its seat in the brain. So, too, the power of spirituality, or the spirit of man, though spiritual, has its seat in the upper part of the heart that is under the left nipple of the breast, near the nipple and slightly above it.

The union of the mind with the heart is the union of the spiritual thoughts of the mind with the spiritual feelings of the heart. Since man has fallen, since his thoughts and feelings have been changed from spiritual into carnal and earthly thoughts and feelings, it is necessary by means of the commandments of the Gospel to lift up the mind and spirit to spiritual thoughts and feelings. When mind and spirit are healed, then they are united in the Lord. In that section of the heart where the power of spirituality or the spirit resides, there will gradually come to be formed the wonderful, spiritual temple of God, the Holy of Holies not made with human hands. Thither the mind, ordained a priest or high priest by the Holy Spirit, descends for the worship of God in the Spirit and in Truth.[6] Then the Christian knows by blessed experience what is said in Holy Scripture: "You are the temple of the living God. As God has said, 'I will dwell in them and walk among them. I will be their God, and they shall be My people.'"[7]

Below the power of spirituality, in the center of the heart, is located the power of jealousy; below it, in the lower part of the heart, is located the power of desire and will. In animals, these two powers act very crudely, since they are not in the least connected with spirituality; in people, they act according to the extent and manner in which their spirit is developed. But they can act rightly and be in complete subjection to the spirit or spiritual power only in a true Christian who has banished not only the obviously sinful but even all natural thoughts and feelings before the knowledge[8] of Christ—the Gospel.

Mind and heart cannot be united other than by the mediation of the Spirit and Truth. This means that the mind and heart cannot be united unless we completely renounce our fallen nature, unless we surrender ourselves entirely to the guidance of the Gospel, unless we attract the grace of the Holy Spirit to heal us by constant and increased[9] obedience to the Gospel commandments, unless we are healed and restored to life by the touch of grace, by the overshadowing of the Spirit.

Not only does every sinful emotion and every sinful thought disrupt this union, even all natural thoughts and feelings, however subtle and disguised by an appearance of righteousness, destroy the union of the mind with the heart, and set them in opposition to one another. Any deviation from the spiritual direction supplied by the Gospel renders all aids and techniques useless; heart and mind will never unite.

The fulfillment of the commandments that precedes the union of the mind with the heart differs from the fulfillment of the commandments that succeeds the union. Before the union, the ascetic fulfills the commandments with the greatest labor and difficulty, forcing and compelling his fallen nature; after the union, the spiritual power that unites the mind with the heart impels him to fulfill the commandments—makes it easy, light, sweet, delightful. "I ran the way of Thy commandments, when Thou didst enlarge my heart," says the psalmist.[10]

For one practicing the Jesus Prayer, it is extremely useful to read through the Notes (Introductions) of Schemamonk Basil (Polianomeroulsky) to the books of Saints Gregory of Sinai, Hesychius of Jerusalem, Philotheus of Sinai, and Nil Sorsky.[11] After reading these notes, the reading of the whole *Philokalia* becomes much clearer and more profitable. In reading the Fathers we should also not lose sight of the fact that the standard of a novice of their time is the standard of a very advanced person in our time. The application of the Fathers' teaching to oneself and to one's own activity must be carried out with great circumspection.

CHAPTER 27

On Divine Meditation

St Dimitry of Rostov and St Tikhon of Voronezh practiced divine meditation—that is, holy reflection on the incarnation of God the Word, on His wonderful life on earth, on His terrible and saving sufferings, on His most glorious resurrection and ascension to heaven; as well as on man, his destiny, his fall, his renewal by the redeemer, and on the other deep mysteries of Christianity.

The holy reflections of the above saints are superbly propounded in their writings. St Peter of Damascus, in common with other ascetic writers, ranks such reflections among spiritual visions, and in the category of visions he assigns them to the fourth degree. Every spiritual vision is a sight of mysteries of some kind, which manifest themselves in the ascetic in accordance with his purification by repentance, as can be seen in the book of St Peter of Damascus. Repentance has its degrees, and spiritual visions have their degrees. The mysteries of Christianity are revealed to the ascetic by degrees, according to his spiritual proficiency. The divine meditations or pious reflections of Saints Dimitry and Tikhon serve as an expression of their spiritual proficiency. Let him who desires exercises in divine meditation read the writings of these saints. Such divine meditation will be the most immune to error and the most profitable for the soul. On the other hand, meditation becomes very wrong and harmful if, before purification by penance[1] and without having any exact grasp of Christian doctrine, the ascetic allows himself self-willed reflection, which cannot fail to be erroneous and therefore cannot fail to produce harmful results and self-deception, cannot fail to lead to the precipice of fatal error.

The saints had been trained with all precision and detail in Orthodox theology, and then by their holy life they had risen to the height of Christian perfection. Divine meditation was natural for them. It is not natural for an ascetic who has no fundamental or precise grasp of theology, and has not been purified by penance.[1] For this reason it was forbidden by the holy

81

Fathers to novices, and in fact to all monks in general who had not been prepared for it by study and had not reached it by their way of life. St John of the Ladder says, "Deep is the depth of the dogmas, and not without risk does the mind of the hesychast caper among them. It is not safe to swim in one's clothes, nor should a slave of passion touch theology."[2] Such words are a warning to hesychasts, and it is common knowledge that only proficient monks are allowed to practice hesychasm.[3]

In ancient times very many monks fell into fatal heresy solely because they allowed themselves to investigate dogmas beyond their powers of comprehension. "A humble monk," St John of the Ladder again teaches, "will not meddle with mysteries, but a proud one will pry into the divine judgments."[4] Very true! In one who is immature and unfit for it, the desire to undertake divine meditation is the suggestion of conceit, is a proud and imprudent desire. Exercise yourself in prayer and in soul-building reading, and this exercise will be an exercise in divine meditation that is right, safe, and pleasing to God.

Just as our eyes of sense when healed of blindness see by their own natural property, so, too, our mind when purified of the disease of sin naturally begins to see the mysteries of Christianity. Rely on God in your efforts. If it is necessary for you and for the general benefit of Christianity that you should be a seer of deep mysteries and a preacher of them to your brethren, God will certainly grant you that gift. But if that is not the will of God, strive for that which is essentially necessary for your salvation and which fully satisfies the demands of that need. Endeavor to acquire pure prayer combined with a sense of penitence and mourning, with the remembrance of death, of God's judgment, and of the frightful dungeons of hell where eternal fire blazes and eternal darkness reigns. Such prayer combined with such recollections is an unerring, excellent form of divine meditation, and of the greatest profit to the soul.

CHAPTER 28

On the Remembrance of Death

A monk should remember every day, and several times a day, that he is faced with inevitable death, and eventually he should even attain to the unceasing remembrance of death.

Our mind is so darkened by the fall that unless we force ourselves to remember death we can completely forget about it. When we forget about death, then we begin to live on earth as if we were immortal, and we sacrifice all our activity to the world without concerning ourselves in the least either about the fearful transition to eternity or about our fate in eternity. Then we boldly and peremptorily override the commandments of Christ; then we commit all the vilest sins; then we abandon not only unceasing prayer but even the prayers appointed for definite times—we begin to scorn this essential and indispensable occupation as if it were an activity of little importance and little need. Forgetful of physical death, we die a spiritual death.

On the other hand, he who often remembers the death of the body rises from the dead in soul.[1] He lives on earth like a stranger in an inn or like a prisoner in jail, constantly expecting to be called out for trial or execution. Before his eyes the gates into eternity are always open. He continually looks in that direction with spiritual anxiety, with deep sorrow and reflection. He is constantly occupied with wondering what will justify him at Christ's terrible judgment and what his sentence will be. This sentence decides a person's fate for the whole of eternity. No earthly beauty, no earthly pleasure draws his attention or his love. He condemns no one, for he remembers that at the judgment of God such judgment will be passed on him as he passed here on his neighbors. He forgives everyone and everything, that he may himself obtain forgiveness and inherit salvation. He is indulgent with all, he is merciful in everything, that indulgence and mercy may be shown to him. He welcomes and embraces with joy every trouble or trial that comes to him as a toll for his sins in time, which frees him from paying a toll in eternity. If the thought comes to him to be proud of his virtue, at once the remembrance of death rushes against this thought, puts it to shame, exposes the nonsense and drives it away.

What significance can our virtue have in the judgment of God? What value can our virtue have in the eyes of God to Whom even Heaven is impure?[2] Remind and remind yourself: "I shall die, I shall die for certain! My fathers and forefathers died; no human being has remained forever on earth. And the fate that has overtaken everyone awaits me too!" Do not fritter away the time given you for repentance. Do not rivet your eyes to the earth on which you are a momentary actor, on which you are an exile, on which by the mercy of God you are given a chance to change your mind and offer repentance for the avoidance of hell's eternal prisons and the eternal torment in them. Use the short spell of your pilgrimage on earth to acquire a haven of peace, a blessed refuge in eternity. Plead for the eternal possession by renouncing every temporal possession, by renouncing everything carnal and natural in the realm of our fallen nature. Plead by the fulfillment of Christ's commandments. Plead by sincere repentance for the sins you have committed. Plead by thanking and praising God for all the trials and troubles sent you. Plead by an abundance of prayer and psalmody. Plead by means of the Jesus Prayer and combine with it the remembrance of death.

These two activities—the Jesus Prayer and the remembrance of death—easily merge into one activity. From the prayer comes a vivid remembrance of death, as if it were a foretaste of it; and from this foretaste of death the prayer itself flares up more vigorously.

It is essential for the ascetic to remember death. This remembrance is essential for his spiritual life. It protects the spiritual life of the monk from harm and corruption by self-confidence,[3] to which the ascetic and attentive life can lead unless it is guarded by the remembrance of death and God's judgment. It is a great disaster for the soul to set any value on one's own effort or struggle, and to regard it as a merit in the sight of God. Admit that you deserve all earthly punishment as well as the eternal torments. Such an appraisal of yourself will be the truest, the most salutary for your soul, and the most pleasing to God.

Frequently enumerate the eternal woes that await sinners. By frequently docketing these miseries make them stand vividly before your eyes. Acquire a foretaste of the torments of hell so that at the graphic remembrance of them your soul may shudder, may tear itself away from sin, and may have recourse to God with humble prayer for mercy, putting all your hope in His infinite goodness and despairing of yourself. Recall and represent to yourself the terrible measureless subterranean gulf and prison that constitute hell. The gulf or pit is called bottomless.[4] Precisely! That is just what it is in relation to men. The vast prison of hell has many sections and many different kinds of torment and torture by which every man is repaid according to the deeds he has done in the course of his earthly life. In all sections imprisonment is eternal, the torments eternal. There, insufferable, impenetrable darkness reigns, and at the same time the unquenchable fire burns there with an ever equal strength. There is no day there. There it is always eternal night. The stench there is insupportable, and it cannot be compared with the foulest earthly fetor. The terrible worm of hell never slumbers or sleeps. It gnaws and gnaws, and devours the prisoners of hell without impairing their wholeness or destroying their existence, and without ever being glutted itself. Such is the nature of all the torments of hell; they are worse than any death, but they do not produce death. Death is desired in hell as much as life is desired on earth. Death would be a comfort for all the prisoners of hell. It is not for them. Their fate is unending life for unending suffering. Lost souls in hell are tormented by the insufferable executions with which the eternal prison of those rejected by God abounds; they are tormented there by the unendurable grief; they are tormented there by that most ghastly disease of the soul—despair.

Acknowledge that you are sentenced to hell for eternal torment, and from that acknowledgment there will be born in your heart such irresistible and mighty cries of prayer that they will inevitably incline God to have mercy on you, and He will lead you into Paradise instead of hell.

You who consider yourselves deserving of earthly and heavenly rewards! For you, hell is more dangerous than for flagrant sinners because the gravest sin among all the sins is pride, self-opinion, self-confidence—a sin of the spirit invisible to mortal eyes and which is often covered with a mask of humility.

The remembrance and consideration of death was practiced by the greatest of the holy Fathers. Of Pachomius the Great, the author of his life says that he "maintained himself constantly in the fear of God with the remembrance of the eternal torments and pains which have no end—that is, with the remembrance of the unquenchable fire and the undying worm. By this means Pachomius kept himself from evil and roused to the better."[5]

CHAPTER 29

The Narrow Way Is Designed by God Himself

Our Lord Jesus Christ spent His earthly life in the greatest humility, subject to constant hardship[1] and maltreatment, persecuted, slandered and libeled by His enemies who finally condemned Him to a shameful death with common criminals. The way of salvation that leads to eternal life is "narrow ... and difficult."[2] It is appointed both by our Lord's holy example and by His holy teaching. The Lord foretold to His disciples and followers that "in the world," that is, during their earthly life, they would have "tribulation" that the world would "hate" them, that they would be persecuted and killed.[3] The Lord compared the position of His disciples and followers in the midst of vicious humanity to the position of "sheep in the midst of wolves."[4] From this it is clear that sorrow and suffering are appointed by the Lord Himself for His true slaves and servants during their life on earth. What is appointed by God is impossible to prevent by any human being, by any kind of wisdom, or prudence, or forethought, or care. Therefore, he who enters the monastic life must give himself up wholly to the will and guidance of God, and must be prepared to endure all such sufferings as the providence of the all-highest may be pleased to permit to His servant during his earthly pilgrimage. Sacred Scripture says, "My son, if you draw near to serve the Lord, prepare your soul for temptation. Set your heart right and be steadfast, and do not strive anxiously in distress. Cleave to Him and do not fall away, that you may be honored at the end of your life. Accept whatever is brought upon you, and in exchange for your humiliation, be patient; because gold is tested in fire and acceptable men in the furnace of abasement."[5]

Why has the Lord reserved for His true slaves afflictions during their earthly life, while for His enemies He has provided prosperity, material success, and material goods? The carnal mind says, "It ought to have been arranged in just the opposite way." This is the reason. Man is a fallen being. He was cast down to earth from Paradise where he had brought death upon himself by transgressing God's commandment.⁶ Immediately after the transgression, death struck the human soul and incurably infected the body. The body, the life of which is the soul, was not separated from the soul immediately after the fall; but the soul, the life of which is the Holy Spirit, immediately after the fall was separated from the Holy Spirit, Who abandoned it as defiled and poisoned by sin, and left it to itself. With such a dead soul, and with a body alive with the life of an animal, the first man was cast down to the earth for a certain time, and the rest of men are born and remain on earth for a limited time. At the end of this time of so-called earthly life, the body also finally succumbs to death, having been harassed by it and having struggled with it during the whole of its earthly life.

Earthly life—this brief period—is given to man by the mercy of the Creator in order that man may use it for his salvation, that is, for the restoration of himself from death to life. Salvation, or the revival of man by the Holy Spirit, is accomplished by means of the Redeemer or Savior, our Lord Jesus Christ. Men born before the coming of the Redeemer were to seek salvation by faith in the promised Redeemer and to receive salvation after the accomplishment of redemption by the Redeemer. Those born after the coming of the Redeemer were to seek salvation by faith in the Redeemer who had come and were to receive salvation even during their earthly life, and final and immutable salvation immediately after the separation of the soul from the body and after the particular judgment. Everyone who believes in the Savior must necessarily acknowledge and confess his fall and his state of exile on earth; he must acknowledge and confess it by his actual life so that his acknowledgment and confession may be living and effective, and not dead and ineffectual. Otherwise, he cannot properly acknowledge the Redeemer, because a Redeemer and Savior is needed only for those who are fallen and perishing; He is quite superfluous and cannot be of any use to those who do not wish to acknowledge and confess their fall, their perdition. To confess one's fall by one's life means to bear all the sufferings of this earthly life as a just recompense for the fall, as a rational and logical consequence of one's sinfulness, and constantly to refuse all pleasures as improper for a criminal and exile who has angered God and has been rejected by God. Temporal earthly life is merely the forecourt to eternal life. And to what kind of life? To eternal life in the prisons of hell amid the most frightful, hellish torments, if during our short life on earth we do not make use of the redemption given free of charge—a redemption the acceptance or refusal of which is left to the free will of each human being. Earthly life is a place of tasting miseries and sufferings, a place of contemplating miseries and sufferings incomparably greater than earthly sufferings. Earthly life offers nothing joyful, nothing comforting, except the hope of salvation. "Blessed are you who weep now," now during the time of your earthly pilgrimage, our Redeemer has said to us, and "woe to you who laugh now."[7]

> The whole Christian life on earth is nothing but penitence expressed in action, in personal repentance. Christ came to call us to repentance. Pay special attention to His words: I came to call sinners to repentance[8] Our Lord offers us here not merry-making, not food, not walks and joyrides, not banquets and dances, but penitence, weeping, tears, lamentation and the cross. You see how a Christian should spend his life on earth! You will see it by reading the Gospel of Christ. There is joy for Christians here, too, but it is spiritual. They rejoice not over gold, silver, food, drink, honor and glory, but in God their Savior, in His goodness and mercy to them, in the hope of eternal life.[9]

The Lord, having taken upon Himself humanity and all human infirmities except sin, also took upon Himself a vivid realization of the fallen state into which the whole human race had cast itself. He spent His earthly life in constant sufferings, without ever uttering a word of displeasure against those sufferings. On the contrary, He called them the chalice given Him by His heavenly Father which He must drink and drain to the dregs unquestioningly. The innocent and all-holy Lord, having suffered in His assumed humanity for guilty and sin-infected mankind, has provided suffering as the way of salvation for all His followers, for all His spiritual tribe and family, in practical realization of their fall and sinfulness, in active acknowledgment and confession of the Savior, in active union with Him, one with Him. At the same time He infuses into the sufferings of His servants from His own sufferings unspeakable spiritual consolation in proof positive of the truth of salvation, and of the truth of the way of suffering which leads to salvation. The innocent and all-holy Lord spent His earthly life in sufferings; still more should the guilty suffer, fully aware that they deserve to suffer. They should rejoice that by means of brief sufferings they are delivered from eternal sufferings and join the ranks of the followers and friends of the God-Man. He who refuses sufferings and does not consider that he deserves them, does not acknowledge his fall and perdition. He who has used his earthly life merely for earthly success foolishly mistakes this briefest spell for eternity and regards eternity as nonexistent—and he prepares himself for eternal misery! He who does not acknowledge his fall and perdition does not acknowledge his Savior and rejects Him. The acknowledgment of oneself as deserving of temporal and eternal punishments precedes the knowledge of the Savior and leads to the knowledge of the Savior, as we see from the example of the robber who inherited Paradise.[10] Perhaps you will say that the robber was a flagrant criminal, and therefore confession was easy for him, but how is a person who has committed no crime to make a confession of that sort? We reply that the other robber who was crucified beside the Lord was also a flagrant criminal, but he did not acknowledge his sinfulness because awareness of sin is a result of love and humility, while unawareness is a result of pride and hardness of heart. God's saints were constantly aware that they were sinners, in spite of the obvious spiritual gifts with which they were so lavishly endowed. On the other hand, the greatest evildoers and criminals have always justified themselves. While drowning in crime, they never stopped proclaiming their virtue.

The Holy Spirit says of the saints of the Old Covenant that they all lived their earthly life "destitute, afflicted, tormented" confessing by their actual life "that they were strangers and pilgrims on the earth."[11] Then—addressing the true servants of God who were his contemporaries and directing them to Jesus, the Author and Perfecter of our faith, Who instead of the glory that was due to and belonged to Him, chose to endure dishonor and the cross— the Apostle Paul utters the following exhortation: "Therefore Jesus also, that He might sanctify the people with His own blood, suffered outside the gate. Therefore let us go forth to Him outside the camp, bearing His reproach."[12] *Outside the camp*, that is, renouncing and abandoning all that the fickle, passing world regards as desirable; *bearing His reproach*, that is, taking our share of the way of the cross appointed by the Lord and followed by Him throughout His life of suffering on earth. All true Christians have responded to this call and, having left the camp that is utterly fickle and alien to all stability and soundness, they followed the path of suffering to the eternal, heavenly city. "If you are without chastening," says the Apostle Paul, "of which all have become partakers, then you are illegitimate and not sons."[13] Here you should note the word *all:* all the saints lived their earthly life in troubles and hardships; not one of them reached heaven by following the broad way of earthly prosperity. "For whom the Lord loves He chastens, and scourges every son whom He receives."[14] "As many as I love, I rebuke and chasten,"[15] said the Lord in the Revelation to St John the Theologian. Instructed by these testimonies of the Holy Spirit and by many others scattered throughout the pages of Holy Scripture, we boldly affirm: troubles sent to a man by the providence of God are a true sign of the man's election by God. When Jesus loved the young man, He offered him the following of Himself and the bearing of the cross.[16] Let us not refuse the call! The call is accepted if, when trouble comes, a Christian admits that he deserves trouble. A Christian follows the Lord with his cross when he thanks and glorifies God for the troubles sent him, when he does not count his life dear to himself,[17] when he completely surrenders himself to the will of God, especially the commandment of love for one's enemies. Suffering is so true a sign of one's election that the Holy Spirit greets those who undergo tribulations with a heavenly greeting. *Rejoice*, He cries to them, *rejoice!* "Count it all joy," that is, supreme joy, "when you fall into various trials."[18] "Blessed are you when [men] revile and persecute you and say all kinds of evil against you falsely for My sake. Rejoice and be exceedingly glad, for great is your reward in heaven."[19] The holy Apostle Peter tells Christians that their vocation is suffering.[20] Such is the divine appointment for man during his earthly life. He must believe in the Redeemer, confess Him with heart and mouth, confess Him by his action by obediently accepting whatever cross Jesus is pleased to lay upon His disciple. He who has not accepted the cross cannot be a disciple of Jesus![21] "Let those who suffer according to the will of God commit their souls to Him in doing good, as to a faithful Creator."[22] The Creator of our souls is the Lord. He creates the souls of those who believe in Him by troubles. Let us give ourselves up to His will and providence, and let us make every effort ourselves to carry out the commandments of the Gospel. When a Christian surrenders himself to the will of God, denies himself and casts all his cares on God, he thanks and glorifies Him for the cross. Then the extraordinary spiritual power of faith suddenly appears in his heart; then unutterable spiritual consolation suddenly appears in his heart; Jesus seals the disciple who has accepted His call with the Spirit—and earthly sufferings become a source of delight for the servant of God. On the other hand, a sorrowless earthly life is a true sign that the Lord has turned His face from a man, and that he is displeasing to God, even though outwardly he may seem reverent and virtuous.

Sang the holy Prophet David, "Many are the troubles of the righteous, but the Lord delivereth them out of all."[23] How true that is! All who truly serve the Lord, who are righteous with the Redeemer's righteousness and not with their own fallen and false righteousness, are permitted to have many troubles. But all these troubles disperse of their own accord. Not one of them can crush the servant of God. They purify, perfect him. Not a word did the Prophet say about the troubles of sinners who live on earth for earthly pleasures and earthly success. Troubles are not given to them. What is the good of troubles for them? They do not bear them with thanksgiving, but they only increase their sins by grumbling, despondency, blasphemy against God, and despair. The Lord provides for them to enjoy earthly goods till the very end, so that they may come to their senses at least on account of their prosperity. He sends troubles only to those sinners in whom He foresees conversion, who according to God's foreknowledge are already inscribed in the book of life among the number of the righteous, made righteous (or justified) by the righteousness of the Redeemer. Intentional and willful sinners, in whom there is no promise of repentance and amendment, the Lord does not consider worthy of troubles, as having rejected the teaching of Christ, as having shown no zeal to follow Christ, as having entered the way of sin neither through impulse[24] nor through ignorance. Sufferings in Christ are Christ's greatest gift, given to those who have wholeheartedly surrendered themselves to Christ's service. Holy David, having mentioned the many sufferings to which the righteous are subjected, said nothing about the sufferings of sinners. Being bastards and not sons, they do not attract to themselves the Lord's discipline. David speaks only about their death, that it is "terrible."[25] Exactly! Terrible indeed is the death of sinners, forgotten, unexpected. It takes them suddenly from the midst of abundant pleasure and hurls them into an abyss of eternal torments. To comfort the servant of God who lives on earth in privations and hardships, David says to him:

> Fret not thyself at him whose way doth prosper,
> at the man that doeth after evil counsels....
> Fret not thyself because of the wicked,
> neither be envious against them that do unlawfulness,
> for they shall soon wither like the grass,
> and quickly fall away even as the green herb.[26]

The Prophet David says in the person of the ascetic whose carnal mind is still shaking: "I was envious of the wicked, seeing the peace of sinners, For there is no fear in their death;"[27] that is, no affliction rouses them from their spiritual torpor, from their deadly sleep, from spiritual death. "They are not in the labor of other folk, neither are they plagued like other men."[28]

By men here is meant servants of the true God who have preserved their human dignity. They exercise themselves in pious voluntary labors and are subjected to the Lord's involuntary discipline. Rejected sinners, living in carelessness, share neither labors nor sufferings. And what is the result? "Therefore hath their pride mastered them utterly; they have clothed themselves in their unrighteousness and impiety."[29] All consciousness of their sinfulness is destroyed in them. An immense, incurable conceit makes its appearance. A sinful life becomes their inseparable property, just as if it were their constant garment or clothing, which in turn becomes their disgrace and consists in ignorance of God, in false conceptions of God and of every doctrine revealed by God. That is the state in which death finds willful impenitent sinners, and it snatches them away and places them at the judgment of God.

Sacred Scripture connects the idea of trial (temptation) with the idea of reproof (exposure)! "My son, do not despise the chastening of the Lord, nor be discouraged when you are rebuked by Him."[30] This is also evident from those previously quoted words of the Lord, "As many as I love, I rebuke and chasten."[31] Why is rebuke connected with trial? It is because every affliction discloses the passions hidden in the heart and puts them in motion. Till trouble comes, a man imagines himself calm and peaceful. But when trouble comes, then passions of which he was unaware rise up and make themselves felt, especially anger, sorrow, despondency, pride, unbelief. Fundamentally necessary and good for the ascetic is the exposure of sin that nestles secretly within him. Besides this, troubles accepted and borne in the proper manner increase faith; they show the man his weakness, induce humility, and reduce self-confidence. The Apostle Paul, in recalling one of his trials, says, "We do not want you to be ignorant, brethren, of our trouble which came to us in Asia; that we were burdened beyond measure, above strength, so that we despaired even of life. Yes, we had the sentence of death in ourselves, that we should not trust in ourselves but in God who raises the dead, who delivered us from so great a death, and does deliver us; in whom we trust that He will still deliver us."[32]

Our heart, doomed after the fall to the production of thorns and thistles, is especially prone to pride, unless it is tilled with troubles. Even a saint richly endowed with spiritual gifts is not immune to this danger. The Apostle Paul says frankly that the great afflictions that befell him were permitted by God's providence in order to preserve him from pride, into which he might have fallen not for some trivial reason, but on account of the abundance of his divine revelations and visions. Before the Apostle knew the cause of his temptations, he prayed to God three times that the temptations which were such a hindrance to the success of his preaching might be removed; but when he knew their cause, he cried, "Therefore I take pleasure in infirmities, in reproaches, in needs, in persecutions, in distresses, for Christ's sake.... But God forbid that I should boast except in the cross of our Lord Jesus Christ, by whom the world has been crucified to me, and I to the world."[33]

Having entered a holy community, let us voluntarily refuse pleasures that depend on us, and let us endure generously such troubles as, quite independently of ourselves, will be permitted us by the providence of God. Let us surrender ourselves with faith wholly to the hands of our Creator and the Builder of our souls. He not only created us, but He also builds[34] the souls of those who wish to be His servants. He builds us by the sacraments of the Church, He builds us by the commandments of the Gospel, He builds us by various troubles and trials, He builds us by His grace. "My Father is the vinedresser," said the Lord. "Every branch in Me that does not bear fruit He takes away; and every branch that bears fruit He prunes [purifies by trials and afflictions], that it may bear more fruit."[35] Notice that the fruit sought and accepted by God from every vine branch, which represents the human soul, is its activity in Christ, that is, its practice of the commandments of the Gospel, and not at all natural action, that is, not at all the doing of natural good, defiled by admixture with evil. "As the branch," said the Lord, "cannot bear fruit of itself, unless it abides in the vine, neither can you, unless you abide in Me."[36] The Heavenly Father purifies only the soul that bears fruit in Christ. The soul that does not bear fruit in Christ, that remains in its fallen nature and bears the fruitless fruit of natural good, and is content with it, does not attract divine care; it is eventually cut off by death, is cast out of the vineyard—out of the bosom of the Church—and is cast into the eternal fire of hell, where it burns eternally without burning out.[37]

The ascetic himself must not willfully and audaciously cast himself into troubles and tempt the Lord. That would be madness, pride, a fall. "Suffer not thy feet to slip,"[38] says Scripture, "nor Him that keepeth thee to slumber."[39] "You shall not tempt the Lord your God."[40] Such is the significance according to the Lord's testimony, of those bold and vainglorious undertakings when the ascetic has the audacity and tries voluntarily to give himself up to temptation. But those troubles and trials that come to us involuntarily, and consequently are permitted and ordered by God's providence, should be accepted with the greatest reverence, as gifts of God, as cures for the infirmities of our souls, as pledges of our election and eternal salvation.

The fruit of troubles, which consists in the purification of our soul and its rising to a spiritual state, should be guarded as precious treasure. This fruit is guarded when, on being subjected to temptation and rebuke, we take all care at the time to abide by the commandments of the Gospel, without being seduced by the passions which are exposed and stirred by temptation. Between the cross and the commandments of the Gospel there is a wonderful relationship! The doing of the commandments draws the cross onto the shoulders of the doer, and the cross perfects and refines our action according to the law of Christ, explains this law to us, gives us a sense of spiritual freedom despite the nailing, and fills us with unutterable spiritual sweetness despite the bitterness of outward circumstances. Divine Scripture encourages, comforts, and exhorts those subjected to various afflictions thus:

> You who fear the Lord, wait for His mercy, and do not turn aside, lest you fall.... You who fear the Lord, hope for good things and everlasting gladness and mercy. Consider the ancient generations and see: Who believed in the Lord and was put to shame? ... Or who called upon Him and was overlooked? Because the Lord is compassionate and merciful, He forgives sins, and saves in time of affliction. Woe to cowardly hearts and weakened hands, and to a sinner who walks on two paths! Woe to a fainting heart, because it does not believe! Therefore it will not be sheltered. Woe to you who have lost your patient endurance! What will you do when the Lord visits you? Those who fear the Lord will not disobey His words, and those who love Him will keep His ways. Those who fear the Lord will seek His approval, and those who love Him will be filled with the law. Those who fear the Lord will prepare their hearts and will humble their souls before Him. We will fall into the hands of the Lord and not into the hands of men; for as His majesty is, so is His mercy.[41]

He falls into the hands of men who, when tempted by men, does not see the hand of God which permits man to tempt, and so, by ascribing the cause to men, can easily fall into man-pleasing and apostasy from God. He who sees God's providence with the eye of faith, when tempted by men, pays no attention to these blind instruments of providence, but with his spiritual intellect and understanding he remains solely in the hands of God, calling upon Him alone in his troubles.

When the Roman governor Pilate, led by carnal wisdom, said to the Lord Who was standing before him, "I have power to crucify You, and power to release You," the Lord replied, "You could have no power against Me unless it had been given you from above."[42] You are such a blind tool that you neither realize nor suspect the work for which you are being used. " 'By your patience possess your souls,'" said the Lord. "He who endures to the end shall be saved.... 'Now the just shall live by faith; but if anyone draws back [if anyone wavers], My soul has no pleasure in him.'"[43]

CHAPTER 30

The Teaching of the Holy Fathers Concerning the Narrow Way

The teaching on patience given by Holy Scripture is expounded very forcibly and in abundance by the holy Fathers, as a kind of food that plays a particularly important role on the spiritual table of the word of life. We shall make a few extracts from the Patristic writings, so that the reader of these poor counsels may have a ready support in troubles when they come, and may be able to prepare himself for them with all his soul before their arrival. A person they take by surprise, unprepared and unarmed, they easily shake and often defeat.

St John of the Ladder says, "He who will not accept a reproof (correction), just or unjust, renounces his own salvation. But he who accepts it with pain, or even without pain, will soon receive the remission of his sins."[1] "Drink at every hour derision and abuse as living water."[2] "When we are bitten by reproofs (corrections), let us remember our sins until the Lord, seeing our efforts (the efforts of those who do violence to themselves for His sake), wipes out our sins and transforms the sorrow that was gnawing our heart into joy. For 'according to the multitude of sorrows in heart [in proportion to them] have Thy comforts refreshed my soul'[3] in their time. Let us not forget him who said to the Lord, 'O what great troubles and adversities has Thou showed me! And yet didst Thou turn and revive me, and broughtest me up from the depths of the earth ... [after my fall] and broughtest me up again.'"[4] "Blessed is he who, though maligned and disparaged every day, masters himself for God's sake. He will join the chorus of martyrs and converse with angels as with friends. Blessed is the monk who regards himself as hourly deserving every dishonor and disparagement."[5] "A little fire softens a large piece of wax. So, too, a small unexpected indignity often softens, sweetens, and wipes away all our fierceness, uncouthness, insensibility, and hardness of heart."[6]

"Annoyance, humiliations, and similar things in the soul of a novice are like the bitterness of wormwood; while praise, honor, and approbation, are like honey and give birth to all manner of sweetness in those who are pleasure-loving. But let us look at the nature of each: wormwood purifies all interior filth, but honey increases gall."[7]

"The very people who seem most patient and able to bear suffering, if left for a time without blame or reproach from their superior as people confirmed in virtue, lose the meekness and patience they previously had. For even land that is good and fruitful and fertile (the hearts of true ascetics), if left without the water of dishonor, can revert to jungle and produce the thorns of conceit and lust."[8]

St Isaac the Syrian says, "If anyone without hardships, struggles, and temptations has drawn near to God, then you imitate him too."[9] "When you find unchanging peace on your way, then fear; because you are far from the right path by which the righteous go with suffering feet. As you make your way to the Heavenly Kingdom and draw near to the City of God, recognize the following as a sign of its nearness: the violence of the temptations that meet you. The more you draw near and the more progress you make, the more temptations increase against you. When on your way you feel in your soul various violent temptations, then know for certain that your soul has secretly reached at that time a higher degree of spiritual life, and that you are being given more grace than before. According to the greatness of the grace, God leads the soul into the shag of trials. During trials we should have two opposite sentiments, with no resemblance to one another: these two sentiments are joy and fear. Joy, because there are signs that we are going by the way that all the saints trod, and especially the Savior of the world. We should have fear out of anxiety lest we are being subjected to trials on account of our pride. A soul that has received a desire to acquire the virtues and that is living in vigilance and the fear of God, cannot be without sorrow for a single day; for the virtues are inseparably connected with sorrows. He who gets out of trouble without any doubt divests himself also of virtue. If you desire virtue, give yourself up to every sort of trouble. Troubles give birth to humility. God does not wish a soul to be without sorrow. He who wants to be without sorrow finds his outlook or way of thinking outside the will of God. Until we attain to true knowledge, which consists in the revelation of mysteries, let us be led to humility by trials. Whoever remains in his virtue without adversities, for him the door is wide open to pride.

"God very often permits people to be tempted, and lets much evil assail them from all sides. He lets their body be afflicted, as in the case of Job; He brings them into poverty, causes them to be ostracized and shunned and strikes them in the matter of their possessions. Only their souls suffer no harm. When walking in the way of righteousness, it is impossible not to meet with trouble, or that the body should not suffer pain and weakness and should remain immutable, if we want to live in virtue. But the person who lives pleasing his own will, giving way to jealousy or anything else that is harmful to him, is already condemned. But if anyone is walking in the way of justice and righteousness, and is traveling to God with many others like himself, and something of the kind happens to him, he should not turn away from the trial that has come to him, but should receive it with joy, without question, and should thank God for sending him this good gift, that he has been granted to fall into temptation for God's sake and has become a par-taker of the sufferings borne by the prophets, apostles and other saints who endured afflictions for the sake of the way of God, whether the afflictions come from men or devils or from the body—for it is impossible for them to come or be sent without God's permission—and let it be to him an occasion for sanctification. Just as it is impossible for God to give grace to a person who wants to be united to Him otherwise than by enduring trials for the truth, so, too, it is impossible for a person without the gift of Christ to make himself capable of this greatness, namely of enduring trial for the divine gift and rejoicing over the trials that have come to him. St Paul bears witness to this. So great is this work—to suffer for one's hope in God—that the Apostle Paul frankly calls it a gift. This is from God, he says, that 'to you it has been granted on behalf of Christ, not only to believe in Him, but also to suffer for His sake.'[10] As also St Peter wrote in his epistle, 'Even if you should suffer for righteousness' sake, you are blessed'[11] because 'you partake of Christ's sufferings.'[12] And so you should not rejoice when you live in full enjoyment and pleasure, and you should not lose courage when in trouble and consider your position far from the way of God. The way of God from the beginning of time and from the creation of the human race has been the way of the cross and death. How did you get your idea that everything is just the opposite? You must realize that you are outside the way of God, that you are far from Him, that you do not wish to walk in the steps of the saints, but want to make some special way for yourself and travel by it without sufferings. The way of God is a daily cross. No one has climbed to heaven by living a life of pleasure.

"Temptation is good for everyone. If temptation was good for Paul, let every mouth be stopped and the whole world be answerable to God.'[13] Ascet-ics are tempted so that their wealth may be increased; the weak, that they may keep themselves from what is harmful for them; those who are asleep, that they may rouse themselves; those who are far away, that they may draw near; His own, that they may be confirmed in confidence. An undisciplined son will not enter into possession of the riches of his father's house because he will not be able to use his wealth profitably. For this reason God first gives troubles and trials, and then gives grace. Glory to the Lord Who by irksome treatment gives the pleasure of health! There is no one who does not suffer during his training, and there is no one who does not find the time difficult when he is given to drink the poison of temptations. Without them it is impossible to acquire firmness of heart. But even the endurance of temptations is not in our power. How can a vessel of earth hold water unless the divine fire give it the strength? If we abase ourselves and ask with humility and with a constant longing for the gift of patience, all will be given us in Christ Jesus our Lord.

"Let not fear force you in its usual way to turn your thoughts over and over in your mind and dwell upon them. On the contrary, rest assured that your Guardian is with you. Let your wisdom convince you with all certainty that with all creation you are under one Lord, Who by a single nod moves everything, shakes, checks, and orders everything. Not a single slave can harm any of his fellow slaves without the permission of Him Who provides for all and Who rules all. And so, take courage! Freedom has been given to some, yet not given in everything. Neither demons, nor carnivorous beasts, nor wicked men can carry out their will to destroy and kill unless the supreme Ruler permits it, and says how much they may do. This Will does not permit the free will of evil creatures to act as they like, otherwise no one clothed in flesh would be able to remain alive. But the Lord does not abandon His creation, and does not let devils and men do as they like with it. And therefore always say to yourself, 'I have a Guardian Who is taking care of me, and not a single creature can appear to me without permission from Above.' Believe me, they dare not appear visibly before your eyes or force your ears to hear their threats. If they were to have permission from Above from the heavenly King, then neither speech nor word would be necessary, but action would immediately follow His will. Likewise say to yourself, 'If this is the will of my Lord, that the evil ones should have power over His creation, then I also accept it, without regarding it as an evil, for I do not wish to oppose the will of my Lord.' In this way you will feel abundant joy in your temptations, for you will realize and feel for certain that the hand of your Lord is ordering and ruling you. And so, strengthen your heart by faith and trust in the Lord, and 'thou shalt not be afraid for any terror by night, nor for the arrow that flieth by day.'"[14]

St Macarius the Great says, "He who wishes to be an imitator of Christ, so as to become a son of God born of the Spirit, must first of all bear generously and patiently all the troubles that befall him, such as bodily illnesses, offenses, wrongs and insults from men, and the attacks of invisible enemies; because it is by the permission of God that various temptations are allowed to holy souls, so that it may become clear which souls sincerely love God. It has ever been the mark of the saints and patriarchs and prophets and apostles and martyrs that they went by the narrow way of trials and troubles, and so pleased God. The soul that desires to please God needs first of all patience and hope, because one of the tricks of the devil is, in time of trouble, to make us despondent and divert us from hope and trust in God. God never allows those who trust in Him to be overwhelmed by temptations so as to reach utter exhaustion; for, says the Apostle Paul, 'God is faithful, who will not allow you to be tempted beyond what you are able, but with the temptation will also make the way of escape, that you may be able to bear it.'[15] The devil does not worry a soul as much as he would like, but as much as he is permitted by God. If men know what weight can be borne by a horse, a donkey, or a camel, and load them accordingly; if a potter knows how long vessels must be kept in the fire so as not to be cracked by being baked longer than necessary and so as not to be unfit for use through being taken out of the fire too soon—if in a man there is so much knowledge, then how much more and incomparably more does the wisdom of God know the amount of temptation each soul must bear so that, by being tested by it, it may become capable of inheriting the Kingdom of Heaven."[16]

St Isaiah the Solitary says, "Diligently attend to yourself and meditate with great reverence on the fact that our Lord Jesus Christ, being God and having unutterable glory and majesty, became man for our sake, and left us 'an example, that you should follow in His steps.'[17] For 'being found in appearance as a man, He humbled Himself'[18] in an extreme, ineffable manner, became poor, endured from many slander and censure, and as it is said, 'He was led as a lamb to the slaughter, and as a sheep before its shearers is silent, so He opened not His mouth. He was taken from prison and from judgment,'[19] and He was subjected to the most shameful death for us. Therefore, for the sake of His commandment and for our sins, we, too, should calmly and patiently bear it, if anyone justly or unjustly grieves us or does us any indignity. If anyone persecutes us even to death, let us behave like sheep led to the slaughter, without resisting, without arguing;[20] on the contrary, in silence and with humility let us pray for our enemies.

"Carefully attend to yourself, and consider it a great attainment and salvation for your soul if you bear patiently for the Lord's sake slander, indignity, and affliction. Think that you deserve much worse punishments for your sins. Consider it a blessing if you bear patiently for the Lord's sake calumny, dishonor, and disappointment. Regard it as a benefit that you are granted to suffer for God's sake, that out of the vast number of afflictions and calumnies of your Lord, you at least to some extent can imitate and follow Him by sharing the most degrading slanders and most cruel tortures endured by Him. Whenever you remember those who offend and persecute you, do not complain of them, but rather pray to God for them, as your greatest benefactors.

"Carefully attend to yourself, so that with complete readiness and faith you may always submit to the will of God and our Lord Jesus Christ, both in life and in death, and in disappointment. Always expect great and terrible trials, sorrows, disappointments, temptations, and deaths, so that they may not defeat you by finding you unprepared.

"Carefully attend to yourself, and hourly expect that there will rise up against you some temptation, or death, or some attack, or some great peril. When they come, then bear everything with courage and firmness of spirit, reflecting that 'we must through many tribulations enter the kingdom of God.'[21]

"Carefully attend to yourself and remain constantly in the presence of God, without expecting anything from anyone, but expecting everything with faith from the one God. Do you need anything? Pray to God that, if it is His will, He may grant it to you. Regard all that you have as received from God, and not from anyone else, and render thanksgiving to Him. Do you lack something? Do not expect to receive it from men, do not grumble at anyone, do not ask anyone for it, but bear everything generously and imperturbably, thinking to yourself thus: 'Although for my sins I deserve many hardships, yet God, if He wishes, can have mercy on me and supply what I need.' If you have such a disposition of spirit, God will supply all your needs."

The Holy Church, among other instructions, exhorts a person about to be professed as a monk in the following way: "May you not prefer anything to God. May you not love father, or mother, or brethren, or sister, or any relation, even yourself, more than God—nor the kingdom of the world, be it comfort or honor. Do not turn away from poverty, malice, humiliation from men, or from anything else, for if you make the excuse that they are difficult, you will be prevented from following Christ. But ever consider the blessings of those who live according to God in hope, and think of all the martyrs and saints from the beginning of time who, by many labors and sweats, and countless bloodsheddings and deaths, acquired these things. Be vigilant in everything, suffer hardship as a good soldier of Christ. For the Lord Himself and our God Who is rich in mercy, became poor for our sake and became like us that we might be enriched with His Kingdom. For we must imitate Him and bear everything for His sake, and advance in His commandments day and night. For the Lord has said, 'Whoever desires to come after Me, let him deny himself, and take up his cross, and follow Me,'[22] which means to be always ready even till our death for every kind of fulfillment of His commandments. You will have to hunger and thirst, and go naked, and be offended and rebuked, and be humiliated and banished, and be oppressed with many other afflictions, but by these things life according to the will of God is shaped. And when you suffer all these things, 'Rejoice,' says the Lord, 'for great is your reward in heaven,'[23] 'to God, alone wise, be glory through Jesus Christ forever. Amen.'[24] "

The Holy Church, having made this exposition of her spiritual way of thought (mind, philosophy) in which is shown the wonderful union of Christ's commandments with the cross of Christ, requires from everyone about to be professed that he should first of all confess the truth of this exposition, and secondly that he should make a vow to follow it. She asks the candidate for monasticism, "Do you thus confess all these things in hope of the enabling power of God, and will you promise to remain in these vows even till the end of your life by the grace of Christ?" Moreover, only those are professed who acknowledge the truth of the above teaching of the Holy Orthodox Church and are prepared to make a vow to prove by their whole life the truth they have heard, acknowledged, and confessed.

Such is the mind of the Holy Church! Such is the mind of all the holy Fathers of the Orthodox Church! We have contented ourselves here with a few extracts. Far more could be given, but that would be merely a repetition of the same teaching in so many different forms. We will conclude the counsels of the Fathers with our own poor advice based on the most beneficial and blessed experiences. When troubles befall you, it is useful to repeat the following short sentences, to repeat them with attention and with all your soul, to repeat them until from the repetition of them your heart is tilled with peace, even comfort and sweetness:

1. I am receiving what I deserve for my deeds. Remember me, O Lord, in Thy Kingdom.
2. Lord, may Thy holy will be done to me and by me, a sinner, now and forever.
3. Lord, I am Thy creature and slave! Whether I will it or not, I am in Thy power. Do with Thy creature according to Thy holy will and according to Thy great mercy.

4. Glory to Thee, O Lord, for everything that Thou hast brought upon me, glory to Thee! Just and most merciful is Thy judgment upon me who deserve all temporal and eternal punishments.

5. I thank and glorify Thee, my Lord and God, for these tiny and trifling troubles which Thy all-good and most wise providence allows me to suffer, by which Thou exposest my passions unknown to me, by which Thou makest easier for me my answer at Thy dread judgment, by which Thou redeemest me from the eternal torments of hell.

It is obvious that these sentences are borrowed from Sacred Scripture and the writings of the Fathers. When repeated attentively and unhurriedly, they act extremely quickly, powerfully, beneficially, salutarily.

CHAPTER 31

Troubles Are the Special Lot of the Monks of the Last Time

The holy Fathers, the monks of the early times of Christianity, were perfect Christians filled with the Holy Spirit. They had revelations from above and uttered prophecies about the monasticism of the last days. All these revelations or prophecies agree with one another and declare that the monasticism of the last times will have an extremely feeble life, that it will not be given that abundance of spiritual gifts which the first monks enjoyed, and that the monks of the last times will even find salvation itself only with great difficulty. A certain Egyptian father once went into ecstasy and became a witness of a spiritual vision. He saw three monks standing on the seashore. From the other shore he heard a voice: "Receive wings and come to Me." After the voice spoke, two of the monks received fiery wings and flew across to the other shore. The third one remained where he was. He began to weep and wail. At last wings were given to him too, but not fiery ones—they were so weak that he flew across the sea only with great difficulty and trouble, often becoming so feeble that he sank in the sea. The first two monks represented the monasticism of early times, while the third represented the monasticism of the last times, poor in numbers and in accomplishments.

Once, the holy Fathers of the Egyptian Scetis were talking prophetically about the last generation. "What have we done?" they said. One of them, the great Abba Ischyrion, replied, "We have carried out the commandments of God." They asked him, "What will those who come after us do?" Abba replied, "They will do half as much as we have done." Again they asked him, "And what will those who come after them do?" Abba Ischyrion replied, "They will not have any monastic activity whatever, but they will be permitted to have troubles and afflictions, and those who persevere will be superior to us and our fathers."

Archimandrite Arcadius, the superior of the Kyrillo-Novo-Yezersk Monastery, who died in 1847, related the following about himself: "Once,

I was in trouble over something or other. Feeling depressed about it, I went to Matins and while standing in church, was thinking about my trouble. I do not know what happened to me. I involuntarily closed my eyes, and then I experienced a kind of oblivion; but I was not asleep, because I heard distinctly every word of what was being read at the time. Suddenly I saw before me the saint of our monastery, Kyril. He said to me, 'Why are you desponding? Surely you know that the monks of the last times must be saved by afflictions?'" On hearing these words, the Archimandrite came to himself. The vision implanted in the soul of the extremely simple elder—for such was Archimandrite Arcadius—deep peace.

And so, afflictions are our special lot, the lot of the monks of today, the lot assigned to us by God Himself. May this knowledge be a source of comfort to us! May it encourage and fortify us in the face of the various troubles and trials that we have to endure. Let us therefore humble ourselves under the strong hand of God, casting all our care and anxiety on Him, for He cares for us,[1] and let us wholeheartedly give ourselves up to our training by troubles (or sufferings), together with the most careful fulfillment of the commandments of the Gospel. Such is the will of God for us.[2]

Our sufferings for the most part are extremely trifling, so that at first sight it seems impossible to regard them as sufferings at all. But that is only the cunning of our enemy who has acquired in the struggle with feeble man uncommon skill and experience, thanks to long practice. The fallen spirit saw that cruel, coarse, obvious temptations provoke in people flaming zeal and courage to bear them. He saw this, and changed his tactics. He changed his coarse temptations to weak but subtle ones which act very powerfully. They do not evoke zeal from our heart, they do not cause it to struggle, but they keep it in a kind of irresolute state and fill the mind with doubt. They weary and gradually exhaust the powers of a man's soul, they throw him into despondency and inaction, and they ruin him by making him an abode of passions on account of his weakness, despondency, and inertia. Satan's cunning and the strain of the struggles waged by him against the monks of today are equally clear to God. God crowns the most recent wrestlers no less than the ancient ones, though the struggle of the former is less obvious than that of the latter. We must not give way to listlessness, despondency, and inertia. On the contrary, let us direct all our attention and all our energy to carrying out the commandments of the Gospel. This obedience will reveal to us the countless snares of the enemy, and that cunning forethought with which his traps are planned and set. We shall see that the outwardly slight troubles and trials of today are directed, like the grim troubles and trials of old, to draw men away from Christ and to destroy true Christianity on earth, only leaving the shell to deceive people more easily.³ We shall see that temptations that are slight but are planned and carried out with hellish wickedness act much more successfully in the eyes of Satan than grave but obvious and direct attacks.

The chief reason why afflictions are particularly burdensome for contemporary monasticism is to be found in monasticism itself, and consists preeminently in lack of spiritual instruction. It must be confessed that lack of spiritual education is the greatest disaster. And this disaster is not quickly discerned. Monks do not quickly realize it. The novice, filled with zeal in which blood (i.e., the flesh) plays the chief part and spiritual knowledge a very small part, is usually content with the education he finds in the monastery or which he wants to give himself. Later, after a most careful study of Sacred Scripture and the writings of the Fathers, it gradually dawns on the ascetics (and only a few even of them) that, for a monk to succeed, spiritual instruction is essential, and that natural education—however outwardly luxurious and splendid it may be, however much it may be extolled by the blind world—remains in darkness, and keeps its followers in darkness, in the realm of fallen spirits.⁴ Direction by the Word of God from a book and not from living lips is the only direction available, and thus a monk of necessity becomes to a considerable extent his own director. But in spite of the real profit which may be gained by private study and self-direction, it is associated with great and frequent errors and lapses, which are the inevitable consequences of ignorance and of being under the dominion of the passions. The novice's ignorance and the prevalence of the passions in him make it impossible for him to understand Scripture properly and stick to it with due firmness. As we fly across the sea of sin, we often grow weak, and out of exhaustion we frequently fall and sink in the sea and are in danger of drowning. On account of the lack of directors who are living vessels of the Spirit, on account of the countless perils with which we are surrounded, our state merits bitter weeping, inconsolable lamentation. We are in need, we have gone wrong, and there is no living voice to guide us out of our delusion and error. A book is silent, while the fallen spirit, wishing to keep us in error, wipes from our memory even the very thought of the existence of a book. "Save me, O Lord!" cried the Prophet foreseeing with the Spirit of prophecy our misery and speaking in the person of one who desires to be saved, "for there is not one godly man left"—there is no Spirit-filled guide and director to show us the way of salvation, no one to whom a soul desiring to be saved can entrust himself with complete confidence. "Truth hath minished from among the children of men. They have talked of vanities every one with his neighbor,"[5] by the suggestion of natural knowledge which is capable only of increasing and broadcasting error and private opinion (or self-opinion; i.e., conceit). We are extremely weak, while the temptations that surround us have increased enormously, and with seductive variety and attraction they are presented to the sick gaze of our mind and heart, which they draw to themselves and avert from God. We are so subject to the influence of distractions that even direction by the Word of God, our one means of salvation, we have abandoned. It is essential to live a recollected life, free from distractions, but our depraved will demands just the opposite. We struggle for material success, for the success of the world! We want honors, we want plenty and luxury! We want distractions and a share of the world's delights! In order to attain this, we are concerned exclusively with the development of our fallen nature. The very idea of a renewed nature we have lost. The commandments of the Gospel are neglected and forgotten. Spiritual activity is quite unknown to us. We are completely engrossed in bodily activity, and that with the purpose of appearing pious and holy in the eyes of the world and to get its reward. We have abandoned the hard and narrow way of salvation; we are going by the broad and easy way. "Save me, O Lord! For there is not one godly man left." "We [monks] have been diminished in number ... more than all the nations, and we are humbled in all the earth today because of our sins. At this time, there is no prince, no prophet, and no leader"[6] to lead us into the battle, invisible to mortal eyes, which is "not against flesh and blood, but against principalities, against powers, against the rulers of the darkness of this age, against spiritual hosts of wickedness in the heavenly places."[7]

"Woe to the world because of offenses! For offenses must come,"[8] said the Lord. Both the coming of offenses, or temptations, is permitted by God, and the moral misery caused by temptations is permitted by God. Toward the end of the world, temptations will be so universal and widespread that, "because lawlessness will abound, the love of many will grow cold,"[9] and "when the Son of Man comes, will He really find faith on earth?"[10] The land of Israel (the Church) will be devastated by the sword—by the deadly violence of temptations—and exceedingly empty.[11] Life according to the will of God is becoming very difficult. That is because, when you live in the midst of temptations and have them constantly before your eyes, it is impossible not to be influenced by them. Just as ice in the presence of warmth loses its firmness and is converted into the softest water, so even a heart overflowing with goodwill, if exposed to the constant influence of temptations, is weakened and changed. Life according to the laws of God is becoming very difficult on account of the widespread, general apostasy. The increasing apostates, by calling themselves and appearing outwardly to be Christians, will all the more easily be able to persecute the true followers of Christ. The increasing apostates surround true Christians with countless snares, and put countless obstacles in the way of their salvation and their good intention to serve God, as St Tikhon of Zadonsk remarks, and they oppose the servants of God by means of coercive authority, and by calumny, and by underhanded double-dealing, and by various kinds of deception, and by means of cruel persecution. The Savior of the world could scarcely find refuge in insignificant and remote Nazareth in order to hide from Herod and from the Jewish scribes, Pharisees, priests, and chief priests who so hated Him. So, too, in the last times a true monk will hardly be able to find some remote and unknown refuge in which to serve God with some degree of freedom, and not be drawn by the violence of apostasy and the apostates into the service of Satan. O disastrous time! O disastrous state of affairs! O moral disaster, unnoticeable for people who live only the life of the senses, yet incomparably greater than all material, glaring disasters! O disaster that begins in time and does not end in time, but passes into eternity! O disaster of disasters, realized only by certain true Christians and true monks, but unknown to those whom it seizes and destroys!

Having been made witnesses of such a spiritual vision, let us sing from the flame of temptations that confession and that song of praise that the three blessed youths sang out of the burning furnace of Babylon. By our love let us unite ourselves with all humanity spread over the face of the earth. From the whole of mankind, as its representatives before God, let us say this confession and doxology to God, let us pour out before Him this humble prayer for ourselves and for all mankind:

> Blessed are You and praiseworthy, O Lord, the God of our fathers, and praised and glorified is Your name unto the ages. For You art righteous in all You did for us, and all Your judgments are true. According to all You brought on us and on the holy city of our fathers, because in truth and judgment You did all these things on account of our sins. For we sinned and acted lawlessly to depart from You. We sinned in every way, and did not obey Your commandments. Neither did we treasure or do as You commanded, that it might go well with us. Everything You brought on us and all You did to us, You did in true judgment. You delivered us into the hands of lawless and rebellious enemies ... For your name's sake, do not hand us over to the end, and do not reject Your covenant. Do not withdraw

your mercy from us ... Yet with a contrite soul and humbled spirit, may
we receive mercy ... Do not put us to shame, but deal with us according to
Your kindness and according to the abundance of Your mercy. Deliver us
by Your wondrous works and give glory to Your name, O Lord.[12]

The holy Fathers said about the monks of the last days, "In the last days,
those who will truly work for God will safely hide themselves from men and
will not perform signs and miracles as at the present time, but they will go by
the way of activity, combined with humility." In actual fact, what is the surest
way of salvation for a monk today? It is the way that can protect him from
the influence of temptations from without and within. It consists outwardly
in renouncing acquaintance and familiar conversation[13] inside and outside
the monastery, in constantly staying as much as possible in your monastery
and in your cell, in heartily[14] studying and doing the commandments of the
Gospel, or, what amounts to the same thing, in studying and doing the will
of God,[15] and in the uncomplaining and patient bearing of all troubles and
sufferings permitted by the providence of God, while acknowledging with
all sincerity of heart that you deserve these troubles. The commandments of
the Gospel teach a monk humility, while the cross perfects him in humility.
Humility eradicates from body and soul all sinful passions, and draws to it
the grace of God. And in this consists salvation.

CHAPTER 32

Sources of Monastic Temptations

Temptations arise from the following four sources: from our fallen nature, from the world, from men, and from demons. Strictly, there is only one source of temptations: our fallen nature. If our nature were not in a fallen state, evil would never arise in us, the temptations of the world would have no influence on us, men would not rise up against one another, fallen spirits would have no occasion or right to approach us. That is why Scripture says, "Each one is tempted when he is drawn away by his own desires and enticed."[1] But the infinite goodness and wisdom of God has so arranged everything for those who are being saved that all temptations, whatever they may be, bring the greatest profit to the true slaves and servants of God, and assist them tremendously in the work of their salvation and spiritual progress. Evil has no good end (aim); it has only an evil end (aim).[2] But God has so wonderfully arranged the work of our salvation that evil, though having an evil aim and acting with the intention of harming the servant of God in time and in eternity, actually furthers his salvation.

Salvation, as a spiritual mystery, which makes man a partaker of the Divine Goodness, is incomprehensible for evil which is blind in regard to the Divine Goodness as something completely foreign to it, and understands only its own, that is, either undiluted evil, or the good of fallen nature mixed with evil and poisoned by evil. St Macarius the Great says, "Evil assists good with a bad intention."[3] And the Apostle Paul has said, "All things work together for good to those who love God."[4]

Fallen nature, vomiting sin out of itself in various forms—here I mean sin not in act but in thought and the feelings of the heart and body—and disputing with the Gospel, gives the ascetic in the light of the Gospel experiential and detailed understanding of the fall, both of his own self and of that which is common to the whole of humanity; gives him experiential knowledge of the necessity of the Redeemer; gives him experiential knowledge that the Gospel cures and revives (quickens) the soul; gives him a broken and humble heart which becomes permanent in the ascetic through his vision of the countless wounds and infirmities inflicted on the individual and on the human race by the fall. The poison of sin, injected into every human being by the fall and which is to be found in every man, acts by the providence of God in those who are being saved in such a way as to be of real and very great profit to them.

The world, by tempting the ascetic, gives him experiential knowledge that earthly life is fickle and illusive, and that all that is sweet, desirable, and great on earth ends in emptiness and misery. From this experiential knowledge the ascetic acquires coldness toward earthly life, toward his guesthouse (earth), toward all that is regarded as desirable by the sons of the world, and he turns the gaze of his mind and heart toward eternity and begins to pray to God with the greatest fervor about his fate beyond the grave.

Men, by tempting the ascetic, give him an opportunity to become a doer[5] of the most sublime commandments of the Gospel, the commandments concerning love for one's enemies. Love for our enemies is the highest degree of love for our neighbor ordained by the Gospel. He who has attained love for his enemies has attained perfection in the matter of love for his neighbor, and to him the gates of love for God have opened automatically. All obstacles have been removed. The eternal bars and locks have sagged and opened. The ascetic no longer criticizes his neighbor; he has forgiven him all his sins. Now he only prays for him as for a fellow member belonging to one body. Now he has acknowledged and confessed that all the troubles that the servant of God encounters are permitted by the nod of God. Now he has submitted to the will of God in all circumstances, both particular and general, and therefore as a beloved confidant and intimate friend of holy peace, as one who has carried out all that God has commanded regarding his neighbor, he enters with freedom into the embraces of divine love. The ascetic could never have attained this unless he had been subjected to various temptations from men, and on account of his temptations had vomited out of himself, as if from the action of a purgative medicine, all the malice and pride with which his fallen nature was infected.

Temptations from evil spirits are usually permitted after training with temptations from fallen nature, from the world, and from men. At first the evil spirits support our fallen nature in its conflict with the teaching of the Gospel, or they take part in temptations caused by the world and by men. Later, by the special permission of God, they themselves open an offensive against the servant of Christ which involves him in a great struggle. A victor in this conflict is crowned with special spiritual gifts, as may be seen from the lives of St Anthony the Great, St John the Sufferer, and other holy monks. Without entering into conflict with the spirits and without properly passing this test, the ascetic cannot part company with them completely, and therefore he cannot attain complete freedom from enslavement to them either in this or the future life. Those who leave this earthly life in such a state cannot avoid being subjected to tortures by fiends at the aerial tolls.[6] St Macarius the Great says, "Souls that have not been tested by troubles caused by evil spirits remain undeveloped (lit. *in childhood*), and are unfit for the Kingdom of Heaven."[7]

Evil is the cause of all troubles and temptations. But the wisdom and omnipotence of God cause temptations and troubles to act in soul-saving ways, and provide the servants of God with an opportunity to carry out the most sublime commandments of the Gospel, to follow Christ by taking up one's cross, and to become the Lord's closest disciples. For the sons of perdition, on the contrary, troubles and temptations act fatally. Evil defeats them; they are unable to conquer it, and their former sins are augmented by new sins. Thus, one of the robbers, who was crucified close to the Lord, crowned his crimes on the cross with blasphemy.[8] The omnipotence and wisdom of God causes evil, acting with an entirely evil aim and intention, to carry out without knowing it the predetermined providence of God. Thus the Jewish clergy, moved by envy and hatred for the God-Man, persecuted Him throughout the whole course of His life on earth, and contrived to have Him sentenced to a shameful form of capital punishment. But by the infinite wisdom and omnipotence of God, the Jewish priesthood was the blind tool of the predetermined plan of God who had decreed that the all-holy Christ, by suffering for guilty humanity, should redeem guilty humanity by His sufferings, and should open for all who wish to be saved the saving way of the cross, which leads those who travel by it to heaven.[9]

In a similar way, evil serves as an instrument of God in relation to all the servants of God, without getting anything out of it for itself. Operating at the beck and call of God, in its ignorance of good, evil never ceases to be both for itself and for those who do it, what it is—evil.

Slaves of God! Know for certain that the troubles that befall you come not of themselves but by God's permission; so take all possible care to bear them with patience and perseverance, offering praise and thanksgiving for them to God. Know that he who resists troubles and tries to escape from the hard way, is acting against his own salvation and is striving in his blindness to frustrate the order and plan of salvation appointed by God for all His servants.

CHAPTER 33

On the Necessity for Courage
in Temptations

One of the greatest merits of a military leader in the wars of this world consists in his not becoming discouraged by all the adverse changes of fortune, but in his remaining unshakable, as if his heart were of rock. His firmness enables him to make the sanest and most advantageous decisions; it also confuses his enemies and reduces their temerity, while infusing courage into his own troops. A general with a character of this kind is apt to have extraordinary successes; all of a sudden, even a whole series of losses and misfortunes is crowned with decisive victory and triumph.

Such should be the mind of a monk—that warrior in the unseen struggle against sin. Nothing, no temptation caused by men or spirits, or arising from fallen nature, should disturb him. Let faith in God Who is almighty, and to Whom he has surrendered himself for service, be the source of his poise and power. Cowardice and agitation are born of unbelief; but as soon as the ascetic has recourse to faith, cowardice and agitation vanish, like the darkness of night before the rising sun.

If the enemy offers you various sinful thoughts and feelings, or if they arise from your fallen nature, do not be alarmed. And do not be surprised at this, as if it were something extraordinary. Say to yourself, "I was conceived in iniquities and born in sins.[1] It is impossible for my nature which is so infected with the poison of sin not to show its infection." Exactly! It is impossible for our fallen nature not to produce its fruit, especially when it begins to be cultivated by the commandments of the Gospel. When land begins to be tilled with the plough, then the very roots of the weeds are ploughed out on to the surface; and if the land is ploughed regularly, the weeds are gradually eradicated and the land gradually becomes clean. In the same way, when the heart is cultivated by the commandments, the most deeply rooted thoughts and emotions,[2] which are responsible for every kind of sin, are dug out of it and brought to the surface; and thus by continual and regular exposure, they are gradually destroyed.

Suppose the passion of lust suddenly arises in you, do not be agitated by it. In exactly the same way, if there should arise anger, resentment (remembrance of wrongs), avarice or dejection, do not be disturbed by it. This is bound to happen. But as soon as any passion makes its appearance, without a moment's delay cut it off by the commandments of the Gospel.[3] If you do not indulge or yield to the passions, you will see their mortification. But if you indulge in them, dally or converse with them, cherish and take pleasure in them, then they will mortify and kill you.

Sinful thoughts and emotions[2] arise from our fallen nature. But when sinful thoughts and emotions[2] begin to come constantly and insistently, this is a sign that they are brought by our enemy, by the fallen angel, or else that he is forcing our fallen nature to multiply them especially. Such thoughts and emotions[2] should be confessed to our spiritual father as often as they occur, even though the confessor may be a simple-hearted man and not noted for sanctity.

Your faith in the holy sacrament of confession will save you; the grace of God present in the sacrament of confession will heal you. By constant and persistent attacks upon us the fallen spirit tries to sow and grow in us the seeds of sin, to habituate us to some form of sin by frequently reminding us of it, to arouse in us a special propensity for it, and to turn this form of sin into a habit as if it were a natural property. A sinful habit is called a *passion* (or vice); it deprives a man of freedom and makes him a prisoner, a slave of sin and of the fallen angel.

Against the persistent and repeated attacks of sinful thoughts and emotions, called in monastic language *conflict*, there is no better weapon for a novice than confession. Confession is almost the only weapon for a novice in time of conflict. In any case, it is the most powerful and most effective weapon. You should confess as often as possible during temptations caused by the devil; confess until the devil and the temptation caused by him leave you. The devil loves to act secretly; he loves to be unnoticed, not understood. "He lurketh in secret like a lion in his den, that he may ravish the poor,"[4] the poor inexperienced feeble monk. He cannot bear to be exposed and discovered. When he is exposed and brought to the light, he leaves his prey and goes away. Thoughts, even though they are sinful, but which come and go without persistently seizing the soul, do not require immediate confession. Reject them, pay no attention to them, mortify them by recalling the commandments of the Gospel opposed to them. Mention them in general terms without bothering to enumerate them in detail in your confession before communion of the Holy Mysteries of Christ. Say that, besides serious sins which you are obliged to confess accurately, you have also sinned by various thoughts, words and deeds, consciously and unconsciously.[5]

CHAPTER 34

On Sobriety or Vigilance

Among His other all-holy and saving bequests, our Lord has commanded us to practice constant prayerful watchfulness over ourselves, a state called in the active writings of the Fathers *holy sobriety* or *vigilance*. "Watch and pray, lest you enter into temptation,"[1] said the Lord to His disciples. "And what I say to you, I say to all: Watch!"[2]

St Hesychius of Jerusalem defines vigilance thus: "Sobriety or vigilance is the way to every virtue and commandment of God."[3] From this it is clear that vigilance comes from the most careful and constant study of the Gospel commandments, and consequently of the whole of sacred Scripture. Vigilance strives unremittingly to abide by all the Gospel commandments in one's actions, words, thoughts, and feelings. In order to achieve its purpose, it unceasingly keeps watch, it unceasingly meditates on the law of God, it unceasingly cries to God for help with the most vigorous prayer.

Vigilance is constant activity. "Sobriety or vigilance," says St Hesychius, "is a spiritual art which, with long and diligent practice and with God's help, releases a man completely from evil deeds and from passionate words and thoughts. It gives the person who practices it a sure knowledge of the incomprehensible God, so far as He can be comprehended, and a solution of divine and hidden mysteries. It accomplishes every commandment of God in the Old and New Testaments, and it gives every blessing of the life to come. It is really purity of heart which, on account of its greatness and value, or to speak more accurately, on account of our listlessness, is now very rare among monks."[4]

"Vigilance is constant silence of the heart, free from all thoughts, always unremittingly and constantly calling upon Christ Jesus, Son of God and God, breathing Him alone, courageously fighting with Him against the enemies, confessing to Him Who alone has power to forgive sins. Such a soul, by invoking Christ, frequently embraces Him Who alone knows the secrets of the heart; and it endeavors in every way to hide its sweetness and inner life from men, so as to prevent the evil one from secretly introducing evil and destroying its good work."[5]

"Vigilance is a firm control of the mind, and posting it at the door of the heart, it sees marauding thoughts as they come, hears what they say, and knows what these robbers are doing, and what images are being projected and set up by the demons, so as to seduce the mind by fantasy."[6]

"The great law-giver Moses, or rather the Holy Spirit—indicating the integrity, purity, far-reaching influence, and high creativity of this virtue (vigilance), and teaching us how we must begin and perfect it—says, Attend to yourself, that there be no secret word or thought of sin in your heart.[7] By secret word or thought is meant a purely mental representation of anything evil or hateful to God, which the Fathers call an attraction[8] offered to the heart by the devil, and which our thoughts follow as soon as it presents itself to the mind, and with which they passionately dally."[9]

Vigilance opposes the very springs and beginnings of sin, the sinful thought and feeling. Vigilance accomplishes the commandments in the very springs of man's being, in his thoughts and feelings. Vigilance reveals to the vigilant soul his fallen nature. It reveals to us the fallen spirits, and reveals that dependence on the fallen spirits into which man fell through doing their will, and into which he falls ever more deeply when he does their will or his own sinful will. Our fall is aggravated, sealed, and becomes our own permanent property, a permanent pledge of eternal perdition through following our fallen will and the will of the demons.

Vigilance is the indispensable property or attribute of true spiritual activity, by means of which all a monk's visible and invisible activity is accomplished according to the will of God, solely to please God, and is kept from all admixture of service to the devil. Vigilance is a cause of purity of heart, and therefore also a cause of the vision of God, which is granted by grace to the pure, and which raises purity of heart to blessed dispassion.[10]

Vigilance is inseparable from unceasing prayer. It is born of prayer, and it gives birth to prayer. From this natural birth one of another, these two virtues are joined in inseparable union.

Vigilance is spiritual life. Vigilance is heavenly life. Vigilance is true humility which concentrates all its hope on God, and renounces all simony and trust in men. For this reason it seems to them the most frightful pride, and is reviled, blasphemed, and bitterly persecuted by them.

It will not be superfluous to notice here that St Hesychius speaks about the commandments of the Old Testament in a spiritual and not in a Jewish sense. When in Christ the veil that lies on their spiritual eyes is annulled, a Jew becomes a Christian. Then the Old Testament acquires the same significance for the reader as the New. The law stated clearly in the New Testament is expressed in the Old in symbols and metaphors. A novice should first study the New Testament. A spiritual understanding of the Old Testament will come in due time; it is a property of those who have made some progress.

Vigilance is obtained gradually. It is acquired by long continued practice. It is born preeminently of attentive reading and prayer, from the habit of keeping watch over oneself, from being alert, from considering every prospective word and action, from being attentive to all our thoughts and feelings, from keeping watch over ourselves so as not to become prey to sin in any way. "Be sober, be vigilant," says the holy Apostle Peter, "because your adversary the devil walks about like a roaring lion, seeking whom he may devour. Resist him, steadfast in the faith."[11]

"Be all eye like the cherubim," said St Euthymius the Great to a monk subject to diabolic temptation, "and guard yourself everywhere with the greatest diligence, because you are walking among nets and snares."[12]

St Barsanuphius the Great and St John the Prophet have given to those who wish to live a sober life pleasing to God excellent advice for practical vigilance. Their advice is that before every undertaking, that is to say, before beginning a conversation or starting any work, we should raise our thought to God and ask Him for enlightenment and help.[13]

In order to remain in vigilance, it is necessary to guard the freshness and brightness of the mind with all care. The mind becomes darkened from imprudent use of food, drink, and sleep, from much talking, from distraction, and from worldly cares. "Take heed to yourselves," said the Lord, "Take heed to yourselves, lest your hearts be weighed down with carousing, drunkenness, and cares of this life, and that Day [the day of Christ's dread judgment, the last day of the world] come on you unexpectedly. For it will come as a snare on all those who are dwell on the face of the whole earth. Watch therefore, and pray always that you may be counted worthy to escape all these things that will come to pass, and to stand before the Son of Man."[14]

Just as the day of the general judgment of all men will come suddenly, so for each man will suddenly come the day of his particular judgment, the day of his death. It is unknown at what hour we shall he called. One has only just begun his life on earth, and he is caught away from it into eternity. Another is taken after going a very short way; another midway; another a considerable distance from the end. Few reach the completion of their days and leave their earthly hut—the body—when it becomes unfit for habitation.

During our earthly pilgrimage, through our sense of immortality having become distorted by the fall, our body seems to us everlasting, filled with a most abundant, most fruitful activity. This feeling is shared alike by child, adolescent, adult, and the aged. All are created immortal, with immortal souls. They ought to be immortal in body, too. Their fall that has struck both soul and body with death, they either know nothing about, or do not want to know, or they know it quite inadequately. Hence their mental outlook and the feeling of their heart in regard to earthly life is false and full of self-deception. Hence people of all ages vainly imagine that man's heritage is eternal. After finishing our earthly pilgrimage, at the gates of death, the way that stretches endlessly into the future seems in the past extremely short, and the vast amount of activity performed not at all for eternity seems a most pernicious, irretrievable loss of time and of opportunity given for our salvation. Very truly do worldly people express their deception by usually calling death an "unexpected calamity" at whatever age it comes to their relatives and friends. And for the decrepit old man or woman, burdened with years and infirmities, who has long been declining to the grave, but who has not given a thought to death, and has in fact dismissed every reminder of it, it is indeed an unexpected calamity. In the fullest sense it is a calamity for all who are unprepared for it. On the other hand, "blessed are those servants whom the master, when he comes, will find watching,"[15] soberly and rightly viewing earthly life, understanding death and preparing for it as something that can come at any age and in any state of health.

We must accomplish the course of our earthly pilgrimage with the greatest attention and watchfulness over ourselves, unceasingly calling upon God in prayer for help. Let the lamp for our journey be the Gospel, as David sang, "Thy law is a lamp unto my feet, and a light unto my paths."[16] We go not only by a narrow way; we travel by night.[17] Constant vigilance of mind is indispensable, so as not to be drawn away by our fallen nature, and by our fathers and brothers who are drawn away by it, and so as to escape all the snares and the furious malice and humanly incomprehensible cunning and wickedness of the fallen angels.

Having guarded ourselves against distractions and worries, let us turn our attention to our body on which mental vigilance is completely dependent. Human bodies differ widely from one another in strength and health. Some by their strength are like copper and iron; others are frail like grass. For this reason everyone should rule his body with great prudence, after exploring his physical powers. For a strong and healthy body, special fasts and vigils are suitable; they make it lighter, and give the mind a special wakefulness. A weak body should be strengthened by food and sleep according to one's physical needs, but on no account to satiety. Satiety is extremely harmful even for a weak body; it weakens it, and makes it susceptible to disease. Wise temperance of the stomach is a door to all the virtues. Restrain the stomach, and you will enter Paradise. But if you please and pamper your stomach, you will hurl yourself over the precipice of bodily impurity, into the fire of wrath and fury, you will coarsen and darken your mind, and in this way you will ruin your powers of attention and self-control, your sobriety and vigilance.

Physical calmness of the blood is absolutely essential for vigilance, and it is procured in the first place by wise temperance. The blood is set into contrary motion by the passions, which in their turn are so varied that they not infrequently oppose one another, and one movement of the blood is often canceled by others. But all these contrary movements of the blood are invariably connected with distraction, daydreaming, and a vast invasion of thoughts and pictures that flatter with self-love.

Whenever the blood is set in violent and unnatural motion, there is always a great invasion of thoughts and daydreaming accompanying it. This motion is a sinful motion, a fruit and product of the fall. Of this movement of the blood it is said that it is unfit to inherit the kingdom of heaven.[18] In other words, a person who allows himself to excite his blood and take pleasure in it is unfit to receive divine grace.

This movement of the blood is all the more dangerous because very few understand it. On the contrary, many take the sinful movement of the blood in themselves as an effect of a good influence, and follow their mistaken impulse as if it were an impulse inspired by holy truth pleasing to God. With an abundant appearance of thoughts and daydreams, beyond the usual order, notice the state your blood then gets into; and you will begin to understand its sinful motion and guard yourself against it.

The waters of Siloam flow gently from their source.[19] God-pleasing virtues flow from obedience to God, and are accompanied by humility, not by excitement, not by fits and jerks, not by twitches and spasms, not by self-will, conceit, or vainglory, which are inseparable fellow travelers of sinful excitement of the blood. The blood is moved differently with angry thoughts and dreams, and differently with impure and sensual thoughts; differently with vainglorious thoughts; differently with greedy, grasping, avaricious thoughts; differently with thoughts and dreams of sorrow and despondency; differently with exasperation; differently with pride; and so on. For this reason fasting is a primary instrument of all the virtues.

Just as we must beware of overeating, so, too, we must beware of excessive temperance or abstinence. Excessive temperance weakens the body, destroys wakefulness, coolness, and freshness which are indispensable for vigilance, and which fade and weaken when the physical powers succumb and fail. Says St Isaac the Syrian, "If you force a weak body to labor beyond its powers, you subject your soul to double darkness, and lead it into confusion (and not relief). But if you give a strong body rest and ease and idleness, all the passions dwelling in the soul are intensified. Then, even if the soul has a great desire for good, even the very thought of the good that is desired will be taken from you.... Measure and time limits in discipline illumine the mind and banish confusion. When the mind is upset by a disorderly or imprudent life, darkness clouds the soul; and with darkness comes disorder and confusion. Peace comes from order; light is born from peace of soul. And from peace, joy fills the mind."[20]

Constant and unfailing vigilance is secured by prudent temperance. Constant vigilance secures a faithful following of the Gospel teaching. The Gospel teaching is the only source of all true, Christian, God-pleasing virtues.

CHAPTER 35

On the Use and Harm of Bodily Discipline

In Paradise, after the transgression of God's commandment by our forefathers, among the punishments to which man was subjected is mentioned the cursing of the earth. "Cursed is the ground for your sake," said God to Adam. "In toil you shall eat of it all the days of your life. Both thorns and thistles it shall bring forth for you, and you shall eat the herb of the field. In the sweat of your face you shall eat bread."[1]

That curse lies on the earth till now, and it is plain for all to see. It does not stop producing weeds, though no one eats them. It is moistened with the farmer's sweat, and only by means of sweating and often bloody labor does it yield those herbs or grasses whose seeds serve as human food and are called bread.

The punishment pronounced by God has also a spiritual meaning. Indeed, God's decree respecting man's punishment is as truly fulfilled in a spiritual as in a material manner.[2] By the term earth or ground the holy Fathers understood the heart. Just as the earth, on account of the curse, does not cease to produce from its injured nature thorns and thistles, so the heart poisoned by sin does not cease to give birth to sinful thoughts and feelings from its own injured nature. Just as no one troubles about the sowing and planting of weeds, but perverted nature produces them automatically, so sinful thoughts and feelings are conceived and spring up of their own accord in the human heart. In the sweat of one's brow material bread is obtained. With intense labor of soul and body the heavenly bread is sown that secures eternal life in the human heart; with intense labor it grows, is gathered and harvested, is rendered fit for use, and is kept.

The bread of heaven is the Word of God. The labor of planting the Word of God in the heart requires such efforts or exertions that it is called a struggle. Man is doomed to eat earth in sorrows and sufferings all the days of his earthly life, and bread in the sweat of his brow. Here by the term *earth* must be understood the carnal wisdom by which man fallen from God is ordinarily guided during his life on earth; subjecting himself through his carnal mind to constant worry and thought about earthly things, constant sorrows and disappointments, constant disturbance and trouble. Only a servant of Christ during his life on earth feeds on heavenly bread in the sweat of his brow by constantly struggling with the carnal mind, by constantly laboring at the cultivation of the virtues.

To till the earth, various iron tools and implements are needed—ploughs, harrows, spades—by which the soil is turned over, mellowed, and softened. So, too, our heart, the center of carnal feelings and of the carnal mind, needs cultivation by fasting, watching, vigils, prostrations, and other oppressions of the body, so that the predominance of carnal and passionate feeling may give way to the predominance of spiritual feeling, and the influence of carnal, passionate thoughts in the mind may lose that irresistible power that it has in people who reject or neglect asceticism.

Who would think of sowing seeds on the earth without working it! That would be simply to waste the seeds, to get no benefit whatever, and to cause oneself real loss. Just so is he who, without controlling the carnal impulses of his heart and the carnal thoughts of his mind by due bodily exercises, thinks to practice mental prayer and to plant Christ's commandments in his heart. Not only will he labor in vain, but he may expose himself to spiritual disaster, self-deception and diabolic delusion, and incur the wrath of God, like the man who went to the wedding feast without a wedding garment.[3]

Land cultivated in the most thorough manner—well manured and finely broken up—but left unsown, will bear weeds with great vigor. So, too, the heart, cultivated by bodily exercises but without making the commandments of the Gospel its own, will all the more vigorously produce the weeds of vainglory, pride, and sensuality. The better the land is tilled and manured, the more apt it is to produce rank and juicy weeds. The greater the monk's bodily asceticism while neglecting the commandments of the Gospel, the greater and more incurable will be his self-opinion.

A farmer who has many excellent farm implements and is delighted at the fact, but does not cultivate his land with them, only dupes and deceives himself without getting the least benefit. So, too, an ascetic who practices fasting, vigils, and other bodily exercises, but neglects to examine himself and guide himself by the light of the Gospel, only deceives himself, trusting vainly and mistakenly in his ascetic labors. He will obtain no spiritual fruit, will gather no spiritual wealth.

The man who would take it into his head to cultivate his land without using farm implements would have a heavy labor expenditure and would labor in vain. Just so, he who wants to acquire virtues without bodily discipline will labor in vain, will waste his time without reward and without return, will exhaust his spiritual and physical powers, and will gain nothing. Likewise a man who is always plowing his land without ever seeding it will reap nothing. Just so, he who is incessantly occupied merely with bodily discipline will be unable to practice spiritual exercises, such as planting in his heart the commandments of the Gospel, which in due time would bear spiritual fruits.

Bodily discipline is essential in order to make the ground of the heart fit to receive the spiritual seeds and bear spiritual fruit. To abandon or neglect it is to render the ground unfit for sowing and bearing fruit. Excess in this direction and putting one's trust in it is just as harmful, or even more so, than neglect of it. Neglect of bodily discipline makes men like animals who give free rein and scope to their bodily passions; but excess makes men like devils and fosters the tendency to pride and the recurrence of other passions of the soul. Those who relinquish bodily discipline become subject to gluttony, lust, and anger in its cruder forms. Those who practice immoderate bodily discipline, use it indiscreetly, or put all their trust in it, seeing in it their merit and worth in God's sight, fall into vainglory, self-opinion, presumption, pride, hardness and obduracy, contempt of their neighbors, detraction and condemnation of others, rancor, resentment, hate, blasphemy, schism, heresy, self-deception, and diabolic delusion.

Let us give all due value to bodily ascetic practices as instruments or means indispensable for acquiring the virtues, but let us beware of regarding these instruments as virtues, so as not to fall into self-deception and deprive ourselves of spiritual progress through a wrong understanding of Christian activity.

Bodily asceticism is necessary even for saints, who have become temples of the Holy Spirit, lest the body, left without discipline, should become alive to passionate movements and be the cause of the appearance in a sanctified person of vile feelings and thoughts, so unnatural and improper for a spiritual temple of God not made by hands. The holy Apostle Paul bore witness to this when he said of himself, "I discipline my body and bring it into subjection, lest, when I have preached to others, I myself should become disqualified."[4]

St Isaac the Syrian says that laxity or relaxation—that is to say, neglect of fasting, vigils, silence, and the other bodily disciplines and aids to the spiritual life, allowing oneself constant ease and enjoyment—harms even elders and the proficient or perfect.[5]

CHAPTER 36

[decorative floral illustration]

Concerning Animal and Spiritual Zeal

A monk must be extremely cautious of carnal and animal[1] zeal, which outwardly appears pious but in reality is foolish and harmful to the soul. Worldly people and many living the monastic life, through ignorance and inexperience, often praise such zeal without understanding that it springs from conceit and pride. They extol this zeal as zeal for the faith, for piety, for the Church, for God. It consists in a more or less harsh condemnation and criticism of one's neighbors in their moral faults, and in faults against good order in church and in the performance of the church services. Deceived by a wrong conception of zeal, these imprudent zealots think that by yielding themselves to it they are imitating the holy fathers and holy martyrs, forgetting that they—the zealots—are not saints, but sinners.

If the saints accused or convicted those who were living in sin or irreligion, they did so at the command of God, as their duty, by inspiration of the Holy Spirit, not at the instigation of their passions and demons. Whoever decides of his own self-will to convict his brother or make some reprimand, clearly betrays and proves that he considers himself more prudent and virtuous than the person he blames, and that he is acting at the instigation of passion and deception and diabolic thoughts. We need to remember the Savior's injunction: "Why do you look at the speck in your brother's eye, but do not consider the plank in your own eye? Or how can you say to your brother, 'Let me remove the speck from your eye,' and look, a plank is in your own eye? Hypocrite! First remove the plank from your own eye, and then you will see clearly to remove the speck from your brother's eye."[2]

What is a plank in this connection? It is the earthly wisdom or carnal outlook, hard as a plank, which deprives the heart and mind of all capacity for true vision, so that one is quite unable to judge either one's own inner state or the state of one's neighbor. Such a person judges himself and others as he imagines himself to be, and as his neighbors appear to him outwardly, by his carnal mind,[3] mistakenly. And so the Word of God is extremely just in calling him a hypocrite.

A Christian, after being healed by the Word of God and the Spirit of God, gains a true view of his spiritual state and of that of his neighbors. The carnal mind, by striking his sinning neighbor with a plank, always upsets and confuses him, often ruins him, never does any good and cannot bring any benefit, and has not the least effect on sin. On the other hand, the spiritual mind[3] acts exclusively on the soul-sickness of one's neighbor, compassionates, heals, and saves him.

It is worth noticing that, after acquiring spiritual understanding, the defects and faults of one's neighbor begin to seem very slight and insignificant, as redeemed by the Savior and easily cured by repentance—those very faults and defects which seemed to the carnal understanding so big and serious. Evidently the carnal mind, being itself a plank, gives them this huge significance. The carnal mind sees in others sins that are not there at all. For this reason, those who are carried away by foolish zeal often fall into slandering their neighbor and become the tool and toy of fallen spirits.

St Poemen the Great relates that a certain monk, carried away by zeal, was subjected to the following temptation. He saw another monk lying on a woman. For a long time he wrestled with the thought that urged him to stop them from sinning. At last he gave them a kick with his foot, saying: "Stop it!" Then he realized that it was two sheaves.

Holy Abba Dorotheus relates that during his stay in Abba Seridas' cenobitic monastery, one brother slandered another brother, carried away by foolish zeal, which is always associated with suspicion and apprehension, and is very prone to fibbing and fabrication. The accuser charged the accused with stealing figs from the garden and eating them early on Friday morning. But when the abbot investigated the matter, it turned out that the slandered monk had not been in the monastery that morning, but in a neighboring village, having been sent there by the steward, and that he returned to the monastery only toward the end of the Divine Liturgy.[4]

If you want to be a true, zealous son of the Orthodox Church, you can do so by the fulfillment of the commandments of the Gospel in regard to your neighbor. Do not dare to convict him. Do not dare to teach him. Do not dare to condemn or reproach him. To correct your neighbor in this way is not an act of faith, but one of foolish zeal, self-opinion, and pride. Poemen the Great was asked, "What is faith?" The great man replied that faith consists in remaining in humility and showing mercy;[5] that is to say, in humbling oneself before one's neighbors and forgiving them all discourtesies and offenses, all their sins. As foolish zealots make out that faith is the prime cause of their zeal, let them know that true faith,[6] and consequently also true zeal, must express themselves in humility regarding our neighbors and in mercy toward them. Let us leave the work of judging and convicting people to those persons on whose shoulders is laid the duty of judging and ruling their brethren.

"He who is moved by false zeal," says St Isaac the Syrian, "is suffering from a severe illness. O man, you who think to use your zeal against the infirmities of others, you have renounced the health of your own soul! You had better bestow your care on the healing of yourself, and if you want to heal the sick, know that the sick need nursing, rather than reprimand. But you, instead of helping others, cast yourself into the same painful illness. This zeal is not counted among men as a form of wisdom, but as one of the diseases of the soul, and as a sign of narrow-mindedness and extreme ignorance. The beginning of divine wisdom is quietness and meekness, which is the basic state of mind proper to great and strong souls and which bears human weaknesses. 'We then who are strong ought to bear with the scruples of the weak,'[7] says Scripture. And again, 'Restore [a sinner] in a spirit of gentleness.'[8] The Apostle Paul[9] counts peace and patience among the fruits of the Holy Spirit."[10]

In another place, St Isaac says, "Do not hate the sinner; we are all sinners and deserve condemnation. If you are moved for God's sake, weep over him. Why should you hate him? Hate his sins and pray for him and you will resemble Christ Who was not angry with sinners but prayed for them. Do you not see how He wept over Jerusalem? But in many cases we become a laughingstock for the devil. Why should we hate those who are mocked like ourselves by the very devil who mocks us? Why, O man, do you hate the sinner? Because he is not so righteous as you are. But where is your righteousness when you have no love? And if you have love, why do you not weep for him instead of persecuting him? Some people, thinking that they have sound judgment in regard to the deeds of sinners, get angry with them; they act like this out of ignorance."

Self-opinion, presumption, or conceit is a great calamity. Refusal of humility is a great calamity. A great calamity is that attitude or state of soul in which a monk, without being called upon or asked, merely from a sense of his own fitness or aptitude, begins to teach, convict, reproach, or blame his neighbors. When asked to give advice or express your opinion, either refuse to do so because you know nothing, or else in extreme necessity speak with the greatest caution and modesty, so as not to wound yourself with pride and vainglory, and your neighbor with a harsh and foolish outburst.

When for your labor in the garden of the commandments God grants you to feel in your soul divine zeal, then you will see clearly that this zeal will urge you to be silent and humble in the presence of your neighbors, to love them, to show them kindness and compassion, as St Isaac the Syrian has said.

Divine zeal is a fire, but it does not heat the blood. It cools it and reduces it to a calm state.[11] The zeal of the carnal mind is always accompanied by heating of the blood, and by an invasion of swarms of thoughts and fancies. The consequences of blind and ignorant zeal, if our neighbor opposes it, are usually displeasure with him, resentment, or vengeance in various forms; although if he submits, our heart is filled with vainglorious self-satisfaction, excitement, and an increase of our pride and presumption.

CHAPTER 37

Concerning Almsgiving

A probationer or beginner in the monastic life should not give material alms to the poor, except in special cases when a neighbor is in urgent need and has no other means of receiving help.[1] The giving of alms to the poor is a virtue of people in the world, whose virtue corresponds to their life, that is to say, it is material and of mixed motive.

Proficient monks, who have acquired the gift of discretion and discernment, or who have been called to it by God, can give alms to the poor. They should fulfill this ministry as their duty, acknowledging that they are instruments of God's providence, blessed with a supply of means to do good, and acknowledging that they themselves are benefited more than those whom they benefit.

A probationer or beginner in the monastic life who gives alms to the poor arbitrarily or at his own discretion is sure to be carried away by vainglory and to fall into conceit. If you have any surplus, give it away to the poor so long as you have not yet entered a monastery. That is what the commandment of the Gospel orders. The Lord said to the young man who wished to attain perfection, "If you want to be perfect, go, sell what you have and give to the poor, and you will have treasure in heaven; and come, follow Me."[2]

The giving away of our possessions precedes the taking up of the cross. While keeping our possessions it is impossible to accept and carry the cross.[3] The cross will be continually taken from our shoulders and replaced by means provided by our material resources, and faith in the one God and the vision of God by faith will be destroyed by reliance on our material resources and attention to them.

The holy martyrs and monks tried quite literally to fulfill the Lord's commandment mentioned above before beginning their struggle. The former distributed their possessions to the poor before going out to the visible tortures, or if they had no time to do that, they entrusted the divinely commanded disposal of their possessions to relatives and friends. The monks acted in exactly the same way before going out to their invisible martyrdom. The monastic life is in the fullest sense a martyrdom, though an invisible one, for those who live that life as they should. By giving away our possessions before entering the monastery, we seal our material life in the world with material kindness, one of the greatest of the material virtues. Another form of almsgiving lies ahead of the person who has entered a monastery: immaterial almsgiving. It consists in not condemning our neighbors when they sin, but showing them mercy and kindness, so that we do not even judge our neighbors and say that some are good while others are bad. Such judgment is invariably linked with the loss of humility and with pride which arrogates to man what belongs to God alone.

Spiritual almsgiving consists in not returning evil for evil, but in repaying evil with good. Spiritual almsgiving consists in our bidding farewell to all insults and offenses offered us by our neighbors, and in admitting that these insults and offenses are real blessings in our regard that purify us of the filth of sin. In brief, monastic almsgiving consists in following Christ, that is to say, in carefully obeying the commandments of the Gospel, and in carrying the cross, that is, in good-natured patience and diligent forcing of oneself to the patient bearing of all the afflictions that divine providence is pleased to allow us during our earthly pilgrimage for our salvation. Without the latter the former cannot exist; there can be no following of Christ without taking up the cross and acknowledging in it the New Testament righteousness and justification of God.

For monks who are proficient and called to it by God, spiritual almsgiving includes teaching our neighbors the word of God. According to the teaching of the holy Fathers, spiritual almsgiving is as high above material almsgiving as the soul is superior to the body.[4] In order to give material alms, one must endeavor to obtain material wealth or property. In order to give spiritual alms, we must endeavor to concern ourselves with amassing spiritual wealth, the acquisition of the knowledge of Christ.

If in some way or other wealth or property should come to you after entering a monastery, try at once to transfer it to heaven by means of almsgiving. Entrust the property that has come to you to your superior or to some other person whose honesty and conscientiousness you are certain of, and leave the disposal of your wealth or property to him. Do not dare to dispose of it yourself by trusting to your own judgment, otherwise you will harm your soul. After handing over your wealth or property to the person who is to dispose of it, do not suspect him or distrust him. Having left the matter to his conscience, do not hurl yourself into anxiety and suspicion and harm your soul. You have done your duty and fulfilled your obligation. You have nothing whatever to do with how the trustee or disposer carries out his duty: "To his own master he stands or falls."[5]

CHAPTER 38

Concerning Poverty or Detachment

Everyone who enters a monastery and takes upon himself Christ's easy yoke, must without fail remain in poverty, content with absolute necessities and guarding against all superfluity in clothing, cell appurtenances or belongings, and money. The possessions, riches, and treasure of a monk should be our Lord Jesus Christ. To Him the eyes of our mind and heart should be constantly turned and directed; on Him our hope should be concentrated; in Him we must put all our trust; by our faith in Him we must be strong, energetic, and vigorous.

Such a state of soul it is impossible for a monk to maintain while retaining possessions. The commandment concerning poverty is given us by our Lord Himself: "Do not lay up for yourselves treasures on earth," He tells us, "where moth and rust destroy and where thieves break in and steal; but lay up for yourselves treasure in heaven, where neither moth nor rust destroys and where thieves do not break in and steal." Having laid down the commandment, the Lord explained the reason why. He said, "For where your treasure is, there your heart will be also."[1]

If a monk has money or some things that are dear to him, then by some inevitable and irresistible law and necessity his hope and trust descend from God to his possessions. He puts all his trust in his goods. He sees power in his capital. In his money or property he sees the means to avoid the influence of those vicissitudes he may meet with in the course of his earthly life. On his possessions are concentrated his love, his heart and mind, his whole being. And his heart becomes attached to material things, hard and dead to all spiritual feeling or sensitivity, like a hard and unfeeling material object.

The accumulation of money and other possessions for a monk is the worship of an idol, according to the definition of the Apostle Paul.[2] Idolatry is invariably associated with rejection of God. The darkened materialist soon reaps the fruits of his self-deception. Death, which in his darkness and reliance on earthly prosperity he had quite forgotten, comes and snatches him away from the midst of his wealth. His capital and full stores on which he was relying are left to others, without bringing him even the least temporary benefit, but having estranged him from God.[3]

The Holy Spirit weeps over the state of a person duped by the delusion of riches who, in terrible and ruinous destitution of spirit, enters upon eternity. He says, "Behold the man that took not God for his helper, but trusted unto the multitude of his riches, and puffed up his vanity."[4]

Thus, from attachment to perishable possessions there develops in the depths of the soul rejection of God which, given a suitable opportunity, will not fail to express itself. This can be seen from the following story, preserved for us by Church History.

"A certain presbyter called Paul was living on a mountain in a desert in order to escape persecution by idolaters. He had with him a considerable quantity of gold. He was joined by five virgins who were nuns, also escaping from persecution. These virgins shone with virtues and were filled with the fragrance of the Holy Spirit. They lived close to the presbyter Paul, exercising themselves with him in prayer and the fulfillment of the divine commandments. A certain ill-intentioned man, learning their whereabouts, informed the chief magician at the court of the Persian emperor Sapor that a Christian presbyter who had a lot of gold was hiding on a mountain with five virgin nuns. 'If you wish to get this gold,' said the informer to the grandee, 'give orders that they are to be arrested and brought before you for trial. Then when they refuse to renounce their faith you can cut off their heads and take the gold for yourself.'

"The grandee at once took this advice. He had the presbyter with the nuns and the gold brought before him for trial. Then the presbyter said to the grandee, 'For what reason are you taking my possessions from me when I am guilty of no crime?'

"Grandee: 'For this reason: that you are a Christian and do not obey the emperor's order.'

"Paul: 'My lord, order me what you will.'

"Grandee: 'If you will worship the sun, take your belongings and go where you like.'

"Paul looked at his gold and said, 'What you order me to do, I will do.' And immediately he worshipped the sun, ate the food offered to the idols and drank the sacrificial blood. The grandee, seeing that his plan had failed, said, 'If you can also persuade your nuns to do as you have done, to worship the sun, and then get married or give themselves to men, you may take your gold and your nuns and go wherever you like.'

"Paul went to the nuns and said to them, 'The grandee has taken my belongings and orders you to obey the emperor's edict. I have already worshipped the sun and eaten the food offered to the idols. I order you to do the same.'

"The nuns said as with one mouth, 'Wretched man! Is not your own perdition enough for you? How can you dare to speak to us? Now you have become a second Judas and, like him, you have betrayed your Lord and Master to death for gold. Judas took the gold and went and hanged himself. And you, wretched man, have become a second Judas in character. For the sake of gold you have ruined your soul and have forgotten about that rich man who, having amassed great wealth, said to his soul, "Soul, you have many goods laid up for many years; take your ease; eat, drink, and be merry." And then he heard, "Fool! This night your soul will be required of you; then whose will those things be which you have provided?"⁵ We tell you straight, as in the presence of God Himself, that you will suffer the same fate, both what happened to Judas, and what happened to the rich man.' So saying, they spat in the apostate's face.

"Then, by order of the grandee, the nuns were cruelly flogged and for a long time. Under the blows they cried, 'We worship our Lord Jesus Christ and will not obey the emperor's edict. But you do what you like.'

"The grandee, trying to find a way of getting the gold into his possession, ordered Paul to cut off the heads of those truly wise virgins with his own hands, thinking that Paul would not want to do that, and that then he would be able to seize the gold.

"Hearing this, wretched Paul again looked at his gold and said to the grandee, 'What you order me to do, I will do.'

"Taking a sword, he approached the nuns. Seeing this, the holy virgins were horrified and with one voice said to him, 'Wretched man! Until yesterday you were our pastor, and now you have come like a wolf to devour us. Is this your teaching which you repeated to us daily when you exhorted us to die willingly for Christ? You had not the least desire to suffer for Him, but without a moment's hesitation, you have renounced Him. Where is the holy Body and Blood which we received from your unclean hands? Know that the sword which you hold in your hand is the gateway for us to eternal life. We are departing to our Master Christ; but you, as we foretold you, will soon be strangled by a rope and will become a son of hell with your teacher Judas.'

"Paul cut off their heads. Then the grandee said to him, 'Not a single Christian has obeyed the emperor's edict as you have done. Therefore I cannot release you without a personal order from the emperor. When I tell him and he learns what you have done, he will grant you great honors. Now enjoy yourself with us and stay near us in the quarters you will be shown. Tomorrow I will report to the emperor about you.'

"That night the grandee sent his slaves secretly to strangle Paul with a rope in the room assigned to him. When morning came, pretending to know nothing, he went to visit him. Finding him hanging by the rope and strangled, he sentenced him as a suicide and ordered him to be carried out behind the city and thrown to the dogs. And he took his money for himself."[6]

A monk who leads a sober and vigilant life and discerns in himself the sins or fall of mankind, will easily notice that on receiving for some reason or other something valuable or a considerable sum of money, reliance on these possessions at once appears in his heart, while reliance on God cools and diminishes. Unless he takes care, attachment to material resources will soon make its appearance. Partiality or attachment to possessions can easily become a passion, on account of which rejection of Christ imperceptibly takes place in the heart, though the lips may continue to confess Him, call upon Him in prayer, and preach His doctrine or teaching.

When some deadly passion gets possession of a person, then other passions abate and grow silent. The devil stops causing him conflicts and temptations, and guards the deadly passion infecting him as his treasure, as a true guarantee of his perdition. A man killed by sin in his secret heart and dragged by it to the very gates of hell, often appears holy and edifying to others, as Paul seemed to the nuns, until experience unmasks him, as it unmasked Paul. Whoever wishes to concentrate his hope and trust and love on God must endeavor to remain in poverty. Any money, valuables, or property that comes to him should be used for obtaining riches in eternity.[7]

The beginning of all spiritual blessings is faith in Christ and the Gospel, a living faith that is proved by the fulfillment of the Gospel commandments in deeds, in life. Naturally "the love of money," which uproots faith from the heart, "is a root of all kinds of evil."[8]

CHAPTER 39

Concerning Human Glory

Like love of money, cupidity, and avarice, vainglory destroys faith in the human heart. Like them also, it makes the heart of a person unfit for faith in Christ and for the confession of Christ. "How can you believe," said the Lord to the representatives of the Jewish people contemporary with Him, "who receive honor from one another, and do not seek the honor that comes from the only God?"[1] Many of the most important Jews believed in the Lord, but the Evangelist records that "because of the Pharisees they did not confess Him, lest they should be put out of the synagogue; for they loved the praise of men more than the praise of God."[2] The Jews had made regulations whereby anyone who confessed that the God-Man was the promised Messiah was forbidden to take part in the assemblies of the synagogue.[3]

Vainglory feeds on human praise and privileges invented by the natural mind and arising from our fallen state. It feeds on wealth, nobility of birth, race distinctions, famous and distinguished names such as are given to those who serve and please the world, and other vain and earthly honors. By its very nature, earthly and human glory is directly opposed to the glory of God. The beginnings of human glory and the ways to it are quite different from the beginnings of the glory of God and the ways to its attainment. The beginnings of vainglory and love of fame originate in false ideas of the opinion and power of things human, vain, transient, changeable, insignificant. The way of the seeker of human glory is a constant and varied effort to court and curry human favor. Right or wrong, lawful or unlawful, seekers of human glory will stop at nothing if only they can attain their object.

The beginning of the desire and longing for the glory of God is based on a living faith in God's omnipotence and His unutterable mercy toward fallen man. By means of repentance and the fulfillment of the commandments of the Gospel, fallen man can be reconciled with God and acquire glory from God. We express ourselves in this way for clarity, in order to explain what is said by God in Scripture to the man whose works proved pleasing to God: "'Well done, good and faithful servant; you have been faithful over a few things, I will make you ruler over many things. Enter into the joy of your lord.'"[4] In accordance with its primary cause, the activity of a person who wishes to win the glory of God consists in carefully and constantly pleasing God, or in following the Lord with the cross on his shoulders, and in pleasing his neighbors in what is permitted and ordered by the commandments of the Gospel. This sort of pleasing does not at all satisfy the children of the world and even rouses their indignation, for they seek and demand unlimited gratification of their passions and their self-deception. And that is why they confer earthly glory on the man-pleaser or sycophant, who is an enemy of God and of the true welfare of his neighbors.

"If anyone serves Me," said the Lord, "let him follow Me; and where I am, there My servant will also be. If anyone serves Me, him My Father will honor."[5] Among other moral principles of the God-Man typical of His all-holy character is the rejection of human glory. "I do not receive honor from men,"[6] said the Lord of Himself. Though He is the King of kings, yet His kingdom is "not of this world."[7] When the crowd wanted to proclaim Him king, He retired to a desert mountain,[8] teaching us also, according to the explanation of blessed Theophylact of Bulgaria, to avoid honors and glory. When during the conversation after the Last Supper the disciples said to the Lord, "Now we are sure that You know all things and have no need that anyone should question You. By this we believe that You came forth from God" the Lord expressed no sympathy with these words, which consisted of human praise and complimentary human opinion. On the contrary, knowing how soon the disciples would be discouraged and teaching unregenerate man not to rely on his fallen nature, so prone to unexpected and sudden change, He retorted: "Do you now believe? Indeed the hour is coming, yes, has now come, that you will be scattered, each to his own, and will leave Me alone."[9]

Christ, Who took humanity upon Himself, by His sufferings and cross ascended as regards His manhood into His glory;[10] but His Divinity was always in glory.[11] We must follow Christ. By obeying His commandments and by patiently accepting all the sorrows and sufferings that come to us, we become partakers of Christ's glory in this and the future life.

[Christ] made Himself of no reputation, taking the form of a bondservant, and coming in the likeness of men. And being found in appearance as a man, He humbled Himself and became obedient to the point of death, even the death of the cross. Therefore God also has highly exalted Him and given Him the name which is above every name, that at the name of Jesus every knee should bow, of those in heaven, and of those on earth, and of those under the earth, and that every tongue should confess that Jesus Christ is Lord, to the glory of God the Father.[12]

That is how we must humble ourselves both inwardly and outwardly so as to become partakers of Christ's glory in this and the future life. Pledges of glory given by the God-Man to His followers during our earthly pilgrimage consist in various gifts of the Holy Spirit. In the future life, the divine glory will embrace Christ's disciples and followers both inwardly and outwardly in such fullness and such majesty as the human mind cannot imagine.[13] For this reason our holy fathers, holy monks, tried to avoid like deadly poison all that leads to vainglory and procures human glory. Divine providence, as can be clearly seen from the lives of God's saints, does not allow God's chosen servants during their earthly pilgrimage to remain at ease in comfort and consolation, in constant earthly prosperity and earthly glory. Their earthly pilgrimage is always filled with troubles and afflictions, voluntary and involuntary. Just as sweet food, when constantly used, harms the stomach, so human glory unmixed with troubles harms the soul. Just as continual clear weather unbroken by rains causes grass and corn to fade and wither and fruit to be worm-eaten, so from constant earthly happiness and prosperity good qualities dwindle away and vanish in a person, while self-assurance, pride, and impure desires are generated in his heart.

St Isaac the Syrian has said, "There is scarcely a man to be found who is able to bear honor, or possibly such a person does not exist; because man is very prone to err and is soon subject to changes."[14] The proneness to change, proved by experience,[15] serves as a reason why God Who has prepared for His servants eternal, unchanging honor and glory in heaven, does not wish them to be constantly honored with vain and temporal honor in this inconstant and unstable world, as St Symeon the Translator noticed in the life of the great martyr Eustace Placidus.[16] Those holy men who, on account of their remarkable natural capacities and spiritual progress, God placed in high positions in the Church, were especially subject to persecutions, dishonors, insults, exasperations, annoyances, and sufferings. Anyone who reads the lives of Athanasius the Great, Gregory the Theologian, Basil the Great, John Chrysostom, and other lights of the Church will be convinced of this. The trials that befell them prevented them from coming to spiritual harm, which might easily have happened owing to their high rank and human honor.[17]

"Carefully attend to yourself," says St Isaiah the Solitary, "so as to avoid desire for power, honor, glory, and praise as spiritual wounds, death, and destruction; as eternal torment."[18] If we look attentively at ourselves and at mankind, it is impossible not to be convinced that the advice given by the holy solitary is right; it is impossible not to see that the desire for human glory and human honors leads a monk away from the narrow way of salvation opened by the God-Man and by which all His followers have gone. More than that, this teaching about the narrow and sorrowful way becomes strange, queer, foolish to those interested in human glory. They laugh at it and at those who advocate it, just as the Pharisees who were lovers of the world laughed at our Lord's teaching concerning self-denial. But the Lord gave us this teaching as the indispensable remedy and means of freeing us from falsehood in the land of exile and self-deception, as the way of escape for those who are captives and from those who take us captive by means of falsehood.[19]

There is no other key to open the gates of the kingdom of God than the cross of Christ. This key is given by God to those who choose and determine to enter the kingdom of God; and they themselves try to obtain it, and they rejoice and exult over obtaining it as a pledge or guarantee of eternal, unutterable beatitude.

Says St Symeon the New Theologian, "A man who has renounced the world and everything in it with undoubting faith in God believes that the Lord is compassionate and merciful and will accept those who come to Him with repentance, gives His servants honor in return for dishonor, makes them rich in the midst of poverty, glorifies them by means of provocations and humiliations, and through death makes them partakers and inheritors of eternal life. The believer like a thirsty stag hastens to climb by these steps to the immortal and heavenly spring or source, as by a ladder. And on this ladder angels ascend and descend to help the climbers, on the summit of which is God, the Lover of men, awaiting such labors and efforts as are within our power; not that He rejoices to see us laboring, but He wishes to give us our reward as if we deserved it."[20]

Beloved brothers, let us avoid vainglory and love of notoriety as denial of the cross of Christ. Denial of Christ's cross is at the same time denial of Christ: "Whoever does not bear his cross and come after Me cannot be My disciple," said the Lord.[21] Fallen men! We cannot know and confess Christ sincerely and practically except from our cross, having first learned and confessed our fall and the necessity of the way of the cross for the attainment of heaven and eternal beatitude. Let us avoid all occasions of vainglory and human glory, as the holy Fathers avoided them, so as not to lose interest in the teaching of Christ and become white-washed sepulchres—Christians in appearance, but in reality apostates.

A tiny grain of dust gets into our eye and disturbs our sight. An apparently insignificant attachment or partiality deprives our mind of right understanding, harms and changes our thought and outlook. Fathers who were strong in spirit and body were afraid of the least sin, the least deviation from the teaching of the Gospel. How much more should we who are weak in spirit and body have a horror of sin which has such a hopeful chance of finding a haven and welcome in our weakness, and which, on getting a foothold in us, assumes the appearance of an insignificant trifle, but having got in, turns out to be a terrible monster.

It was not without reason that the holy Fathers observed extreme simplicity in their clothing, in the furniture and appurtenances of their room or cell, in their monastic buildings and even in the construction and adornment of their churches.[22] The thought and heart of a weak person correspond with his or her outward circumstances. This is something quite incomprehensible for inexperienced and inattentive people. If a monk wears elegant clothes, if his cell is carefully furnished with an air of taste and luxury, if even the churches of a monastery are magnificent buildings, shining with gold and silver, and provided with rich vestries, then the monk's soul will certainly be vainglorious, full of conceit and self-satisfaction and he will be a stranger to compunction and the realization of his sinfulness. Filled with vainglorious pleasure and gratification, which is taken for spiritual joy, such a soul remains in darkness, self-delusion, hardness, and deadness, as if in the midst of a triumphant festival. On the other hand, when a monk's clothing is simple, when he lives like a pilgrim in his cell as if he were in a tent or hut and has only what is essential in it, when the church serves as a place of prayer and thanksgiving, confession and weeping, without distracting and enrapturing him by its splendor, then his soul borrows humility from his outward surroundings, is detached from everything material, and is transported in thought and feeling to that inescapable eternity that confronts all men. Such a soul endeavors by repentance and the fulfillment of the Gospel commandments to prepare himself in good time for a blessed reception in eternity. His modest cell, simply furnished, is entered and visited equally by grand people and by simple folk. But visitors cannot enter a carefully furnished cell for fear lest they should upset the exact arrangement of the cell. In the person of a poor, simple man, often rich in faith, Christ is rejected.[23]

Especially pernicious is vainglory; still more pernicious is human glory. For a monk to receive honor and glory from worldly people and carnal wisdom is a sign that this monk is a vessel rejected by God, since on the contrary, reproaches and persecutions from men constitute for a true monk a sign of his election by God. Both are mentioned by the Lord Himself: "Woe to you," He said, "when all men speak well of you, for so did their fathers to the false prophets." On the other hand, "Blessed are you when men hate you, and when they exclude you, and revile you, and cast out your name as evil, for Son of Man's sake. Rejoice in that day and leap for joy! For indeed your reward is great in heaven. For in like manner their fathers did to the prophets."[24]

Let us follow the advice of the holy solitary cited above. But if by the judgments of God a monk has to bear the heavy burden of earthly titles and honors, let him pray to God with insistent and tearful prayers that the earthly greatness may not influence his mind and outlook, and that pride may not enter his soul and cause him to look down on his neighbors. It was of this that our Lord warned His disciples when He says: "Take heed that you do not despise one of these little ones, for I say to you that in heaven their angels always see the face of My Father who is in heaven. For the Son of Man has come to save that which was lost."[25] He shed His precious blood for all and everyone, and in this way He set a single, identical, equal value on all men, and showed that all are equally important and precious.

CHAPTER 40

Concerning Resentment or
Remembrance of Wrongs

A profound and hidden mystery is the fall of man. It is quite impossible for a person to understand it by his own powers. This is because among the consequences of the fall is mental blindness, which prevents the mind from seeing the depths and darkness of the fall. Our fallen state deceptively appears to be a state of triumph, and the land of exile seems to be an exceptional field of progress and enjoyment. Gradually God discloses the mystery to those ascetics who serve Him sincerely and with all their soul.

What a different picture, brethren, and how terrible is the sight that meets our gaze when the mystery is disclosed to us! When by divine guidance the abysses of hell are laid bare in the depth of the heart, how is it possible not to be filled with fear! How can we not be filled with fear especially when our weakness and infirmity is proved to us by countless bitter experiences! How is it possible not to be filled with horror at the thought that some deadly passion can lie hidden in the heart for a long time, then suddenly appear and ruin a person forever! That is true. But whoever fears sin, whoever does not trust himself, is not in danger from sin. And so, wishing to acquaint beloved brethren with the mysteries of sin so as to safeguard them from it, we shall not omit to point out here the fearful, invisible havoc that the passion of resentment produces in the soul.

"God is love,"[1] says St John the Theologian. Consequently, resentment or rejection of love is rejection of God. God withdraws from a resentful person, deprives him of His grace, is definitely estranged from him, and gives him up to spiritual death, unless he makes shift in good time to be healed of that deadly moral poison, resentment.

In Antioch, a capital in the East, in the first centuries of Christianity, there lived two friends, Sapricius the presbyter and a citizen called Nicephorus. For a long time they lived in intimate friendship. Then the sower of evil, the devil, sowed enmity between them. This animosity grew to such proportions that it turned into implacable, bitter hatred. Of the two friends, Nicephorus recovered—"came to himself," as it is said in his Life—and realizing that hatred is sown and intensified by the devil, he sought to be reconciled with Sapricius. Sapricius stubbornly rejected the offer of reconciliation, though it was repeated more than once.

While the mutual relations between these two persons were in this state, there suddenly arose a persecution against Christians in Antioch, in the reign of the Roman emperors Valerian and Gallien. Sapricius, as a Christian presbyter, was arrested and brought before the Roman provincial governor of Antioch. Pressed to offer sacrifice to idols, Sapricius confessed Christ, and for confessing Him endured supernaturally terrible agonies. When various tortures could not shake Sapricius' firmness in confessing Jesus Christ as God, then the governor gave orders that his head should be cut off.

Hearing of Sapricius' trial and wishing to receive the forgiveness and blessing of a martyr who had finished his course and was already about to be crowned by death at the hands of the executioner, Nicephorus rushed to meet the martyr. He fell at the martyr's feet, saying, "Martyr of Christ, forgive me who have sinned against you." But Sapricius did not even give him the slightest reply, because his heart was full of rancor and malice. However many times Nicephorus repeated his request, the bitter and blinded Sapricius replied only with a silence full of hatred and by turning away his face.

They reached the place of execution. Here Nicephorus again implored Sapricius for forgiveness. "I beg you, martyr of Christ," he said, "forgive me if as a man I have sinned against you. Scripture says, 'Ask, and it will be given to you.'² So I ask: Grant me forgiveness."

Even to this request at the very gates of death, Sapricius remained unbending. Suddenly the grace of God that had strengthened him in his martyrdom left him. When the torturers were about to behead him, he suddenly asked them, "What do you want to execute me for?" They replied, "For refusing to offer sacrifices to the gods, and for disregarding the imperial edict concerning a certain man called Christ." Wretched Sapricius said to them, "Don't kill me. I will do what the emperors order. I will worship the gods and offer them sacrifice."

On hearing these terrible words of Sapricius, St Nicephorus implored him with tears, saying, "Don't do that, beloved brother, don't do that! Don't reject our Lord Jesus Christ, don't lose the heavenly crown which you have woven for yourself by patiently enduring so much suffering. Look, standing at the doors is the Lord Christ, who will soon appear to you, and He will repay you with an eternal reward in return for temporal death; and that is why you have come to this place."

Sapricius paid not the slightest attention to these words, and rushed headlong to eternal perdition. Then seeing that the presbyter had finally fallen and renounced Christ the true God, St Nicephorus moved by divine grace began to call to the torturers with a loud voice, "I am a Christian. I believe in our Lord Jesus Christ Whom Sapricius has rejected. Cut off my head." St Nicephorus' desire was fulfilled.[3]

Evidently, rejection of a commandment of the Gospel by Sapricius was regarded by the Holy Spirit as a rejection of Christ in his heart and in an instant He had withdrawn from the wretched man. Without confessing Christ in his heart, he could not hold out and maintain merely verbal confession. In the case of Nicephorus, the careful fulfillment of the commandment gave him the fitness and high calling of a martyr, to which he was suddenly led by the grace of the Holy Spirit Who filled his heart which had been prepared for the Spirit of God by the fulfillment of the divine commandment.

Here is another story. In the Kiev-Petchersk lavra (monastery) two monks, Hieromonk Titus and Hierodeacon Evagrius, lived in harmony and spiritual friendship. Their mutual love was a matter of edification and amazement for other brethren. The enemy who hates goodness and whose habit it is to sow tares among the wheat and turn wheat into tares, especially when people sleep (that is, do not attend to themselves and do not guard against being robbed, supposing that the good they have acquired is safe and secure), turned the monks' love into enmity. Titus and Evagrius were so disaffected one against the other that they could not even look at one another. The brethren asked them many times to make peace and be friends, but they would not even hear of peace.

After this quarrel had gone on for a considerable time, Hieromonk Titus became seriously ill. So dangerously ill was he that his recovery was despaired of. Then he began to weep bitterly over his sin, and he sent to Evagrius to ask for his forgiveness, laying the blame on himself with great humility. But Evagrius not only refused to forgive, but he even said many hard and cruel things about Titus, and even uttered curses. However, seeing that Titus was dying, the brethren brought Evagrius to him for reconciliation. On seeing him, the sick man got out of bed and bowed to the deacon, falling at his feet and saying with tears, "Forgive me, father, and bless me."

Evagrius turned away from him and uttered the following frightful words in the presence of everyone, "I will never make peace with him, neither in this life nor in the future life." As he said this, Evagrius tore himself away from the brethren who were holding him and fell down. The brethren were going to lift him up, but he proved to be dead. They could neither bend his arms, nor shut his mouth, nor close his eyelids. On the other hand the sick Hieromonk Titus rose from his bed perfectly well, as if he had never been ill.

All present were overcome with horror, and they asked the healed priest how his healing had occurred. Blessed Titus replied to them, "When I was seriously ill, I saw angels withdrawing from me and weeping over the ruin of my soul poisoned with rancor and resentment. And I saw devils rejoicing that I was perishing on account of my anger. So I begged you to go to our brother and ask him to forgive me. But when you brought him to me and I bowed to him, and he turned away from me, then I saw a stern angel holding a fiery spear who struck the unforgiving brother so that he fell and died. But the same angel gave me his hand and raised me up. And here I am, well!"

The brethren wept much over Evagrius who had died such a dreadful death. And they buried him in the very position in which he had grown stiff, with open mouth and outstretched arms.[4]

Brethren, let us be alarmed at our weakness. Let us be alarmed at sin which so easily deceives us, so easily slinks into us, captures and fetters us. Let us be alarmed at our fallen nature which never ceases to produce the tares of sin. We must constantly watch ourselves, check our conduct and spiritual state with the Gospel, and on no account allow any sinful tendency to grow strong and propagate in our soul by regarding this tendency as unimportant. "When led into the beginning of evil, do not say to yourself: It will not overcome me. To the extent that you are led you are already overcome," says St Mark the Ascetic.[5] And we should also know that "the devil makes little sins appear trifling, for otherwise he cannot lead us into great sins," as the same Saint has said.[6]

We must never neglect tares that spring up from the heart, or sinful thoughts that appear to the mind. Thoughts should at once be rejected and banished, and sinful feelings uprooted and destroyed by opposing them with the commandments of the Gospel and by having recourse to prayer. Tares are easily got rid of when they are young and frail. But when they take root with time and habit, then their removal calls for the greatest efforts. A sinful thought when accepted and appropriated by the mind enters into the composition of the mind or understanding and deprives it of soundness; while a sinful feeling that lingers in the heart becomes, as it were, a natural property and deprives the heart of spiritual freedom.

Let us be convinced beyond a doubt of this unfailing truth: God cares indefatigably for a monk and for every Orthodox Christian who surrenders himself heart and soul to the service of God and to the will of God. He keeps him, builds and trains his soul, and prepares him for a blessed eternity. All the sorrows and sufferings caused us by people never come to us except with God's permission for our essential good. If these sorrows and troubles were not absolutely necessary for us, God would never allow them. They are indispensable, in order that we may have occasion to forgive our neighbors and so receive forgiveness of our own sins. They are indispensable, in order that we may discern the providence of God watching over us, and acquire a living faith in God. Such a living faith makes its appearance in us when we learn from numerous experiences that it is the all-powerful hand of God that always delivers us from our troubles and difficult circumstances, and not our skill or ingenuity. They are indispensable, in order that we may acquire love for our enemies, for it is love that finally purifies the heart from the poison of malice and makes it capable of loving God and of receiving that special, abundant grace from God.

The connection between love for our neighbor and love for God is clearly seen in the two stories quoted above. From these stories it is seen that love for our enemies is the highest rung on the ladder of love for our neighbors, through which we enter the vast palace of love for God. Let us force our heart to accept from our neighbors all kinds of offenses and injuries that they may inflict upon us, so as to receive forgiveness of our countless sins by which we have offended the Divine Majesty.

Let us not be overcome by unbelief and give ourselves up to all kinds of cares, anxieties, imaginations, daydreaming, subterfuges, and maneuvering to guard ourselves from our enemies and to work against their ill will or evil intentions. This is forbidden by the Lord Who says, "I tell you not to resist an evil person."[7] When oppressed by difficult and painful circumstances, let us have recourse to God in prayer; for in His complete power are we and our enemies and our circumstances and the circumstances of all men. He can by His absolute power and supremacy dispose of and arrange everything; He can instantly overcome and annihilate all the greatest difficulties. Let us pray for our enemies with great care, and by this prayer obliterate the malice from their hearts and replace it with love. "He who prays for people who offend and wrong him crushes the demons; but he who resists or opposes the former is wounded by the latter," says St Mark the Ascetic.[8]

"Above all," says the Apostle Paul, "[take] the shield of faith with which you will be able to quench all the fiery darts of the wicked one."[9] These darts or arrows are the various actions in us of the demons who stir into motion the weakness and infirmities of our fallen nature: the inflaming of the heart with anger, heated and angry thoughts and fancies, impulses to revenge, vast numbers of anxious and troubled imaginings; and plans, for the most part absurd and impossible, for resisting or opposing one's enemy, for defeating and humiliating him, and for securing for oneself the most solid and stable situation, proof against all dangers.

He who has obtained faith has obtained God as his manager or operator Who will act for him. He has become above and beyond all the cunning and wiles not only of men, but also of the demons. Such a person receives the ability to attain true, pure prayer, undistracted by any cares or anxieties about oneself, or by any fears and apprehensions, free from all daydreams and pictures presented to the imagination by the evil spirits out of malice. By his faith in God the pious monk has entrusted himself to God. He lives in simplicity of heart and free from care and anxiety. He thinks and is concerned about one thing only; namely, how he can become in all respects an instrument of God and accomplish the will of God.

CHAPTER 41

The Meaning of the Term "World"

The word *world* has two special meanings in Holy Scripture. In one sense
it signifies all mankind in the following and similar passages of Scripture: "For God so loved the world that He gave His only begotten Son, that
whoever believes in Him should not perish but have everlasting life. For
God did not send His Son into the world to condemn the world, but that
the world through Him might be saved."[1] "Behold! The Lamb of God who
takes away the sins of the world!"[2]

In the second sense, by the term *world* is meant those people who lead a
sinful life opposed to the will of God, who live for time and not for eternity.
Thus we must understand the word *world* in the following and similar passages: "If the world hates you, you know that it hated Me before it hated you. If
you were of the world, the world would love its own. Yet because you are not
of the world, but I chose you out of the world, therefore the world hates you."[3]
"Do not love the world or the things in the world. If anyone loves the world,
the love of the Father is not in him. For all that is in the world—the desire of
the flesh, the lust of the eyes, and the pride of life—is not of the Father but is
of the world. And the world is passing away, and the lust of it; but he who does
the will of God abides forever."[4] "Adulterers and adulteresses![5] Do you not
know that friendship with the world is enmity with God? Whoever therefore
wants to be a friend of the world makes himself an enemy of God."[6]

Blessed Theophylact the Bulgarian thus defines *world*: "It is usual for
Scripture to call *the world* the life of sinful people of carnal outlook living in
it. That is why Christ said to His disciples, 'You are not of the world.' They
formed a part of the people living in the world, but as they did not live in sin,
they did not belong to the world."[7]

Most people have lived and live a sinful life, abominable in God's sight,
hostile to God. For this reason and because the number of enemies of God is
incomparably greater than the number of true and faithful servants of God,

therefore the majority is called in Scripture *the world*. That is how we must understand the words of the Evangelists: "That was the true Light which gives light to every man coming into the world. He was in the world, and the world was made through Him, and the world did not know Him. He came to His own, and His own did not receive Him."[8] "And this is the condemnation, that the light has come into the world, and men loved darkness rather than light, because their deeds were evil."[9] "Blessed are you when men hate you, and when they exclude you, and revile you, and cast out your name as evil, for the Son of Man's sake…. Woe to you when all men speak well of you, for so did their fathers to the false prophets."[10]

The majority of people did not recognize the Savior. The majority of people hate and hound with calumnies and persecutions the true servants of God. And so great is this majority that the word of God judged it right to attribute the rejection of the God-Man and the persecution of His servants to the whole of mankind. The fact that very few people live lives pleasing to God, and very many gratify their sinful and carnal appetites, the Lord puts beyond all doubt. "Wide is the gate and broad is the way that leads to destruction, and there are many who go in by it. Because narrow is the gate and difficult is the way which leads to life, and there are few who find it."[11] "God's wisdom is vindicated by very few of His children."[12] A few chosen souls recognized Him, a few gave Him His due.

True servants of the true God! Study and learn the real situation appointed for you by the providence of God during your earthly pilgrimage. Do not allow fallen spirits to deceive and seduce you when they set before you earthly prosperity in an attractive, false picture, and suggest that you should desire and strive for it, so as to steal and rob you of your eternal treasure. Do not expect and do not seek praise and approval from human society. Do not hanker after fame and glory. Do not expect and do not seek an untroubled life with plenty of latitude and scope, replete with every convenience. That is not your lot. Do not seek and do not expect love from people. Seek earnestly and demand from yourself love and compassion for others. Be content with the fact that a few true servants of God whom you meet from time to time in the course of your life love you, and with love and interest approve of your conduct and glorify God for you. Such meetings were not frequent even in the flourishing times of Christianity; latterly they have become extremely rare.

Save me, Lord, for there is not one godly man left,
for truth hath minished from among the children of men.
They have talked of vanities every one with his neighbor.[13]

The Holy Abba Dorotheus superbly explains these words of the holy Apostle Paul: "The world has been crucified to me, and I to the world."[14] It is essential for those who are living the monastic life to know this explanation. Here it is: "The Apostle says, 'The world has been crucified to me, and I to the world.' What distinction is there between these two clauses? How is the world crucified to a man, and a man to the world? When a man renounces the world and becomes a monk—leaves his parents, property, gains, trade, business, giving to others and receiving from them—then *the world* is crucified to him, for he has left it. And that is the meaning of the Apostle Paul's words, 'The world is crucified to me.' Then he adds, 'And I to the world.' How is a man crucified to the world? When having freed himself from outward things, he struggles also against pleasures, or against his desire for things, against his own wishes and likings, and mortifies his passions—then he is himself crucified to the world, and he can say with the Apostle, 'The world has been crucified to me, and I to the world.'

"Our fathers, as we have said, having crucified the world to themselves, gave themselves up to asceticism and crucified themselves to the world. And we think that we have crucified the world to ourselves just because we have left it and have come to a monastery. But we do not want to crucify ourselves to the world, for we love its pleasures, we are attached to it, and are interested in its glory; we are attached to food and clothing. If we have any good working tools, we are attached to them, too, and we allow some trifling tool to produce worldly attachment in us, as said Abba Zosimus. We think that by leaving the world and coming to a monastery we have left everything worldly. Yet for the sake of fiddling things we fill ourselves with attachments. This comes from our great stupidity in that, after leaving great and valuable things, in the matter of some trifling things we gratify our passions. Each of us left what he had. The man who had much, left much; and the one who had something, left what he had, each according to his power. And on coming to a monastery, as I said, we cherish our attachment to paltry and trivial things. Yet this is exactly what we should not do; but just as we renounced the world and the things of the world, so we ought to renounce our fondness and attachment to things."[15]

After this explanation it is very understandable why St Isaac the Syrian, who wrote his instructions for monks of the most sublime life—that is to say, for hermits, recluses, and solitaries—defines *the world* thus: "*The world* is the general name for all the passions. If a man has not first learned what the world is, he cannot understand by how many members he is detached from it and by how many he is tied to it. There are many who think themselves free from the world in their life because in two or three respects they refrain from it and have renounced contact with it. This is because they have not understood or perceived with discernment that they are dead to the world only in one or two members, while the rest of their members are living within the carnal mind and belong to the world. Therefore they are not even aware of their passions; and since they are not aware of them, they are not anxious to be cured of them. According to research in spiritual science, the term *world* is used as a common name that embraces separate passions. When we wish to call the passions by a common name, we call them *the world.* But when we want to distinguish them by their special names, we call them passions. Each passion is a particular activity of the 'elemental spirits of the world.'[16] Where the passions have ceased to act, there the elemental spirits of the world are inactive. The passions are the following: love of riches, desire for possessions, bodily pleasure from which comes sexual passion, love of honor which gives rise to envy, lust for power, arrogance and pride of position, the craving to adorn oneself with luxurious clothes and vain ornaments, the itch for human glory which is a source of rancor and resentment, and physical fear. Where these passions cease to be active, there the world is dead. In so far as some of these passions are forsaken, just so far does the ascetic live outside the world which to that extent is destroyed through being deprived of its parts. Someone has said of the saints that while alive they were dead; for though living in the flesh, they did not live for the flesh. See for which of these passions you are alive. Then you will know how far you are alive to the world, and how far you are dead to it. When you understand what the world is, then you will understand these distinctions, and how far you are tied to the world, and how far you are detached from it. In brief, *the world* is the carnal life and the carnal mind."[17]

"The world is a harlot that attracts those who direct their gaze to it with love and longing for its beauty. He who is only partly allured by love for the world and entangled by it cannot escape from its hands before it strips him of life (eternal). When the world completely strips a man and carries him out of its house on the day of his death, then he realizes that the world is a liar and deceiver. While a man is struggling to escape from the darkness of the world and so long as he is in it, he cannot see its meshes. Not only its disciples— children and captives that the world holds in its fetters—but also the renounced and the ascetics and those who had risen above it does the world now begin in various ways to entangle in its service, trampling on them and making them litter for its feet."[18]

On the basis of these conceptions of the world taught us by Sacred Scripture and the holy Fathers, we offer our beloved brother monks this advice and our most urgent entreaty: Let us beware of serving the world, which is a servitude that even ascetics can fall into if they do not strictly attend to themselves, and which can happen through the medium of trifling attachments and trivial objects. Let us take all measures and all precautions to guard ourselves from love of the world. Let us not regard as harmless even the seemingly most insignificant attachment. Let us not consider unimportant the least deviation from the commandments of the Gospel. Let us not forget that thundering warning of the holy Apostle James: "Adulterers and adulteresses! Do you not know that friendship with the world is enmity with God? Whoever therefore wants to be a friend of the world makes himself an enemy of God."[19] In the spiritual sense, every attachment is adultery for a monk, since he is pledged to love God with all his being. And that is what the Psalmist also tells us, "O love the Lord, all ye His saints."[20] "They that go far from Thee will perish; Thou hast destroyed all them that are unfaithful against Thee."[21]

While serving the world it is impossible to serve God. In fact, such double service does not exist. Even though to the distorted sight of the slaves of the world it seems as if such service is real, actually there is no such thing. What appears to be is something different—hypocrisy, pretense, sham, deception of oneself and others. A friend of the world invariably becomes, though he may not notice it himself, the most bitter enemy of God and of his own salvation. Love of the world steals into the soul like a thief, profiting by the darkness of the night—negligence and inattention to oneself. Love of the world is capable of committing the greatest iniquities, the greatest crimes.

We can see a frightful example of this in the Jewish priesthood at the time of the earthly life of the God-Man. It had fallen into love of the world. It was corrupted with a love of honors, glory, and human praise. It had a passion for money and property. It had fallen into materialism and corruption. It was given to extortion and every kind of injustice. And in order to keep its position among the people, it was clothed in a mask of the strictest service of God, the most detailed fulfillment of the appointed rites and traditions of the elders. What was the result of this love of the world? Utter estrangement from God, preceded by a blind and fanatical hatred of God. The Jewish priesthood obdurately opposed the God-Man when He revealed Himself to the world. It opposed Him even though it was fully convinced of His divinity, as is attested by Nicodemus, one of the members of the supreme Jewish council—the Sanhedrin.[22]

The Jewish priesthood determined to resort to murder, and committed it. They certainly knew that in so doing, they were acting in defiance of the Messiah, and in their darkness they admitted this in those scoffings and mockeries with which they sprinkled the world-saving sacrifice on the altar of the cross. "He saved others; Himself He cannot save," said the high priests, scribes, elders, and Pharisees,[23] not realizing that they were pronouncing judgment on themselves. They admit that they are delivering to crucifixion the One they are reviling Who, in a miraculous way, with divine power and authority, saved others.

As soon as they heard the news of His birth, the Jewish priesthood hated the God-Man and took steps to get rid of Him. This is clearly seen from the Gospel. When the magi brought news to Jerusalem of the birth of the Jewish King-Messiah, the reigning Jewish king was troubled, and all the Jewish capital was troubled with him.[24] It was natural, remarks blessed Theophylact the Bulgarian, for the Jewish ruler to be troubled at the news of the birth of a new Jewish King Who might subsequently seize his throne and deprive him or his descendants of power. But why should Jerusalem be troubled at the news of the birth of the Messiah—Jerusalem that for so many centuries had expected the promised Messiah, their Deliverer, their glory—Jerusalem whose whole religion consisted in faith in the coming Messiah and in preparations to welcome Him?

The reason why Jerusalem was troubled was because the religious life of the people of Jerusalem was corrupt. The capital understood with an intuition worthy of a capital city's delicate feelings that the new King, the King of righteousness, would require true virtue and the rejection of immorality, and would not be deceived or satisfied with sham, hypocritical virtue. On account of their love of the world, the monster Herod was more tolerable and acceptable to the people of Jerusalem as their king than God. Gauging correctly the spiritual attitude of the tyrant as that of an actor and humbug, as were also the members of the Sanhedrin, at the first question as to where the Messiah was to be born, without the least hesitation or delay, the chief priests and the scribes promptly told Herod the exact place of the Messiah's birth, and delivered the Messiah into the hands of a murderer. The Christ is to be born "in Bethlehem of Judea," they said. To reinforce their statement, they added, "for thus it is written by the prophet," and they recited a prophecy of striking clarity.[25] If they had had an opposite disposition, they would have given an evasive answer and concealed the place.

The Gospel attributes to lovers of the world all the crimes committed by men, beginning with the murder of Abel by Cain.[26] During the earthly life of the God-Man, lovers of the world crowned their crimes by rejecting Christ and murdering God;[27] and in the last times of the world, they will crown all by welcoming the antichrist and giving him divine honor.[28] How terrible is the love of the world! It enters a person gradually and imperceptibly; but once it gets in, it becomes his cruel and absolute lord. Gradually men develop a disposition and acquire a state of soul that aspires to kill God; gradually they will develop a disposition and acquire a temper and character capable of welcoming the antichrist.[29]

The holy martyr Sebastian excellently exposed the futility of love of the world and its pernicious consequences in his conversation with those martyrs who wavered in the contest through love for their parents and families. St Sebastian said to them, "O staunch warriors of Christ! By your self-sacrificing heroism you were courageously approaching your triumph. But now you want to destroy your eternal crown for the sake of the wretched caresses of your relatives. Now let the courage of the soldiers of Christ teach you to arm yourselves not with iron but with faith. Do not throw down the signs of your victory for the sake of women's tears, and do not release the neck of the enemy (the devil) who was under your feet, lest he should get power and rise again to the attack. If his first onslaught against you was savage, the next will be still more savage. He is enraged and infuriated by his first defeat. Raise up from earthly attachments the glorious standard of your struggle, and do not lose it on account of the idle wailing of children. Those whom you see weeping would have rejoiced now if they knew what you know. But they suppose that the life in this world is the only one there is, and that after ending it by the death of the body, there is no life for the soul. If they knew that there is another life which is deathless and painless, where unceasing joy reigns, they would count temporal life nothing, and would long for the eternal. This present life is fleeting, and so fickle and uncertain that it has never been able to maintain fidelity even to its lovers. All who have trusted in it from the beginning of the world, it has destroyed. All who have desired it, it has deceived. All who have been proud of it, it has insulted. To all it has lied. All have been disillusioned and disappointed, for it has proved utterly false. O, if only it had merely deceived, and not also led into cruel error! Worst of all, it leads its lovers into all kinds of lawlessness. It makes overeating and drunkenness delightful for gluttons, it moves pleasure-lovers to lust and all kinds of impurity. It teaches thieves to steal, the irritable to get angry, liars to bluff and cheat. It sows discord between husbands and wives, enmity between friends, quarrels between the meek, injustice among the just, stumbling blocks among brothers. It takes justice from judges, purity from the chaste, understanding from the sensible, morality from the well-principled. Let us also remember the grave crimes to which it leads its lovers. When a brother has killed his brother, a son his father, or a friend has done his friend to death, at whose instigation have such crimes been committed? At whose command? In hope of what? Is it not for the sake of this present life which people love inordinately, and therefore hate one another, and ill-treat one another, each seeking the best and happiest life for himself? Why does a robber murder a traveler, a rich man outrage a poor man, a proud man insult a humble man, and every wrongdoer persecute the innocent? All this is done by those who serve this life and wish to live for a long time and enjoy its love. This world that suggests all evil to its lovers and servants, delivers them to its daughter, from whom is born eternal death to which the first men were subjected because, being created for eternal life, they gave themselves up to the love of temporary things, and became enslaved to gluttony, pleasure, and the lust of the eyes, and from there fell into hell, without taking any of their earthly goods or pleasures with them.

"This temporary life,"' continued St Sebastian, addressing his fellow martyrs, "is beguiling you to turn back through the bad advice of your friends when you are on your way to eternal life. It teaches you, respected parents, by your senseless wails to divert your sons and prevent them from going to the heavenly army to incorruptible and immortal honor and to friendship with the eternal King. It induces you, chaste wives of the saints, to seduce the minds of the martyrs, and lead them away from their good intention by advising them to choose death instead of life, slavery instead of freedom. If they take your advice, they will live with you for a short time; then they will have to be separated from you by death, and separated in such a way that you will be able to meet them again only in eternal torments, where the flame consumes the souls of the faithless, where the snakes of Tartarus gnaw the mouths of blasphemers, where adders torture the breasts of idolaters, where is heard the bitter weeping, grievous groaning, and incessant wailing of those in torment. Let them escape these torments, and you, try to avoid them yourselves. Allow them once again to rush to the crowns prepared for them. Have no fear; they will not be separated from you. They are going to prepare happy homes for you in heaven where with them and your children you will enjoy the blessings of eternity. If fine stone houses comfort you here, how much more will the beauty of the heavenly homes console you where the tables are of pure gold, where bridal halls shine with the light of glory as if they were made of lovely jewels embellished with precious stones, where ever-blossoming gardens produce unfading flowers, where green meadows are watered by sparkling streams, where the air is always salubrious with refreshing breezes that give a sense of unutterable fragrance, where day never changes to night and light never fails and joy is unbroken. No sighing, no weeping, no sorrow is there, nor is there any ugliness to offend the eye. No bad odor of any kind mars that atmosphere, and no sound of anything sad or sorrowful or terrible is ever heard. For the eye, there is only beauty; for the nose, sweet aromas; for the ear, only rejoicing. There choirs of angels and archangels unceasingly sing, praising in harmony the immortal King. Why is such a life despised and temporary life loved? For wealth? But riches are soon spent. Those who want to have riches with them eternally should listen to what money says: 'You so love me,' it says, 'that you wish never to lose me. After your death I cannot follow you, but during your life I can go ahead of you. If you wish to send me ahead of you, let the grasping moneylender and the hardworking farmer serve as examples. One gives money to his neighbor, so as to get back his money doubled. The other sows various seeds in the earth so as to get a hundredfold increase. The borrower gives back to the moneylender twice the amount he borrowed, while the earth returns to the sower a hundredfold increase of his seeds.' If you entrust your riches to God, will He not repay you with an infinite increase? Send your riches ahead of you, and try to get there yourselves as soon as possible. What advantage is there in this temporary life? If a person were to live even a hundred years, yet when the last day of his life comes, will not all his past years and all the pleasures of life seem as if they had never existed? Only meager traces will remain, memories like the recollection of a traveler who has stayed with us for a single day. Truly he who does not love the sublime eternal life is mad, a complete stranger to true joy and happiness. Truly senseless is he who is afraid to lose this fleeting existence in exchange for the life that is life indeed where delights, riches, and joys begin in such a way that they never cease but remain unending for all eternity. Those who do not want to be lovers of that everlasting life spend their temporary lives in vain, fall into eternal death, and stay bound in hell in unquenchable fire, perpetual misery, unceasing torments; where cruel spirits live whose eyes flash darts of fire, whose teeth are like elephants' tusks in size, whose tails torture like the tails of scorpions, whose eyes are like the eyes of roaring lions, the very sight of whom causes great terror, cruel pain, and bitterest death. O, if only it were possible to die in the midst of these horrors and torments! But the most frightful thing of all is that they never cease to live there, so as to die unceasingly. They are never annihilated and so their torment is without end. They remain whole so as to be eternally devoured by gnawing snakes; their chewed limbs are forever being renewed so as to serve afresh as food for poisonous snakes and the undying worm." [30]

The right use of earthly life consists in preparing oneself for eternal life. Brethren, let us accomplish our brief earthly pilgrimage, making it our one business to please God, borrowing from the world only what is essential. "Now godliness with contentment," says the Apostle Paul, "is great gain. For we brought nothing into this world, and it is certain we can carry nothing out. And having food and clothing, with these we shall be content. But those who desire to be rich fall into temptation and a snare, and into many foolish and harmful lusts which drown men in destruction and perdition."[31]

Love of glory and love of pleasure also lead men to the same sort of moral misery and disaster as love of money. Love of the world consists of these three capital or primary passions.

CHAPTER 42

On Avoiding Acquaintance with the Opposite Sex

Our holy fathers, holy monks of all times, carefully guarded themselves from acquaintance with the opposite sex. Women were forbidden to enter men's monasteries. This good and holy custom is maintained even now on the whole of Mt Athos. Monks who lived an especially attentive life guarded themselves with special care against acquaintance and meetings with women. This may be seen from the lives of saints such as Arsenius the Great, Sisoes the Great, John the Silent, and other fathers of the most sublime holiness. They acted in this way not merely from self-will or personal choice, but because they discovered it was essential according to the guidance that they read clearly as in a mirror in their attentive life.[1]

Some monks say that, though they are often in the company of women, they feel no harm. We should not believe those monks. Either they are not speaking the truth and are hiding their spiritual disorder, or they are leading a most inattentive and listless life and so cannot see their own state; or else the devil is robbing them by dulling their understanding and sense of harm, so as to make their monastic life fruitless and prepare them for eternal perdition.

St Isidore of Pelusium has shown superb discernment on this subject in his letter to Bishop Palladius: "If 'evil company corrupts good habits,'[2] as Scripture says, conversation with women does so in quite a special way. Even though the subject of conversation is good, yet its influence is such that it secretly corrupts the inner man with impure thoughts, and even if the body remains pure, the soul is defiled. As far as possible avoid conversations with women, good man. If you are obliged to have dealings with women, keep your eyes cast down, and teach those with whom you speak to look chastely. Having said a few words to strengthen and enlighten their souls, be off at once so as not to relax and weaken the vigor of your soul by a long conversation. You may say, 'Though I often talk to women, yet no harm comes to me from it.' Granted that it is so, yet I want all to be quite sure that stones are ground by water, and are broken up and worn away by the drops of rain that constantly fall on them. Just think! What is harder than stone, and what is softer than water, and especially drops of water? Yet nature is changed by the constant action. If such a hard nature is overcome, suffers, and diminishes from contact with such a substance as water which is nothing in comparison with it, how can long habit fail to conquer and pervert the human will which is so easily shaken?"[3]

Seraphim of Sarov compared a monk living piously and guarding his chastity to an unlighted wax candle. He says that a monk who has frequent dealings with women is like an unlighted candle when it is placed among many lighted candles. Then the unlighted candle begins to melt owing to the effect of the warmth emitted by the lighted candles standing round it. A monk's heart, says the Saint, cannot fail to be weakened if he allows himself frequent association with women.[4]

The union of the sexes in its essential form is natural (to fallen nature). Virginity is supernatural. Consequently, he who wishes to maintain his body in virginity must without fail keep it at a distance from that body with which nature requires that it should unite. The bodies of man and woman contain an invisible power that mutually attracts body to body.[5] The man who approaches a woman is inevitably subject to the influence of this power. The oftener the approach, the more it is augmented and therefore the stronger the influence. The stronger the influence, the weaker becomes our free will by which we resolve, with God's help, to conquer nature. The figures of women, their glances, their voices, their tenderness and sweetness, make a very strong impression on our souls by the action of nature, especially when Satan cooperates with nature. At the actual time when we are keeping company with women and when the impressions are made, we may not feel it; but when we withdraw into solitude, then the impressions made on the soul rise up within it with extraordinary force and produce a severe conflict of lust.

St Jerome relates of himself that when he was living in Rome and was frequently in the society of the pious ladies and maidens of the capital of the world, he did not feel the slightest lascivious movement either in his mind or in his body. But when the blessed man went to the Bethlehem desert and gave himself up to the strictest monastic exercises, then the figures of women he had seen in Rome suddenly began to appear in his imagination. Then in his elderly body exhausted by thirst, fasting, vigils, and labors, the lusts of youth made their appearance. Victory was very difficult to obtain because, as is usual in such cases, fallen nature was reinforced by the open collaboration of the devil.[6]

What occurred with blessed Jerome occurs with all monks who pass from a social life to a life of silence. They learn from experience the importance of impressions, of which they have no idea so long as they live a life of distraction. All the impressions to which the soul was subject in the midst of human society rise up like dead men from their tombs in the heart of the solitary and urge him to commit sin in his thoughts and feelings, till by the mercy of God and by God's decree all the hordes that came out of Egypt have fallen in the desert. Then a new generation of Israel enters the promised land.[7]

Pure souls that have had no experience of actual sin are subjected to the influence of impressions with special ease. They may be compared to expensive lacquered and varnished tables such as stand in the drawing rooms of wealthy people. A little scratch on such a table becomes very noticeable and destroys its value. On the other hand, people who have not guarded themselves may be compared to kitchen tables on which vegetables and other provisions are daily chopped and cut up. A thousand new grooves or scratches mean nothing for such tables which are covered with innumerable scores. A pure soul the devil tries to corrupt by means of carnal impressions or sensations. This explains why the holy fathers avoided women with such elaborate care. St Arsenius the Great said many hard words about the distinguished Roman lady who traveled all the way from magnificent Rome to the Egyptian desert on purpose to see him and suddenly appeared before him. The hard words of Arsenius consist in his hard but holy outspokenness, "I ask God," he said to the Roman lady, "to wipe the memory of you from my heart."

By these words the Saint expressed all the burden and danger of the struggle with sensations, a struggle that can lead a monk to the gates of hell, and which Arsenius evidently knew from experience.[8] In the same sense, we must also understand the following words of St Macarius the Great:

The heat of a lighted lamp melts butter, and the fire of lust is stirred up by the company of women. A woman's face is a cruel dart that inflicts a wound in the soul. If you wish to be pure, avoid the society of women like poison, because in their society there is a strong pull of sin, like the pull of ravenous beasts. It is not so dangerous to be near a fire as to be near a young woman. Avoid while you are young the turbulent action of impure passion and the society of women. Those who fill their stomach and at the same time hope to acquire purity are deceiving themselves. More terrible is the shipwreck from the look of a beautiful face than shipwreck from a storm at sea. The face of a woman, if formed in the mind, will force one to neglect the very custody of the heart. Flame placed in straw will produce a fire; so impure passionate desire flares up from dallying with the remembrance of a woman.[9]

Macarius the Great could not have said this unless he had experienced the cruel struggle with impressions and sensations received unexpectedly in complete ignorance. St Tikhon of Voronezh has spoken very exactly and truly in his instructions to monks: "Beware of women, beloved, lest you get burned. Eve is always true to her character—she always tempts or entices."[10]

An elder asked his disciple, "Why do the holy Fathers forbid monks, especially young ones, even a short acquaintance with women?" The disciple replied, "Lest by a brief acquaintance with a woman, a monk should fall into fornication with her." The elder replied, "Right! A fall into fornication is the crowning end. Brief acquaintance with women is forbidden a monk by the Holy Spirit." But this acquaintance, though it does not always end in a bodily fall, always leads to disorder and spiritual barrenness. A woman is guided by her feelings that are the feelings of fallen nature, and not by wisdom and spiritual understanding which are completely unknown to her. In a woman, the understanding is the servile tool of the feelings. Carried away by her feelings, she is very soon infected with passionate attachment, not only to a young monk and those of mature years, but even to an elder or old man— she makes him her idol, and then she usually becomes his idol. A woman sees perfection in her idol, endeavors to convince him of it, and always succeeds.

When a monk is infected with conceit and pride as a result of pernicious and incessant suggestions and praises, then the grace of God leaves him. Left to himself, his mind and heart become darkened, and in his blindness he becomes capable of the most senseless behavior and a fearless disregard of all the commandments of God. When Delilah[11] made the judge and ruler of Israel, the mighty Samson, sleep in her lap, then he lost the conditions whereby divine grace accompanied and cooperated with him, and she handed Samson over to the insults and tortures of the Philistines.[12]

It should be noted that a woman who has become acquainted for quite a short time with a monk living in a well-ordered monastery or receiving instruction from a spiritual elder considers it her first duty to draw her lover out of such a monastery and draw him away from his elder or spiritual father in spite of the obvious benefit to the monk of the strictness of the monastery and the instructions of the elder. She wants to have exclusive possession of the object of her passion. In her madness, she regards herself as sufficient and able to take the place of the elder whom she considers and declares to be most inadequate and incapable. She will spare no means to attain her ends—neither means supplied by the world, nor means provided by Satan. Her attachment or infatuation, and often even vicious passion, she calls a living faith, purest love, the feeling of a mother for her son, of a sister for her brother, of a daughter for her father; in a word, she gives it every holy appellation, trying in this way to keep in sacred inviolability her acquired possession—the unfortunate soul of the monk entrusted to her. In a woman, blood prevails; it is in the blood that all the passions of the soul act with special power and subtlety— preeminently vainglory, sensuality, and cunning. The two first are protected by the last.

Here we are not in the least censuring or depreciating the female sex. It is honored by God with the honor of the humanity and image of God, as also is the male sex. It is redeemed by the precious blood of the Savior. Redeemed and renewed, it constitutes together with the male sex one new creature in Christ.[13] Here women are represented as they are when they act according to the anarchic laws of fallen nature, as prompted by their ungoverned blood. Having proved capable of causing Adam to be expelled from Paradise by means of lying and seduction, as Adam bore witness of his wife before God,[14] even now they continue to display and evince this faculty, luring monks who are subject to them from a pious life as from Paradise.

A monk is obliged to love all his neighbors, among whom also are women, with true evangelical love. He undoubtedly shows them this true love when, realizing his weakness and theirs, he guards himself and them from soul-destroying harm, and behaves in their regard with extreme caution, not allowing himself even a brief acquaintance, refraining from all familiarity, and guarding his senses, especially sight and touch.

CHAPTER 43

Concerning the Fallen Angels

The holy Apostle Paul says to all Christians, "For we do not wrestle against flesh and blood, but against principalities, against powers, against the rulers of the darkness of this age, against spiritual hosts of wickedness in the heavenly places."[1]

This struggle is terrible. It is a matter of life and death. The outcome of this conflict must be either our eternal salvation or our eternal perdition. The malicious spirits, rankling with bitter hatred for the human race, wage this warfare with extreme obduracy and infernal skill. The holy Apostle Peter says, "Your adversary the devil walks about like a roaring lion, seeking whom he may devour."[2] But true lovers of God cannot possibly be separated from God by the fallen angels, even though they employ all their powers to effect this separation.[3] They use all their ingenuity to separate us from God because this separation means our perdition. In order to stand firm against the spirits of evil and overcome them by the grace of God, it is necessary to know exactly who they are, how to deal with them, and the conditions of victory and defeat.

The malicious spirits are fallen angels. God created them with the other angels. He created them pure, good, and holy, and He lavished upon them many gifts of nature and grace. But darkened by pride, the spirits ascribed to themselves their abundant skills, their exquisite virtues, the very gifts of grace. They excluded themselves from the category of creatures, and affirmed that they were self-existent beings, forgetting about their creation; and on this disastrous basis they spurned their sacred duties to God their Creator. They were drawn away to this presumption and self-deception by one of the chief angels whom the holy Prophet Ezekiel calls a *cherub*,[4] and whom all the saints in general number among the highest angels. This cherub became so inflated with presumption and pride that he considered himself equal to God,[5] openly rebelled against God, became the adversary of

God, the raging enemy of God. The spirits who refused obedience to God fell from heaven. They creep over the earth and fill the space between earth and heaven; hence they are called the spirits of the air, since the air is their habitat. They descended to hell, to the interior of the earth. All this is recorded in Holy Scripture.[6]

The number of fallen angels is very considerable. Some suppose, basing themselves on the evidence of the Apocalypse,[7] that a third of the angels fell from heaven. Many of the highest angels fell, as is seen from the words of the Apostle Paul cited above; he calls them principalities and powers. The head and prince of the kingdom of darkness composed of fallen spirits is the fallen cherub. Excelling in the talents of every fallen angel, he excels them all in malice and evil. Naturally the spirits allured by him as well as those who obey him voluntarily must constantly borrow evil from him and consequently be in servitude to him. Leaving to the choice of the fallen angels their voluntary continuance in evil, God—in His omnipotence and wisdom, which infinitely surpasses the intelligence of all intelligent creatures—does not cease to remain their supreme, sovereign Lord. They are in the will of God as though in unbreakable chains, and they can do only what God permits them to do.[8]

In place of the fallen angels, God created a new rational creature—man; and He placed him in Paradise, which was in a lower heaven and which was previously under the jurisdiction of the fallen cherub.[9] So Paradise came under the control of the new creature—man. How very understandable that the new creature became an object of envy and hatred to the fallen angel and his satellites? The reprobate spirits, led by their chief, tried to seduce the newly created men to make them share their fall, and so as to have adherents or associates of the same mind; and they endeavored to infect them with the poison of their hatred for God. In this they succeeded.

Although man was deceived and seduced, yet he voluntarily refused obedience to God, voluntarily consented to the diabolic blasphemy against God, voluntarily entered into fellowship with the fallen spirits and into obedience to them. So he fell from God and from the company of holy spirits to whom he belonged not only in soul but also in his spiritual body, and he joined the company of spirits fallen in soul and body to the state of irrational and dumb animals.

The crime committed by the fallen angels against men finally decided the fate of the fallen angels. The mercy and grace of God was finally withdrawn from them, and they set the seal on their fall. The fallen spirit is doomed to creep and crawl in thoughts and feelings that are exclusively carnal and material. It is incapable of raising itself from the earth. It cannot rise to anything spiritual. Such is the meaning, according to the explanation of the holy Fathers, of the sentence pronounced by God on the fallen angel after that angel had infected newly created man with eternal death: "On your belly you shall go," said God to the demon, "and you shall eat dust all the days of your life."[10]

Although man was reckoned among the fallen angels, his fall, on account of the way in which it took place, assumed quite a different character from that of the angels. The angels fell consciously, deliberately, intentionally; they themselves were the cause of the evil within them. Having committed one transgression, they madly rushed to another. For these reasons they were completely deprived of good, were filled to overflowing with evil, and have only evil as their nature. Man fell unconsciously, unintentionally; he was deceived and seduced. For this reason his natural goodness was not destroyed, but was mixed with the evil of the fallen angels. But this natural goodness, being mixed with evil, poisoned with evil, became worthless, inadequate, unworthy of God Who is perfect, purest goodness. Man for the most part does evil, meaning to do good, not seeing the evil wrapped in a mask of goodness on account of the darkening of his mind and conscience. The fallen spirits do evil for the sake of evil, finding enjoyment and fame in doing evil.

God in His unspeakable goodness has given fallen man a Redeemer and redemption. But redeemed man has also been given freedom either to avail himself of the redemption granted him and return to Paradise, or to refuse redemption and remain in the company of the fallen angels. The time assigned to man to express his mind and choice is the whole of our life on earth. By redemption man is restored to fellowship with God; but he is given full liberty to express his will, so it is left to his choice to remain in this fellowship or to break it off, and he is not deprived of the possibility of fellowship with the fallen angels, a fellowship into which he entered voluntarily. While man is in this uncertain state throughout the whole of his earthly life, the grace of God does not cease to assist him till the very moment of his departure to eternity, if he wants it; and the fallen angels do not cease to make every endeavor to hold him in their fellowship as their prisoner and as a slave of sin, in eternal death and ruin.

The reprobate spirit often tried to tempt even the holy martyrs and saintly monks after they had accomplished the greatest penances and miracles just before their end, in sight, so to speak, of the heavenly crowns.[11] Very true is the thought which we meet in the writings of many of the holy Fathers that a monk is in danger of being exposed to some temptation till his very grave, and never knows where it may spring from or what form it may take.

Holy Church teaches us that every Christian receives from God at holy baptism a holy guardian angel who invisibly guards the Christian, guides him to every good work throughout the whole course of his life, and reminds him of the commandments of God. So, too, there is a prince of darkness who wants to drag the whole human race to its ruin and who assigns to each person one of the evil spirits who follows the person everywhere and tries to draw him into every form of sin.[12]

From what has been said, it is clear that a monk should keep vigilant watch over himself throughout his life, and should be filled with both fear and courage. He should be in a constant state of caution and fear on account of his enemy and murderer, and at the same time he should always be bold and courageous from the conviction that continually near him is his mighty helper, his guardian angel. St Poeman the Great says, "The great help of God surrounds a man; but he is not allowed to see it."[13] The reason why he is not allowed to see it, of course, is lest he should rely on that help and become careless and negligent and give up his vigorous ascetic life with its struggles and exploits.

The fallen angel, doomed to creep on earth, uses all his ingenuity to make man crawl on earth, too. Man is extremely prone to this, on account of the self-deception that nestles within him. He has a sense of his eternity, but as this feeling is distorted by his falsely named reason and evil conscience, man's earthly life also seems to him everlasting. On the basis of this illusory, false, ruinous judgment, man gives himself up entirely to the cares and labors of arranging his life on earth, forgetting that he is a passing pilgrim in this world, and that his permanent abode is either heaven or hell. Sacred Scripture says to God in the person of fallen man, " My soul cleaveth to the dust; O give me life, according to Thy word."[14] From these words it is clear that attachment to the earth deadens the soul with eternal death; it is revived by the word of God which, by tearing it away from the earth, lifts its thoughts and feelings to heaven.

"The devil," says St John Chrysostom about the fallen angel, "'is shameless and insolent. He attacks from below. Yet even so he often wins, but that is only because we do not try to raise ourselves to where he is powerless to wound us. For he cannot raise himself high, but creeps over the earth; and that is why the serpent is his type or image. And if God set him crawling at the beginning of things, he is all the more so now. But if you do not know what it means to attack from below, I will try to explain it to you. It means to steal upon you and master you by using low things, by means of pleasures, riches, and all that is earthly. So if the devil sees someone soaring to heaven, first he is not in a position to attack him; and second, if he does risk attacking, he soon falls, because he has not a leg to stand on. Do not be afraid of him; he has no wings. He only crawls over the earth and creeps among earthly things. So have nothing in common with earth; then there will be no need even of labor. The devil cannot fight openly, but just as a snake hides in thorns, so he mostly lurks in the delusions of wealth. If you cut out the thorns, he will soon be scared and take to flight. If you can exorcize him with divine charms, you will easily strike him. And we do have, we surely have spiritual charms: the name of our Lord Jesus Christ and the power of the cross."[15]

St Macarius the Great, learning that a certain monk named Theopemptus was being tempted by impure thoughts induced by the devil, gave Theopemptus the following advice: "Fast till evening, so as to feel real hunger. Learn by heart the Gospel and other books of Holy Scripture, so as to remain always in the thought of God. If an evil thought comes to you, do not accept it. Never allow your mind to be dragged down, but always raise it on high, and God will help you."[16]

A brother asked Abba Sisoes, "What shall I do in order to be saved and please God?" The elder replied, "If you want to please God, quit the world, relinquish the earth, leave creatures, and come to the Creator. Unite yourself with God by prayer and weeping, and you will find rest in this and the future life."[17]

St Barsanuphius the Great wrote to a certain brother, "If you want to be saved, force yourself to die to everything earthly. Regard yourself as nothing, and strive for what lies ahead, lest under the pretext of a good work the devil involve you in untimely worries."[18]

The wily serpent, skilled in the struggle with men and their destruction, does not always resort to powerful expedients to attain his end. Why use them when they may arouse in a monk vigorous resistance and afford him a glorious victory, as is proved by many experiences? Weak expedients act more surely. They are for the most part not noticed, and even if noticed, they are ignored on account of their outward insignificance and apparent harmlessness. Generally speaking, nowadays in the devil's warfare against Christianity and monasticism, powerful expedients are in fact not seen, but only weak shifts. No longer do the Saracens and Latins attack Orthodox monasteries; no longer are monks burned and killed in order to destroy Orthodox monasticism. It is destroyed by imperceptible snares in which it is caught extremely easily according to the custom of our time. Earthly occupations—when a monk devotes himself to them with enthusiasm, even without obvious sins— are quite capable of depriving him of success and progress and of desolating his unfortunate soul. Such a soul becomes an abode of demons, according to the witness of the Gospel.[19] When the heart of a tree is infected with rot, then the tree is gradually and imperceptibly ruined, though its exterior for a long time continues to maintain its beauty, without showing the inner death that is eating it away. Weak expedients, without touching the exterior of monasticism, destroy its essence. What is a monk? Is he not a Christian who has separated himself from everything and become united in heart and mind in order to belong to God alone, and has entered into inseparable fellowship with Him? But where is the monk when he is estranged from God and attached to the earth?

Among the number of weak expedients, yet whose effect is extremely powerful, belong various forms of handwork and bodily labor, when a monk engages in them excessively and with attachment, and this happens time after time with self-appointed occupations, not undertaken by obedience. In these occupations attachment to them imperceptibly creeps in. At first, special attention and zeal is shown for the work. Then the monk devotes all his powers of soul and body to the work, while he forgets and forsakes God. Meanwhile the snake tries to make the monk imagine that his occupation is innocent, even soul-saving and generally useful. By the serpent's cunning, praises and approbations for his work begin to reach the monk's ears from all sides. He is infected with conceit. His soul, unenlightened by the word of God, is wrapped in the darkness of ignorance and stupidity. He acts under the full control of the fallen spirit.

When a soul abandons his spiritual exercises—or what amounts to the same thing, performs them listlessly, perfunctorily, and coldly—and employs himself solely or principally, with attachment and enthusiasm, in earthly occupations, then the passions belonging to our fallen nature have free play in the heart with nothing to disturb them. They grow, enlarge, increase in scope and freedom. Then the monk enjoys an illusory calm, consoling himself with conceit and vainglory, and thinking it is the consolation of grace. Those who do not wrestle with their passions leave them undisturbed. And even if the passions are disturbed for a short time, one who is unaccustomed to self-scrutiny pays no attention to it, and merely tries to calm the passions by some earthly distraction. Such calm, or more accurately, spiritual sleep—without compunction, without remembrance of death and judgment, heaven and hell, without concern to obtain God's mercy in good time and be reconciled and united with Him—the holy Fathers call insensibility, deadening of the soul, death of the spirit while the body is still alive.[20] During the terrible slumber of the soul, the passions and especially those of the soul grow to incredible dimensions, and acquire strength and power beyond natural capacities. The monk perishes without his noticing it.

St John Cassian, who visited the monasteries of Egypt at the end of the fourth or beginning of the fifth century at a time when monasticism was particularly flourishing and shone with a galaxy of spiritual lights, relates that the monks of the Egyptian desert called Kalamon, which was at a very considerable distance from worldly settlements and was practically inaccessible to people of the world, showed far less success and progress in the monastic life than the monks of the desert of Scetis, which was not far from worldly habitations or even from the crowded city of Alexandria. The cause of this, St John Cassian sees in the following: the desert of Scetis was the most barren, and so its monks were not distracted either by cultivation of the land or by contemplation of the beauties of nature. They remained in the silence of their cells occupied with the simplest kinds of handwork, continuing constantly in prayer, in reading and studying the word of God, and in discerning the thoughts and feelings that arose within them. By leading such a concentrated life, they soon obtained success, and their progress reached the highest degree of perfection. On the other hand, Kalamon was an extensive, fertile island, an oasis in the desert resembling Paradise, with plenty of magnificent trees and large numbers of plants of various kinds suited to the tropical climate. The island was surrounded on all sides by a vast sea of sand, so it could be justly called a sandy steppe, in the midst of which was Kalamon. It was extremely difficult of access. The monks of Kalamon, attracted by the conveniences of the place, were largely occupied in gardening and agriculture. The beauty of nature offered many opportunities for distraction. By giving a considerable part of their attention to the earth, they could not apply it wholly to heaven.[21]

In the "Life of St Sava," who was Archbishop of Serbia, it is said that when he visited the holy solitaries of Athos, he found them entirely free of all earthly occupations. They were not employed in agriculture, vine-growing, or the sale of their own handwork. They had no earthly cares or worries whatever. Their one occupation was prayer, tears, and the turning of the mind and heart to God.[22] St Arsenius the Great was so careful to avoid distraction to some subtle passion such as pride and vainglory, that he wrote neither letters nor books, although he was fully capable and was equipped with learning and spiritual attainment.[23]

The great monks of antiquity such as Anthony the Great, Macarius the Great, and others who were endowed by God with great strength of body and soul, did much handwork. But their handwork was so simple, and it became so habitual, that it did not hinder them in the least from being occupied in prayer at the same time. They so accustomed themselves to their simple handwork that their mind was free to be immersed in profound prayer and to be lifted up in vision while their hands continued to work automatically. Their work was so simple and so much a matter of habit that it demanded no attention from the mind whatever.[24] Very many of the ancient monks made rope, others made baskets or rugs and mats. It can be easily seen that even some of our present-day handicrafts need very little attention when we have the skill, for example knitting socks or stockings. Those who are skilled in this work produce it without looking at it at all, and while knitting they freely occupy their mind with other objects. But other occupations—for instance, painting—require great attention. Those who are skilled in painting, even though they can practice it with prayer, yet it is impossible for them to immerse themselves wholly in prayer because their craft requires them frequently to give their full attention to it. Painting arouses great feeling and interest for it in the soul, and then our ardor and aspiration cannot fail to be divided between God and our handicraft.

From the examples given, we can judge also about other forms of handwork. It is vital that the monk's heart should be detached from his handwork, especially in the case of intellectual occupations liable to divert a person from humility and God, and draw him to pride and ego worship. With occupations of this kind we should take special care to do our work for the glory of God and for the common good, and not for our vainglory and self-love. It is impossible to work for God and mammon at the same time. It is impossible to work for God and at the same time indulge our own inclinations, predilections, and passions.

From what has been said here, we give our beloved brother monks the advice to observe extreme caution with regard to earthly occupations, knowing that the malicious and wily serpent is creeping over the earth, always ready to wound us and pour his deadly poison into us. Novices and probationers should devote themselves with all care and diligence to their appointed obedience for God's sake and for their own salvation, without delighting in its successful accomplishment, without boasting of it, and without developing vainglory, conceit and pride whereby obedience is changed from an instrument of salvation into an instrument and means of perdition.

One should constantly pray to God for the successful accomplishment of an obedience, and ascribe success solely to the mercy and grace of God. And when a monk is given freedom to use a considerable part of his time at his own discretion, he should guard himself from attachment to any kind of material occupation and to all that is earthly and corruptible as from deadly poison. He should unceasingly raise his mind on high. To raise the mind on high does not mean to imagine heavenly dwellings, angels, the splendor of God, and all that sort of thing. No! Such dreaming only gives occasion to diabolic delusion. Without any reverie let the monk raise his thought with spiritual feeling to the judgment of God; let him be filled with salutary fear from the conviction that God is present everywhere and knows everything; let him weep and confess to God Who is present in his cell and looking at him; let him ask in good time for forgiveness and mercy, remembering the multitude of his sins and his imminent death. If the time given for repentance and for obtaining a blessed eternity is wasted in temporal occupations and for earthly gains and acquisitions, it will not be given a second time. Its loss is irreplaceable. Its loss will be bewailed in hell with futile and eternal tears. If during his earthly pilgrimage a person does not break his connection with evil spirits, he will remain in fellowship with them even after his death, more or less belonging to them, depending upon the degree of intercourse. Unbroken intercourse with fallen spirits consigns one to eternal perdition, while insufficiently broken relations render one liable to severe torments on the way to heaven.

Look, brethren, look what the devil is doing, has done, and will do— leading the mind of man from the spiritual heaven to material things, chaining the heart of man to earth and earthly pursuits and occupations! Look and be alarmed with a healthy fear! Look and beware with necessary soul-saving caution! The fallen spirit busied certain monks with obtaining various rare and costly things; then, by attaching their minds to these things, he estranged them from God. Others he employed in various studies and arts, anything so long as the aim was earthly; then, having drawn all their attention to passing studies, he deprived them of the vital and necessary knowledge of God. Others he employed in obtaining for the monastery various improvements, buildings, cultivation of flower gardens, kitchen gardens, pastures, meadows, cattle breeding or dairy farming, and forced them to forget God. Others he occupied in decorating their cells with flowers, pictures, the making of furniture or rosaries, and withdrew them from God. Others he attached to a lathe, and taught them to ignore and neglect God. Others he taught to give special attention to their fasting and other bodily exercises and to attribute special significance to dry bread, mushrooms, cabbage, peas, or beans; and in this way sensible, holy, and spiritual exercises were turned into senseless, carnal, and sinful farces. The ascetic was corrupted and reduced to carnal and falsely-called knowledge, conceit, and contempt for his neighbors which snuffs out the very conditions for progress in holiness and provides the conditions for ruin and perdition. Others he inspired to attach an exaggerated importance to the material side of church services, while obscuring the spiritual side of the rites; thus, by hiding the essence of Christianity from these unfortunate people and leaving them only a distorted material wrapper or covering, he enticed them to fall away from the Church into the most foolish form of clouded perception, into schism.

So easy is this kind of conflict for the fallen spirit that now he employs it everywhere. It is so easy for the devil to ruin men by this kind of warfare that he will make use of it in the last days of the world to draw the whole world away from God. These are the tactics the devil will use, and he will use them with marked success. In the last days of the world, through the influence of the lord of the world, men will be full of attachment to the earth and to everything carnal and material. They will give themselves up to earthly cares and material development. They will busy themselves solely with the affairs of earth as if it were their eternal home. Having become carnal and material, they will forget eternity as if it did not exist, they will forget God and abandon Him. "As it was in the days of Noah," our Lord foretold, "so will it be also in the days of the Son of man: They ate, they drank, they married wives, they were given in marriage, until the day that Noah entered the ark, and the flood came and destroyed them all. Likewise as it was also in the days of Lot: they ate, they drank, they bought, they sold, they planted, they built; but on the day that Lot went out of Sodom it rained fire and brimstone from heaven and destroyed them all. Even so will it be in the day when the Son of Man is revealed."[25]

In order to stand firm against fallen spirits, we need to see them. A struggle is possible only with an opponent who can be sensed by feelings of body or soul. When an enemy is invisible, when his weapons are invisible, when no sensation or feeling gives evidence of his presence and activity, then he is equivalent to a nonexistent enemy. Then what battle can there be?

Spirits, invisible to our bodily eyes, are visible to the eyes of our soul, to our mind and heart. But the holy fathers who had attained purity and perfection saw the spirits with their bodily eyes as well. For us who cannot see the fallen spirits with our bodily eyes, it is necessary to learn to see them with the eyes of the soul. To explain how spirits appear to men and how they can be seen by men, we will relate the two following stories.

St Macarius the Great lived the life of a solitary in Scetis in the Egyptian desert. At some distance from his cell was a large community of monks under his direction who lived the life of hermits. Their cells were about a stone's throw apart. Once, the Saint was sitting on the path leading to the monks' cells. Suddenly he saw a devil coming in the form of a man, carrying a lot of crockery. The elder asked, "Where are you going?" The devil replied, "I am going to disturb the brethren." The elder asked, "What have you got in those crocks?" The devil replied, "Food for the brethren." The elder asked, "Food in all the crocks?" He said, "Yes. If one kind of food does not suit a person, I give him another, and then a third, and so on with all the foods one after another, so that each may taste at least one." So saying, the devil went on his way, while the elder stayed on the path and waited for him to return. When he saw him coming back, the elder said to him, "Be well!" "How can it be well with me?" he replied. "Why is that?" asked the elder. "Because," replied the devil, "all the monks were ill-disposed toward me, and not one of them received me." The elder said, "And so don't you have a single friend among them?" The devil replied, "I have one friend there who listens to me. But when I come to him and he sees me, he begins to whirl in all directions." The elder asked, "What is his name?" The devil said, "Theopemptus." So saying, he went off. St Macarius searched out Theopemptus and went into his cell for a talk. He found that the monk had not recognized the devil who had appeared to him, had conversed with him, and had enjoyed the thoughts he had brought to him without realizing or suspecting that he had thereby entered into fellowship and most intimate intercourse with the fallen spirit. The Saint taught Theopemptus how to struggle with the devil, and turn demons from friends into enemies.[26]

From this story it is clear that Theopemptus saw the devil, as also the devil attested, but he saw him only with his mind in various sinful thoughts. The devil's coming to Theopemptus was made known by a special influx of obtrusive and seductive thoughts with which he did not know how to deal. This produced a state of perplexity, unrest, and confusion. He conversed with the thoughts evidently without realizing that they were offered by the devil, but supposing that they arose in his own soul. He tried to calm them by reasoning and arguing with them, but he was finally carried away by them and took pleasure in them.

In a second example, another great servant of God, St Macarius of Alexandria, once saw with his bodily eyes a lot of child-size black demons, running and flying about in the church. It was the custom in that community for one monk to read the Psalms slowly in the middle of the church while all the rest of the monks sat and listened attentively to him.[27] The Saint saw that beside each monk sat a demon who made sport of him. The demons put their fingers on the eyes of one monk, and he immediately began to doze. They put their fingers on the mouth of another, and he began to yawn. To some, they appeared in the form of women; before others, they erected build-ings, brought various things, and engaged in various occupations. When the divine service was over, St Macarius called each brother to him and asked him privately what he had been thinking or dreaming about during divine worship. It turned out that each had been thinking or dreaming about what the spirits had portrayed before him.[28]

From this story it is evident that spirits influence us not only by means of idle and sinful thoughts but also by idle and sinful dreams, even by touch and various kinds of contact. All this becomes quite clear in due time from personal experience to a monk leading an attentive life in accordance with the Gospel commandments. "The devils enter our senses and members," says St John Karpathios, "torment our flesh with the heat of passion, make us look, hear, and smell lustfully, inspire us to say what should not be said, fill our eyes with adultery, and throw us into confusion, acting from outside and within us."[29]

In order to explain to some extent for everyone how spirits, those gas-like or vapory intelligent beings, can enter the members of our body, produce in them their own peculiar effect, attack the very soul, and influence it, we shall point out similar action of certain gases. Take the case of suffocation caused by heavy carbonic gas, invisible to our eyes of our senses, which enters and poisons our system by means of the sense of smell. Take the case of alcohol (spirits); from the use of wine or other liquor, alcohol passes from the stom-ach through the body to the head, and affects the brain and the mind in a manner that is incomprehensible to us. The alcohol or spirits, then, passing from the stomach into the blood in a way we now understand produces heat-ing of the blood (or what amounts to the same thing), brings it into physical union with caloric,[30] that subtle gaseous material, and subjects both body and soul to the influence of this material. Gaseous materials have the property of entering into hard substances and into other gases, and of passing through them. Thus, a sunbeam passes through the air and through all known gases belonging to the earth, through water, through ice, through glass. Heat eas-ily penetrates through iron and through all metals and produces a change in them; it passes also through those gases through which light passes. Air passes through wood, but it does not pass through glass. Steam and various smells (i.e., gases) pass through air.

St Macarius the Great says, "Ever since through the transgression of the commandment (by the first people in Paradise) evil entered into men, the devil has obtained free access always to converse with the soul as man con-verses with man, and to instill into the heart all that is harmful."[31]

The devil converses with a person without using a voice, yet with words; because thoughts are the same as words, only not uttered by a voice, not clothed in sounds without which men cannot communicate their thoughts to each other. In the same Word, Macarius the Great says, "The devil acts so cunningly that all evil appears to us as if it were born of itself in the soul and not from the extraneous action of an alien spirit acting maliciously and endeavoring to remain hidden."[32]

Clear signs of the coming to us and action upon us of the fallen spirit are the sudden appearance of idle and sinful thoughts and fancies, heaviness of the body and an increase of its animal needs, hardening of the heart, arrogance and haughtiness, vainglorious thoughts, rejection of repentance, forgetfulness of death, despondency and boredom, or a special inclination for earthly occupations. The coming of the fallen spirit is always associated with a sense of confusion, disturbance, gloom, and perplexity.

"Thoughts coming from demons," says Barsanuphius the Great, "are above all filled with confusion, disquiet, and sadness, and they secretly and subtly draw the soul after them. For the foes wear the clothing of sheep, that is, they suggest thoughts apparently right and true, but 'inwardly they are ravenous wolves,'[33] that is, they ravish and 'deceive the hearts of the simple'[34] by what seems good but in reality is evil and harmful."[35] This subject is treated in a similar way by all the great guides of monasticism.

With monks who stand firmly against the rejected spirits in the warfare that is invisible to the eyes of our senses, in due time, but only with the permission of God Who does all for our good, the spirits enter into open combat.[36] Since they are volatile beings without flesh and bones,[37] they assume the forms of various wild beasts and animals, reptiles and insects, in size both very large and very small. They try to terrify monks, unsettle and derange them, give them a high opinion of themselves, even cast them into that ruinous state called diabolic delusion. Humble surrender to the will of God, discernment and readiness to endure all the sufferings that God may permit, complete disregard and distrust of all words, actions, and apparitions of fallen spirits effectually frustrate their endeavors. Attention to them and trust in them always cause the greatest harm, and often the monk's ruin.

By struggling aright with the spirits, the soul of a monk derives abundant profit, and makes special progress. St Macarius the Great says, "For babes in spirit, the prince of this world is a rod that punishes and a whip that causes wounds. Yet in this way, as was said above, by means of trials and temptations, he procures great honor and glory for them. For he thus helps them to attain perfection, while he prepares for himself the most grievous torment.... The devil, being a slave and creature of God, does not tempt as much as he likes, nor does he let loose his fury as much as he wishes, but in so far as God permits and allows him. For God, knowing perfectly everything about everyone and how much strength each person has, allows each to be tempted according to his powers."[38]

One who has a living faith in God and who surrenders himself to God with self-renunciation, remains untroubled in all trials and temptations caused by evil spirits, and sees in the fiends only the blind tools of divine providence. Without paying any attention to them during trials caused by them, he surrenders himself entirely to the will of God. Surrender to the will of God is a calm, restful haven in all trials and afflictions.[39]

CHAPTER 44

The First Way of Struggling with the Fallen Angels

In the previous chapter we explained as well as we could how the fallen angels struggle with men. That was mostly necessary and comprehensible for monks who have attained some proficiency. Here we offer a way of struggling with the spirits suitable for beginners and which is practically all their experience will allow them to grasp.

The way for a beginner to struggle with an invisible spirit that is visible only to the mind in thoughts and visions is to reject the sinful thought or vision immediately without entering into conversation or argument with it and without paying any attention to it, so that the thought or fantasy may not have time to make any impression on the mind and so get possession of the mind. At first, for the most part, a mere formless thought that only brings a reminder of sin acts imperceptibly on a monk of some spiritual proficiency and experience. Only if the mind dallies with the thought does a sinful figment appear to bolster the thought. To a beginner or novice in whom the flesh and blood is very wanton, thought and sinful fantasy appear together. If he delays even momentarily in the matter of attention and begins a conversation with the thought, though apparently without consenting to it and seemingly contradicting and opposing it, he will invariably be defeated and seduced by it. Even the most experienced monk, though he has spent a century in monastic exploits, is insufficiently experienced in comparison with the fallen angel whose experience in struggling with the servants of God has been cultivated for thousands of years. What sense can there be, then, for an inexperienced novice or probationer to struggle with this angel when he is even without an experiential, living knowledge of the very existence of the fallen angel? Engagement with this invisible foe is certain defeat for a beginner.

Our first mother Eve, in spite of the fact that she was in a state of innocence and holiness, had scarcely entered into conversation with the serpent when she was seduced by his cunning into transgressing God's commandment and fell.[1] She should never have entered into conversation with the wily serpent. She should never have discussed the value of God's commandment. Having no experiential knowledge of evil or of the tempter—ill-intentioned beings usually hide their evil intentions by simulation, hypocrisy, and cunning—she was easily allured by the advice of the murderer[2] who veiled his murderous counsel under a mask of good intention. It is to this sort of deception and catastrophe that inexperienced monks expose themselves. "Our soul," says St Hesychius of Jerusalem, "being simple and good—for that is how it was created by its good Lord—is delighted by the fantastic suggestions of the devil. Once it is seduced, it rushes to evil that is presented to it as good and mingles (unites) its own thoughts with the fantasy of the devil's suggestion."[3]

All the Fathers agree that a novice should reject sinful thoughts and fantasies at their very inception, without entering into argument or converse with them. Especially one should act in this way with regard to unchaste thoughts and fantasies. For repelling sinful thoughts and fantasies, the Fathers offer two expedients: (1) immediate confession of thoughts and fantasies to the elder, and (2) immediate recourse to God with most fervent prayer to dispel the invisible enemies.

Says St John Cassian, "Ever watch the serpent's head, that is, the beginning of thoughts, and at once confess them to your elder. You will learn to crush his dangerous beginnings if you are not ashamed to disclose them all without exception to your elder."[4]

This way of dealing with diabolic thoughts and fancies was in general use among all novices in the flourishing times of monasticism. Novices living constantly in close contact with their elders confessed their thoughts at all times, as may be seen from the life of St Dositheus.[5] Novices who visited their elder at a certain time confessed their thoughts once a day, in the evening, as may be seen from *The Ladder of Divine Ascent*[6] and other Patristic books. Confession of one's thoughts and direction by the counsel of a Spirit-filled elder were considered indispensable by the ancient monks, without which it was impossible to be saved.

Says the holy Abba Dorotheus, "I know of no other fall for a monk except when he entrusts himself to his own heart. Some say that a person falls on account of this or that; but for my part, as I have already said, I know of no other fall except when a person goes his own way or follows his own will. Have you seen a fallen person? Know that he followed his own will. There is nothing more perilous, nothing more ruinous than this. God preserved me and I always dreaded this disaster.'"[7]

The directions of a Spirit-filled elder lead the novice constantly by way of the commandments of the Gospel, and nothing so separates him from sin and the demon who is the source of sin as constant and repeated confession of sin in its very beginnings. Such confession establishes between man and the devil an implacable but salutary enmity. Also, by destroying all duplicity or wavering between love for God and love for sin, such confession gives extraordinary power to the monk's good will and therefore unusual speed to his progress. This can also be seen from the life of St Dositheus.

Those monks who were unable to take action against sin by constant and frequent confession of sinful thoughts on account of their not having an elder, opposed it by constant and frequent prayer, as for example St Mary of Egypt.[8] The act of prayer must be most decisive and determined, without any preliminary intercourse with the thought, still more without taking any pleasure in it. As soon as you feel the enemy coming, stand up for prayer, bend your knees, raise your hands to heaven or stretch them out over the earth. With this lightning, strike the enemy in his face, and he will not be able to hold out against you; he will soon learn a lesson and take to flight helter-skelter.

Renunciation of duplicity—that is, of wavering between love for God and love for sin—is indispensable. By this repudiation, our free will and ardor for God is preserved, grows, and increases, whereby we attract to us the special mercy of God. "If we constantly hold the sword[9] in our hands," says Poemen the Great, "then God will be constantly with us; if we are courageous and generous, God will show us His mercy."[10] A superb example of wrestling by prayer against sinful thoughts may be seen in the "Life of St Mary of Egypt."

Says St Isaac the Syrian, "Not to contradict or argue with the thoughts cunningly sown in us by the enemy, but to cut off all intercourse with them by prayer, is a sign of a mind that has found wisdom and power by grace. Its true understanding of the situation frees it from much (vain and superfluous) labor. By taking this shortcut, we cut out the devious circuits of a long ramble. For we do not at all times have the power to reduce to silence all opposing thoughts by argument and to conquer them. For the most part, we receive wounds, and the healing of these injuries may take a long time. You are challenging foes with six thousand years experience behind them! Your conversation with them will provide them with the means of bringing about your downfall, for they are far superior to you in wisdom and knowledge. But even if you win, your mind will be defiled by their vile thoughts, and their foul stench will linger in your memory. By using the first method (i.e., by refusing discussion), you will be free from all these effects and from fear. There is no help apart from God."[11]

In particular we should especially avoid conversation and argument with salacious thoughts. By such argument, the ascetic mostly gives himself up, mistakenly supposing that the lustful thoughts and fantasies have sprung up in his own soul of themselves and can be controlled by the power of his own reasonable admonishment—not understanding, on account of his inexperience, the invasion of the demon who readily enters into conversation and argument with us, knowing for certain that sensual thoughts and fantasies will find sympathy in the soul of a novice and will arouse and excite the sensuality latent within him. He decoys and draws us into conversation and argument—now yielding and retreating, then again attacking—in full hope of obtaining a decisive victory over us. St John of the Ladder has said, "Do not expect to overthrow the demon of fornication by arguments and disputes; for with nature on his side, he has the best of the argument. He who has resolved to contend with his flesh and conquer it himself struggles in vain. For unless the Lord destroys the house of the flesh and builds the house of the soul, the man who wants to destroy it watches and fasts in vain. Offer to the Lord the weakness of your nature, fully acknowledging your own powerlessness and inability, and you will receive imperceptibly the gift of chastity."[12] "This demon, much more than any other, watches for critical moments. And when we are physically unable to pray against it, then the unholy creature launches a special attack against us."[13]

"For those who have not yet obtained true prayer of the heart, violence in bodily prayer helps—I mean stretching out the hands, beating the breast, sincere raising of the eyes to heaven, deep sighing and groaning, frequent prostrations. But often they cannot do this owing to the presence of other people, and so the demons especially choose to attack them just at this very time. And as we have not yet the strength to resist them by firmness of mind and the invisible power of prayer, we yield to our enemies. If possible, go apart for a brief spell. Hide for a while in some secret place. Raise on high the eyes of your soul, if you can; but if not, your bodily eyes. Hold your arms motionless in the form of a cross, in order to shame and conquer your Amalek by this sign. Cry to Him Who is mighty to save, not with cleverly spun phrases but in humble words, preferably making this your prelude: 'Have mercy on me, for I am weak.' Then you will know by experience the power of the Most High, and with invisible help you will invisibly drive away the invisible ones. He who accustoms himself to wage war in this way will soon be able to put his enemies to flight solely by spiritual means; for the latter is a recompense from God to doers of the former; and rightly."[14]

"When we are lying in bed, let us be especially sober and vigilant in prayer, because then our mind struggles with the demons without our body, and if it is sensual, it readily becomes a traitor. Let the remembrance of death and the Jesus Prayer continue as you sleep and remain to get up with you."[15]

The impure fiend shamelessly attacks even saints and Spirit-filled men. This may be seen from the lives of St Macarius of Alexandria, St Pachomius the Great, and other servants of God. Even for holy persons, prayer of the heart alone was not always sufficient to resist the enemy (who has a support in our fallen nature), and in time of intense conflict they sometimes had to resort to bodily asceticism, to reinforcing prayer of the heart with the participation of the body in prayer, to bridling the body by work till it was exhausted.

Against some monks of extremely attentive and recollected life who have preserved bodily virginity, the spirit of impurity hurls himself with special fury. This happened in the case of a young monk, upset by the advice of an inexperienced elder, of whom St John Cassian tells in his discourse on discretion. St Poemen the Great says, "As a royal guard or armor bearer stands in the king's presence in constant readiness, so the soul must be always ready against the demon of fornication."[16] For this reason, monks struggling with violent passions should be always ready to resist the fiend. And even while in bed for sleep and refreshment, they lie clothed and with their belts on, as if they were armed. They are indeed armed with fervor and vigilance, so that if the enemy makes his appearance they can at once rise and repulse him. That is why in some well-ordered monasteries on Mt Athos that ancient and holy custom has been kept whereby all the brethren are obliged to sleep fully dressed. Such a custom is indicated by the Gospel itself.[17]

You should know, pious monk, that when Satan comes to you with his temptation, your omnipresent Lord is here, too, looking at you, at your mind and heart, and waiting to see how your contest will end:[18] by your remaining faithful to the Lord or by your betraying Him?[19] By your showing love for the Lord and entering into fellowship with Him, or by your showing love for Satan and entering into fellowship with him? One or the other invariably occurs as a result of collision with the invisible enemy. True monasticism is invisible martyrdom. A monk's life is a chain of continual struggles and sufferings. The victor is given eternal life—the betrothal of the Holy Spirit. The monk whom God wishes to enrich with spiritual knowledge and spiritual gifts is allowed to endure violent conflicts. "He who overcomes shall inherit all things," says Scripture, "and I will be his God and he shall be My son."[20] And so, let us not be discouraged or despondent!

CHAPTER 45

The Second Way of Struggling
with the Fallen Angels

St Nil Sorsky, following the teaching of St Isaac the Syrian, offers the following method of dealing with sinful thoughts. But this is only for when
the conflict is not violent and when it yields to this treatment. This method
consists in changing evil thoughts into good ones, and converting passions
into virtues. For instance, if a thought of anger and resentment comes to
us, it is useful to remember meekness and forgiveness, and the Lord's commandments that strictly forbid anger and resentment.[1] If a thought or feeling
of sadness comes, it is useful to remember the power of faith and the words
of the Lord Who has forbidden us to give way to fear and sadness, declaring
and assuring us by His divine promise that even the hairs of our head are
numbered, and that nothing can happen to us without the providence and
permission of God.

St Barsanuphius the Great has said, "The Fathers say, if demons entice
your mind to fornication, remind it of chastity; and if they allure it to gluttony, remind it of fasting. Act in this way also in regard to the other passions."[2]
Do this when thoughts of avarice, love of money, pride, vainglory, and other
sinful thoughts and fancies arise. This method, we repeat, is very good when
it proves sufficiently powerful; it is shown us by the Lord Himself.[3]

But when the passions are roused, and the mind is darkened and confused
at the enormity of the temptation, and thoughts assail with persistence and fury,
then—not only against lustful thoughts, but also against thoughts of anger,
sadness, despondency, sloth, despair, greed, in fact against all sinful thoughts—
the surest and most reliable weapon is prayer with the body's participation in
it. Once again it is the Lord Himself Who has given us an example of this and
enjoined it. In His agony before His death in the garden of Gethsemane, the
Savior of the world bowed His knees and fell on His face and prayed pros-
trate. And to His disciples, who did not understand the great anguish that was
approaching, He said, "Watch and pray, lest you enter into temptation."[4]

CHAPTER 46

Concerning Dreams

Demons use dreams to disturb and injure human souls. Likewise, inexperienced monks, by paying attention to their dreams, harm themselves. It is therefore essential here to determine the exact significance of dreams in a person whose nature has not yet been renewed by the Holy Spirit.

During sleep, the state of a sleeping person is so designed by God that the whole man is in complete repose. This repose is so complete that a person loses consciousness of his existence and is in a state of oblivion or self-forgetfulness. During sleep, all voluntary activity and labor governed by the will and reason stops. Only that activity continues that is essential for existence and cannot be relinquished. In the body, the blood continues its circulation, the stomach digests food, the lungs maintain respiration, the skin perspires. In the soul, thoughts, fantasies, and sensations continue to be produced, only without dependence on the will and reason, but by the action of our unconscious nature. A dream consists of such fantasies accompanied by their peculiar thoughts and sensations. It often seems strange, as if it bore no relation to the person's voluntary and purposeful thoughts and imaginings, but appears spontaneously and whimsically in accordance with a law and demand of nature. Sometimes a dream bears an incoherent impression of voluntary thoughts and fancies, while sometimes it is a result of a particularly moral state of mind. Thus, a dream in itself cannot and should not have any significance. The desire of certain people to see in the ravings of their dreams a prediction of their future or the future of others or some other meaning is ludicrous and quite illogical. How can that be which has no cause for its existence?

The demons, who have access to our souls during our waking hours, have access also during sleep. And during sleep they tempt us to sin by mixing their fantasy with our fantasy. Also when they observe in us a regard for dreams, they try to increase our interest in our dreams. Then by arousing greater attention to these ravings, they gradually lead us to put our trust in them. Such trust is always accompanied by conceit, and conceit makes our mental view of ourselves false, whence all our activity becomes unsound. This is just what the demons want. To those who are advanced in this self-opinionated state, the demons begin to appear in the form of angels of light, in the form of martyrs and saints, even in the form of the Mother of God and of Christ Himself. They applaud the way these dupes are living, promise them heavenly crowns, and in this way they lead them to the height of self-opinion and pride. This height is at the same time the abyss of perdition.

We need to know beyond a shadow of doubt that in our present state, while still unrenewed by grace, we are unfit to see dreams other than those concocted for our harm by the guile of the demons. As during our waking state thoughts and fancies constantly and unceasingly arise within us from our fallen nature or are brought about by demons, so during sleep we see only dreams due to the action of our fallen nature or the action of demons. Just as our consolation during our waking state springs from compunction born of a realization of our sins, remembrance of death and God's judgment (only these thoughts arise in us from the grace of God planted in us by holy baptism and are brought to us by God's angels in proportion to our repentance), so, too, during sleep, very rarely, in extreme need, angels of God picture or represent to us our end, or hellish torment, or the threatening judgment at death and beyond the grave. From such dreams, we come to the fear of God, to compunction, to weeping over ourselves. But such dreams are given extremely rarely to an ascetic or even to a flagrant and outrageous sinner by the inscrutable and special providence of God. They are given extremely rarely not on account of the stinginess of divine grace—no! It is because all that happens to us outside the general run leads us to pride and self-opinion and undermines our humility that is so essential for our salvation. The will of God, the fulfill-ment of which is man's salvation, is expressed in Holy Scripture so clearly, so forcibly, and in such detail that to assist the salvation of men by breaking the ordinary course of things is quite superfluous and unnecessary.

To one who asked for the resurrection of a dead man (that he might be sent to his brothers to warn them to cross from the broad road to the narrow way), it is said, "They have Moses and the prophets; let them hear them." But when the petitioner retorted, "No! ... but if one goes to them from the dead, they will repent," he received the reply, "If they do not hear Moses and the prophets, neither will they be persuaded though one rise from the dead."[1]

Experience has shown that many who were granted in their sleep visions of sufferings—the fearful judgment and other horrors beyond the grave—were shaken by the vision for a short time, but then became dissipated, forgot what they had seen, and led a careless life. On the other hand, those who have had no visions of any kind but have carefully studied the divine law, have gradually come to the fear of God, have attained spiritual proficiency and victory, and in joy born of an intimation of salvation have passed from the earthly vale of sorrows to a blessed eternity.

St John of the Ladder discusses the part played by demons in the dreams of monks in the following manner: "When we leave our homes and relatives for the Lord's sake, and sell ourselves into exile for the love of God, then the demons try to disturb us with dreams, representing to us that our relatives are either grieving or dying, or are held captive for our sake and are destitute. But he who believes in dreams is like a person running after his own shadow and trying to catch it.

"Demons of vainglory prophesy in dreams. As tricksters, they guess the future and foretell it to us. When these visions come true, we are amazed; and we are elated with the thought that we are already near to the gift of foreknowledge. A demon is often a prophet for those who believe in him; but he is always a liar for those who despise him. Being a spirit, he sees what is happening in this lower air; and noticing that someone is dying, he foretells it through dreams to the more superficial sort. The demons know nothing about the future from foreknowledge. If they did, then the sorcerers and fortune-tellers would also have been able to foretell our death.

"Demons often transform themselves into angels of light and take the form of martyrs, and make it appear to us during sleep that we are in communication with them. Then, when we wake up, they plunge us into unholy joy and conceit. But this is the sign of diabolic delusion and that you are being deceived. For angels reveal torments, judgments, and separations; and when we wake up, we find we are trembling and sad.

"As soon as we begin to believe the demons in dreams, then they make sport of us when we are awake, too. He who believes in dreams is completely inexperienced. But he who distrusts all dreams is a wise man. Only believe dreams that warn you of torments and judgment. But if despair afflicts you, then such dreams are also from demons."[2]

St John Cassian tells of a monk, a native of Mesopotamia, who led a most solitary and ascetic life, but perished through being deceived by diabolic dreams. Observing that the monk paid little attention to his spiritual development and gave all his attention to bodily efforts which he esteemed and consequently himself, too, the devils began to set dreams before him, which by their diabolic cunning came true in actual fact. When the monk's confidence in his dreams and in himself had grown strong, the devil set before him a magnificent dream: Jews enjoying the beatitude of heaven, while Christians were tortured with the torments of hell. Then the devil (in the guise of an angel, of course, or of some Old Testament saint) advised the monk to accept Judaism so as to be able to have a share in the beatitude of the Jews. This the monk did without the least hesitation.[3]

Enough has been said to explain to our beloved brethren, contemporary monks, how foolish it is to pay attention to dreams, still more to believe and trust them, and what terrible harm can come from relying on them. From paying attention to dreams, faith and trust in them invariably creeps into the soul. Therefore, even paying attention to them is strictly forbidden.

When nature is renewed by the Holy Spirit, it is governed by entirely different laws from fallen nature persisting in its fallen state. The ruler or governor of renewed man is the Holy Spirit.[4]

Speaking of those who are renewed, St Macarius the Great says, "The grace of the Divine Spirit illumines them, and is settled in the depth of their mind. Thus the Lord is as their soul."[5] And both awake and asleep they remain in the Lord,[6] without sin, without earthly and carnal thoughts and fantasies. Their thoughts and fantasies that while during sleep are outside the control of the human will and reason, act in them under the control of the Spirit and not as with others unconsciously at the demand of nature. Thus the dreams of those who are renewed have spiritual significance. So St Joseph learned in a dream of the mystery of the incarnation of God the Word;[7] in a dream he was told to escape to Egypt,[8] and in another dream to return to Israel.[9]

Dreams sent by God bring with them an irrefutable conviction or certainty. This conviction can be understood by God's saints, but it is incomprehensible to those who are still struggling with the passions.

CHAPTER 47

On the Close Affinity Between Virtues and Vices

I t is essential for our beloved brethren to know that all good thoughts and virtues have a close affinity one to another; so also are all sinful thoughts, fantasies, sins, and passions closely related to one another.

On account of this affinity, a voluntary submission to one good thought induces a natural submission to another good thought. The acquisition of one virtue brings into the soul another virtue, akin to and inseparable from the first. On the other hand, deliberate submission to one sinful thought induces an involuntary submission to another. The acquisition of one sinful passion attracts to the soul another passion akin to it. The deliberate commission of one sin leads to an involuntary fall into another sin born of the previous one.

Evil, say the Fathers, "cannot bear to remain unmarried" in the heart.[1] We will explain this by examples. He who has cast out of his heart all resentment and remembrance of wrongs naturally feels tender compassion and compunction of heart. He who refuses to judge his neighbors naturally begins to see his own sins and infirmities that he never saw when he was occupied in criticizing his neighbors. He who praises or excuses his neighbor for the sake of the commandment of the Gospel naturally feels well-disposed and is kind to his neighbors. Immediately after poverty of spirit, mourning and weeping over one's state naturally appears. One who is poor in spirit and weeping over his state naturally becomes meek. He who denies the righteousness of his fallen nature, and renounces it, will naturally hunger and thirst for the divine righteousness. To be entirely without righteousness is unnatural for man.

On the other hand, he who criticizes his neighbor naturally despises and feels scorn for him. He who feels scorn has acquired pride. Through despising one's neighbor, and having a high opinion of oneself (and these two states are inseparable), hatred for one's neighbor makes its appearance. From hatred and resentment and remembrance of wrongs, hardness of heart develops. On account of the hardening of the heart, carnal sensations and a carnal mind and outlook begin to predominate in a person, whence arises sensual passion that kills faith in God and hope in Him. Then a tendency to love of money and human glory appears, which leads to complete forgetfulness of God and apostasy from Him.

On the basis of this affinity both between the virtues and the sins, the Holy Spirit reveals the law for the true service of God: "Therefore have I held straight to all Thy commandments; I have hated every wrong way.... I refrained my feet from every evil way, that I may keep Thy word."[2] The wrong way, the way of unrighteousness, is sinful thoughts and imaginings; through them sin enters the soul.

Beloved brother, do not regard as permissible for you any intercourse or conversation with bad thoughts or any enjoyment of mental images opposed to the spirit of the Gospel. Agreement with the Lord's enemies, union with them, cannot fail to involve a breach of fidelity to the Lord, a breach of union with Him. "For whoever shall keep the whole law, and yet stumble in one point, he is guilty of all."[3] Just as the breaking of one commandment is at the same time a breach of the whole of God's law or God's will, so the fulfillment of one diabolic suggestion is at the same time a fulfillment of the devil's will in general. An ascetic who has carried out the devil's will loses freedom and becomes subject to the violent influence of the fallen spirit to the degree in which he has done the devil's will. Mortal sin definitely enslaves a person to the devil, and emphatically breaks his fellowship with God, until he heals himself by repentance. Distraction or rape by thoughts and fantasies causes less enslavement and separation, but does cause it. Therefore it is essential to refrain from all thoughts and fantasies not in accordance with the teaching of the Gospels, while any distraction or seduction that occurs should be immediately remedied by repentance.

We implore our beloved brethren to pay attention to this. Those who are ignorant of this and those who do not pay attention to it suffer the greatest harm and deprive themselves of spiritual victory. For instance, while guarding themselves from adulterous thoughts and reveries, many think nothing of taking pleasure in thoughts and fantasies of love of money and vainglory. Yet according to spiritual law, thoughts and dreams of possessions, honors and human glory are adulterous thoughts. All sinful thoughts and fantasies have this significance in regard to our relations with God, since they seduce us from the love of God.[4] According to spiritual law, those who take pleasure in sinful thoughts and fantasies will never be freed from sensual passion, however hard they may struggle against it.

St Macarius the Great says, "We must guard the soul and watch it in every way to see that it does not hold communion with vile and evil thoughts. As a body that is joined to another body is infected with uncleanness, so also the soul is corrupted by uniting with vile and evil thoughts, and by consenting and agreeing with them unanimously, with thoughts that lead not to this or that sin, but that hurl the soul into every kind of evil, such as unbelief, lying, vainglory, anger, envy, jealousy. That is what it means to "cleanse" oneself "from all filthiness of the flesh and spirit."[5] You should realize that corruption and aberration are lurking in the caverns of your soul through the action of idle and wanton thoughts."[6]

CHAPTER 48

Concerning the Special Opposition
of the Fallen Spirits to Prayer

The fallen spirits obdurately oppose all the commandments of the Gospel, but especially prayer as the mother of virtues. The holy Prophet Zechariah saw in his vision "Joshua the high priest standing before the Angel of the Lord, and Satan standing at his right hand to oppose him."[1] So also now the devil continually confronts every servant of God with the purpose of robbing and defiling his offering of prayer and sacrifice, and finally stopping and frustrating it. "The fallen spirits jealously worry and torment us," says St Anthony the Great, "and never stop setting in motion all kinds of evil to prevent us from inheriting their former thrones in heaven."[2] In particular, "the fiend is very jealous of a person praying," says St Nil Sorsky, "and uses every wile to frustrate his activity."[3]

The devil employs all his efforts to hinder prayer or to make it powerless and ineffective. For this spirit—cast down from heaven for pride and rebellion against God, infected with incurable envy and hatred for the human race, burning with thirst for the destruction of men, sleeplessly engaged day and night in man's ruin—it is intolerable to see weak and sinful man detach himself by prayer from everything earthly, and enter into conversation with God Himself and go out from this conversation sealed with the mercy of God, in hope of inheriting heaven and seeing even his frail body transformed into a spiritual body. This spectacle is unbearable for a spirit who is forever condemned to creep and crawl, as in mud and stench, in thoughts and feelings exclusively carnal, material, sinful, and who must finally be cast down and confined for all eternity in the prisons of hell. He raves and rages, uses cunning and hypocrisy, commits crimes and outrages. It is necessary to be attentive and wary. Only in extreme need, especially if obedience requires it, may the time appointed for prayer be given up to some other occupation. Without an extremely important reason, never abandon prayer, beloved brother! He who abandons prayer abandons his salvation; he who is careless about prayer is careless about his salvation; he who quits prayer renounces his salvation.

A monk must be very cautious, because the enemy is trying to surround him on all sides with his wiles and snares to deceive, incite, confuse, seduce him from the way enjoined by the commandments of the Gospel, and ruin him in time and eternity. With an attentive and watchful life, this insensate, malicious, and crafty persecution on the part of the enemy is soon discerned. Soon we notice that for the very time set apart for prayer he prepares other occupations and provides them with important and unavoidable protractions, if only he can rob the monk of prayer. But the enemy's wiles are turned to profit by a watchful ascetic. Seeing a murderer constantly near him with a drawn dagger raised to strike, the helpless, powerless monk who is truly poor in spirit unceasingly cries for help to the all-powerful God with vigorous shouting and tears, and obtains it.[4]

When the apostate spirit cannot snatch the time assigned to prayer, then he tries to rob and smirch prayer during its performance. For this purpose he acts by means of thoughts and mental images. Thoughts he mostly clothes in a mask of righteousness and truth, so as to give them more power and conviction, while he presents mental images in the most seductive light. Prayer is robbed and ruined when during its performance the mind does not attend to the words of the prayer but is occupied with idle thoughts and fancies. Prayer is smirched and defiled when, during prayer, the mind is distracted and the attention turns to sinful thoughts and fantasies presented by the enemy. When sinful thoughts and fantasies appear to you, do not pay the slightest attention to them. The moment you see them with your mind, enclose your mind in the words of the prayer all the more earnestly, and implore God with the most fervent and attentive prayer to drive your murderers away from you.

The evil spirit organizes his hordes with peculiar skill. Before him in the advance guard stand thoughts, clothed in all forms of truth and righteousness, and fantasies or mental images that an inexperienced ascetic can take for harmless and even inspired apparitions, for holy and heavenly visions. When the mind accepts them and by subjecting itself to their influence loses its freedom, then the commander-in-chief of the foreign paratroops throws into the front line flagrantly sinful thoughts and fantasies. "After the dispassionate thoughts," says St Nil Sorsky citing earlier great Fathers, "come the passionate thoughts. The unchallenged entry of the former is the cause of the forced entry of the latter."[5]

The mind, having voluntarily lost its freedom through collision with the advance guard, is disarmed, enfeebled, enslaved; it cannot possibly hold its own against the main forces; it is promptly defeated by them, subjugated and enslaved to them. It is essential during prayer to enclose the mind in the words of the prayer, rejecting without distinction every thought, both flagrantly sinful ones and also apparently good ones. No matter what the clothing or armor of thought may be, if it distracts you from prayer, that in itself proves that it belongs to the foreign or Philistine army and that the uncircumcised or unclean spirit has come "to defy Israel."[6]

For his invisible warfare or conflict with man, especially by means of sinful thoughts and imaginations, the fallen angel relies on the mutual affinity of the sins one with another. This conflict never ceases day or night, but it becomes especially intense and furious when we stand for prayer. Then, according to the expression of the holy Fathers, the devil gathers the most monstrous thoughts from everywhere and pours them on our soul.[7] First he reminds us of all who have wronged or offended us. He tries to present all the insults, wrongs, and injuries inflicted on us in the most lurid colors. He points our the necessity for retaliation and resistance[8] to them by demanding justice, common sense, the public good, self-preservation, self-defense. It is obvious that the enemy tries to shake the very foundation of prayer, namely forgiveness and meekness, so that the building erected on this foundation may collapse of its own accord. And this is just what happens, because a person who is full of resentment and who does not forgive his neighbor's sins is quite unable to obtain compunction or concentrate when he prays. Angry thoughts dissipate prayer; they blow it aside, just as a violent wind scatters seeds thrown by a sower on his field; so the field of the heart remains unsown, and all the ascetic's hard work comes to nothing. It is a well-known fact that forgiveness of wrongs and offenses—changing condemnation of our neighbors into kindness and mercy so that we excuse them and blame ourselves—provides the only solid basis for successful prayer.[9]

Very often, at the very beginning of prayer, the enemy brings to mind thoughts and imaginations of earthly success; at one time he represents human glory in an alluring picture as the just or lucky renewal of virtue, as if this were at last known and recognized by men who will henceforth be guided by virtue; at another time he represents in a similarly alluring picture the abundance of earthly riches, as if on this basis Christian virtue must flourish and increase. Both these pictures are false. They are painted in direct opposition to the teaching of Christ. They cause terrible harm to the eye of the soul that looks at them and to the soul itself that plays the wanton from its Lord through sympathy with the devil's picture.

Outside the cross of Christ there is no Christian success. The Lord said, "I do not receive honor from men.... How can you believe, who receive honor from one another, and do not seek the honor that comes from the only God?"[10] When doing your good deeds, do not be like the hypocrites,[11] who do good for the sake of human glory, who accept human praise as a reward for their virtue, and so lose their right to eternal reward.[12] Do not let your left hand (i.e., your own vainglory) know what your right hand (i.e., your will guided by the commandments of the Gospel) is doing, and your Father Who sees the unseen will reward you openly with the gift of the Holy Spirit.[13] The Lord also said, "No one can serve two masters; for either he will hate one and love the other, or else he will be loyal to one and despise the other. You cannot serve God and mammon [i.e., possessions, riches][14].... Whoever of you does not forsake all that he has cannot be My disciple."[15]

It is worth noticing that in tempting the God-Man, the devil offered Him the vainglorious thought of winning fame for Himself by a public miracle, and gave Him a vision of a most consequential and commanding position. The Lord refused both offers.[16] He leads us up to the height of success by the narrow way of self-renunciation and humility, and He Himself blazed this trail and opened this saving way. We must follow our Lord's example and teaching; we must reject thoughts of earthly glory, success, and earthly plenty; we must refuse joy brought by those fancies and reflections that destroy in us contrition of spirit, concentration, and attention during prayer, and that lead to self-opinion and distraction. If we consent to thoughts of resentment and condemnation, thoughts and fantasies of vainglory, pride, love of money, and love of the world, and if we do not reject them, but dawdle in them and take pleasure in them, then we enter into fellowship with Satan, and the power of God which protects us will leave us.[17] Seeing the withdrawal of God's power from us, the enemy rushes at us with two most grievous conflicts: the conflict with thoughts and fantasies of lust, and the conflict with despondency or sloth.[18] Defeated in the first conflict and deprived of God's protection, we cannot stand against the second conflict either. This means, the Fathers tell us, that God allows Satan to defeat us until we humble ourselves.

It is obvious that thoughts of resentment, criticism, earthly glory, and earthly success are due to pride. Rejection of these thoughts is rejection of pride. Rejection of pride enables humility to settle into the soul. Humility is the mind of Christ, His way of thought,[19] and that pledge of the heart which springs from this thought pattern through which all the passions are killed in the heart and expelled from it—the fire of the Holy Spirit.[20]

Invasion by the twin passions of lust and listlessness (sloth) is followed by the invasion of thoughts and feelings of sadness, dejection, unbelief, hopelessness, hardness, stubbornness, darkness and blindness, blasphemy and despair. Delight in desires of the flesh produces a particularly serious impression on us. The Fathers call these sensual desires defilers or desecrators of God's spiritual temple. If we take pleasure in them, then for a long time the grace of God will leave us, and all sinful thoughts and imaginations will get a more powerful hold over us. They will plague and torture us until we attract grace to us again by sincere and genuine repentance and by refraining from taking pleasure in the enemy's baits and lures. All this an attentive monk will not fail to be taught by experience.

Having learned the ropes—the order, rule, routine, and racket that the enemy follows in his struggle with us—we can organize a corresponding resistance.[21] We will not judge and condemn our neighbor under any pretext whatever. We shall forgive our neighbors all the most grievous offenses they may have caused us. Whenever a thought of resentment against anyone appears, we will at once pray for that person and ask God to show him mercy both in time and in eternity. We will renounce and deny ourselves, our souls, our lives; that is to say, we will refuse to seek human glory, or to chase needlessly after a comfortable earthly position, and all earthly privileges, and we will surrender ourselves entirely to the will of God, thanking and praising Him for our past and present, and leaving our future to Him.

This new line of action will serve as a preparation and foundation for our prayer. Before beginning our prayer, let us humble ourselves before our neighbors, let us blame and accuse ourselves for having been a stumbling block to them and for continuing to tempt them by our sins. Let us begin our prayer with a prayer for our enemies, let us unite ourselves in prayer with all men, and let us ask God to have mercy on us together with all men everywhere, not because we are fit or worthy to pray for mankind, but to fulfill the commandment of love that says, "Pray for one another."[22]

Although a true servant of God is allowed to undergo a struggle with the many forms of solicitation and temptation to sin offered by Satan and arising from our nature warped by the fall, yet God's right hand is constantly supporting and guiding him. The very struggle brings the greatest profit, giving the combatant spiritual experience, a clear and exact understanding of the corruption of human nature, of sin, of the fallen angel, leading the wrestler to contrition of spirit, to weeping and mourning over himself and all mankind.

St Poemen the Great related of St John Kolov, a Father filled to overflowing with the grace of the Holy Spirit, that he prayed to God, and afterward the conflict within him caused by the infirmities of fallen nature or by the passions came to an end. He went and told this to a certain elder advanced in spiritual discernment, saying, "I see myself in unbroken peace, without any conflict or struggle."[23] The discreet elder answered John, "Go and pray to God that the warfare may return, because through conflict the soul comes to proficiency and victory. And when the struggle comes, do not pray for it to be taken away, but that the Lord may give patience in persecution."[24]

Let us surrender ourselves wholly to the will of God. Let us devote ourselves wholeheartedly to doing the will of God. With unceasing prayer, let us ask God for the gift of carrying out His will, and also for that gift whereby the will of God may always be welcomed by us. Whoever surrenders himself to the will of God finds that God is with him inseparably. This is felt and experienced and the truth of it is attested by every soldier of Christ who fights lawfully, by every athlete and combatant who is guided by the Gospel.[25]

CHAPTER 49

On Keeping the Eye of the Soul from All That Is Harmful to It[1]

The Savior of the world has said, "The lamp of the body is the eye."[2] By *lamp* the Savior meant the spiritual power of the human soul, the spirit of man; by *body* the Savior meant all man's activity and the quality of his life that is formed by and depends on this activity.

The following words of the Apostle Paul have a meaning similar to that of the Savior's words just quoted: "May the God of peace Himself sanctify you completely; and may your whole spirit, soul, and body be preserved blameless at the coming of our Lord Jesus Christ."[3] The spirit is mentioned first because the integrity and perfection of both soul and body is entirely dependent on the spirit. The spirit, or speaking power, is the highest faculty of the human soul. It is this that distinguishes the human soul from that of animals, which are called dumb because they are without this faculty.[4]

"When your eye is good," that is, when the spiritual power is unconfused by sin or fellowship with Satan, then "your whole body also is full of light," that is, your activity will be right and will be holy in quality. "But when your eye is bad, your body also is full of darkness. Therefore take heed that the light which is in you is not darkness."[5] See to it that your spirit, which is your natural light and the source of light for your life, does not become dark and a source of darkness. This eye becomes evil through accepting falsehood. A result of this acceptance is wrong activity, while the quality of life becomes a state of sinfulness and self-deception. By accepting false thoughts the mind is corrupted, the conscience loses its reliability, and all the spiritual feelings of the heart are likewise infected with abnormality and sinfulness. Man becomes useless, an enemy of his own salvation, a murderer of his own soul, an enemy of God.

Holy Scripture, or rather the Holy Spirit speaking by means of Scripture, utters the following pronouncement against men who are mentally depraved, completely ignorant of the faith, describing them as "men of corrupt minds, disapproved concerning the faith."[6] It is quite impossible for a person of depraved mind to have faith. In such a person, the place of faith is occupied by falsely named reason, and the preaching of the cross is for him a subject either of scandal or derision, as it was for the Jews at the time of the God-Man.[7]

Depravity of mind always goes hand in hand with corruption of the other spiritual faculties. So depravity of mind and depravity of spirit are identical as far as results go. Acceptance of false doctrine or false thoughts about God, or distorting the dogmatic and moral teaching revealed by God by means of false doctrine, culminates in depravity of the human spirit, and man becomes a son of the devil.[8] But even conversation and contact with thoughts belonging to the realm of Satan without accepting or assimilating them—the mere contemplation of thoughts and fantasies offered by demons—injures the eye of the soul. Its visual power loses, in proportion to the degree of fellowship with Satan, its accuracy and purity. St Hesychius of Jerusalem says, "Just as we injure ourselves by looking at something harmful with our physical eyes, so we injure ourselves by looking at what is harmful with our mind."[9]

We must therefore pay special attention to guarding the eye of the soul and take particular care to prevent its being injured, lest its diseased condition become the cause of our spiritual ruin. As an example of how a damaged eye of the soul can have a harmful effect on our salvation, we will cite the following that we saw in actual experience: some people were reading novels or romances; their mind and heart was attuned accordingly. Later, struck by some change of life, or by some rousing inner impulse, or even by some indication of the mercy and love of God, these people wanted to live a pious life. Then the ruinous effect of their previous reading became clear. Their habit of constantly enjoying sensuality diverted them from a sense of repentance and brought even into their spiritual life a delight in sensuality that is abhorrent to God. Such a person's soul is inaccessible to the Holy Spirit and easily becomes a dwelling of Satan.

With special clarity this is observable in the female sex. Those women who have read many novels or romances, and then give themselves up to piety and even to asceticism, mostly want their new life also to be a romance; they want to be lovers spiritually. They want this because their will, injured by misuse, draws them by force to that sensuality they have made their own, while their mind—weakened, darkened, perverted, captivated by thoughts received from reading—has neither the power nor the ability to guide their will and restrain its wrong tendencies.

Those who have been soaked in the reading of novels are extremely prone to self-deception and diabolic delusion. Having acquired a taste for the pleasure of sensuality, it can act not only in a coarse manner but also in the most refined and subtle forms, not understood and not noticed by a person who has not yet thrown off the yoke of the passions.

A certain monk during his worldly life, not knowing what wisdom and discretion is needed in submitting the soul to impressions that stay alive in it, out of idle curiosity read some books written against the Christian Faith. When he entered a monastery and laid upon himself a reasonable monastic discipline, the impressions received previously in the world began to manifest their presence in his soul by thoughts of doubt, perplexity, and blasphemy. This showed that the eye of his soul had been blighted by intercourse with thoughts from the realm of Satan.

The holy Apostle Paul has said, "Do you not know that you are the temple of God and that the Spirit of God dwells in you? If anyone defiles the temple of God, God will destroy him. For the temple of God is holy, which temple you are."[10] Though our bodies are also God's temple, yet more particularly our praying power, our spirit, our mind and heart constitute God's temple. Under the name of heart are understood all the sensations, feelings, and emotions of the spirit. When the mind and heart become God's dwelling—and they become His dwelling first of all—then naturally the soul and the body also become His dwelling, since they are completely dependent on the mind and heart. God's temple is corrupted and destroyed when the body falls into sensual lust, and when the mind and heart enter into adulterous intercourse[11] with Satan by means of Satanic thoughts, sensations, feelings, and emotions.

The words "God will destroy him" mean that God will withdraw from a person who has corrupted God's temple within him and made himself unfit for God to live in him. The consequences of His withdrawal are well known; death of the soul that begins in time followed by burial in the prisons of hell in eternity.[12]

The spirit of a person is corrupted, is struck with blindness and darkness, as we have already said, by accepting false doctrine—teaching coming from the world and Satan—which is teaching opposed to the divinely revealed teaching, the teaching of Christ, the teaching of the Ecumenical and Orthodox Church. The following teachings are recognized as false doctrine: the doctrine that denies the existence of God, or atheism; the doctrine that denies Christ and Christianity, though it admits the existence of God, but denies all intervention or converse between God and men, or deism; the doctrine that does not deny Christianity outright, but distorts the divinely revealed teaching by arbitrary, human, blasphemous doctrines which destroy the essence of Christianity. Such as are all heresies; the doctrines that do not deny Christianity per se but rather reject works of faith, or the moral, evangelical, and ecclesiastical tradition. They accept pagan activity, and thereby destroy faith and ruin the essence of Christianity. Contemporary progress for the most part is like this, as evidenced by dialectic materialism, prosperity, affluence and advance in immorality. All of this takes place in complete ignorance of Christianity, and consequently in complete withdrawal and estrangement from God.

The temple of God is not finally corrupted or destroyed, but is defiled or profaned; the eye of the soul is not struck with total blindness, but is injured and receives a more or less serious wound when a monk reads an immoral or heretical book, visits immoral or irreligious society, exposes himself to the influence of sinful pitfalls and temptations, when he dallies with sinful thoughts and takes pleasure in them, when he allows himself the diversion or distraction of some worldly habit, such as are all worldly games and amusements. But if a monk lingers in all this, and justifies his distraction instead of admitting and repenting of it, he falls into the greatest spiritual disaster. He injures the very core of his being—his praying power, his spirit, his mind and heart.

We must guard the eye of our soul, and keep guarding it. All that we do outside the teaching of the Gospel and not in accordance with the divine law invariably produces a harmful impression on us. Every thought, word, and act, both good and bad, invariably leaves a corresponding stamp, mark, or impress on us. We need to know this thoroughly and really understand it.[13]

CHAPTER 50

Concerning Repentance and Mourning[1]

When we began to offer our beloved brethren our poor counsels, we said that monasticism is simply the duty of fulfilling with exactitude the commandments of the Gospel, that the monastic life is simply a life lived in accordance with the commandments of the Gospel, wherever it may be, whether among crowds of people or in the most profound desert. Our solitude is in God. In God, our mind and heart can find a safe and calm haven, where neither the waves nor the winds of the sea of life have any effect. Without this, the world that is hostile to God will accompany us into the densest forests, into the gorges of mountains, and into our caves, where it will make us its servants.

Monastic life that is not based on the commandments of the Gospel is like a building without a foundation; it will collapse. Monastic life that is not inspired by the commandments of the Gospel is like a body without a soul; it will reek with the stench of pharisaism, and the more it is clothed outwardly in bodily discipline and asceticism, or pretends to be, the more it will stink. The intelligent reader will find endorsement of this truth in all our proffered counsels heretofore.

In bringing these poor counsels to an end, we feel bound to explain to our dearly beloved brethren about that most important spiritual activity which should embrace the whole of a monk's life, which should be the soul of his life, the soul of his spiritual and bodily discipline. He who has read attentively our previous counsels will, of course, have discovered this activity from what has been said. But we consider it our duty to speak about it separately and as far as possible in detail.

A monk's life is nothing less than active and constant repentance. We must not fail to immerse ourselves in thoroughgoing repentance if we do not wish to bear the name and calling of a monk idly and to our condemnation. Only when he is filled and guided by a sense of repentance does a monk advance aright. When the sense of repentance leaves his heart, it is a true sign that the monk is distracted by false thoughts suggested by Satan or arising from his fallen nature. Constant lack of repentance is a sign of a completely wrong attitude or outlook.

A man-made church or temple of God during every service is filled with the smoke of incense. So the air in the church is constantly filled with aromas coming from the smoking incense. Even the vestments and other appurtenances are redolent with the fragrant perfume. All who come to the church for prayer or for a service are bound to breathe it. So, too, a temple of God not made by human hands but created and renewed by God—that is to say, a Christian and especially a monk—should be constantly filled to overflowing with a sense of repentance. This sense of repentance should be stirred and aroused every time a monk prays; it should accompany and support his prayer and give it wings to ascend to God. Otherwise, his prayer will not be able to lift itself above the earth and free itself from distraction.

A monk's whole conduct and behavior should be imbued with a sense of repentance, even the very way he fulfills the commandments of the Gospel. He should fulfill them as a debtor, as unprofitable servants,[2] and he should put them into the treasury of the heavenly King as worthless payment of his irredeemable debt, which can be paid only by the mercy of the heavenly King. St Mark the Ascetic has said, "Those who do not regard themselves as debtors in respect of every commandment of Christ honor God's law in a bodily manner, not understanding either what they say or on what it is based."[3]

From the fallen human spirit, God accepts only one sacrifice— repentance. Other sacrifices, even the strictest asceticism such as might be called a whole burnt offering or holocaust, are rejected as being defiled by sin and needing purification by repentance before they can be offered in sacrifice. This is the one sacrifice of fallen man that God does not despise by refusing it.[4] When Zion is renewed by repentance and the walls of our spiritual Jerusalem are built, then we can confidently offer on the altar of our heart sacrifices of righteousness—our sentiments and feelings renewed by the grace of God. Then a person becomes fit to offer even himself as a holocaust pleasing to God.[5] The holy martyr Sadok says, "Whoever is spiritual awaits a martyr's death with joy, longing, and great love, and he is not afraid of it because he is ready; but to a carnal person the hour of death is terrible."[6]

Repentance is a commandment of the Gospel. The immediate consequence of repentance, according to the Gospel, should be our entry into the kingdom of heaven. Therefore, the whole space of time from our adoption by Christ till our entry into eternity (and the heavenly kingdom becomes

the secure possession of those who are granted salvation), or the whole of
our earthly life, should be a field of repentance. The first sermon and commandment uttered by God incarnate to our fallen humanity that He came
to save was about repentance: "Jesus began to preach and to say, 'Repent, for
the kingdom of heaven is at hand.'"[7] After His resurrection and before His
ascension to heaven, the Lord opened the apostles' minds and enabled them
to understand the Scriptures. Then He told them that, in accordance with
the Scriptures, it was inevitable that Christ should suffer and rise from the
dead on the third day, "and that repentance and remission of sins should be
preached in His name to all nations, beginning at Jerusalem."[8]

To believe in Christ and to accept Christianity, a realization of one's sinfulness and repentance are necessary; to remain a Christian, it is necessary
to see one's sins and realize them, then to confess them and repent of them.
When the Jews who were disposed to accept the faith asked the holy Apostle
Peter what they must do, he replied, "Repent, let every one of you be bap-
tized in the name of Jesus Christ for the remission of sins; and you shall
receive the gift of the Holy Spirit."[9] So, too, the Apostle Paul preached everywhere that men should turn to God in repentance and have faith in our Lord
Jesus Christ.[10]

It is impossible while living in sin and loving sin to be adopted by Christ
and become His: "For everyone practicing evil hates the light and does not
come to the light, lest his deeds should be exposed."[11] "For what fellowship
has righteousness with lawlessness? And what communion has light with
darkness? And what accord has Christ with Belial?"[12] In order to approach
Christ and enter into union with Him by means of holy baptism, it is essential
first of all to repent. And after holy baptism, we are given freedom either to
stay in union with the Lord or to break this union by intercourse with sin.
Not only that, but in our fallen nature holy baptism does not destroy our aptitude for producing evil mixed with good, so that our will and pleasure may
be constantly tested, so that our choice of divine good and our preference of it
to evil and our corrupted good may be free, proved positively by our submission to all the sorrows and sufferings of the way of the cross.[13]

By holy baptism, original sin is expunged, as are also sins committed
before baptism. It also eliminates the violent power sin has over us till our
rebirth; it gives us the grace of the Holy Spirit by which we are united with
God in Christ, and we receive power to subdue and conquer sin. For the simple reason that we are not delivered from the struggle with sin, we cannot be
entirely free from sin during the whole of our earthly life, and even "a righteous man may fall seven times" [i.e., often] and rise again" by repentance,

says Scripture.[14] He falls on account of his weakness and limitations, because he does not always notice sin, which subtly and imperceptibly rears its head from his fallen nature, and which is artfully and imperceptibly offered and suggested by the fallen spirits. Repentance becomes his secure possession, his constant weapon, his invaluable treasure. By repentance, the righteous man maintains his fellowship with Christ. He is healed by repentance from the wounds caused by sin.

St John the Theologian says, "If we say that we have no sin, we deceive ourselves, and the truth is not in us. If we confess our sins, He is faithful and just to forgive us our sins and to cleanse us from all unrighteousness. If we say that we have not sinned, we make Him a liar, and His word is not in us."[15] The Theologian says this of involuntary sins due to weakness and frailty, of slight sins which even the saints cannot avoid. But of a deliberately sinful life, he says the following: "Whoever abides in Him [in our Lord Jesus Christ by communion and obedience] does not sin. Whoever sins has neither seen Him nor known Him. Little children, let no one deceive you. He who practices righteousness is righteous, just as He is righteous. He who sins is of the devil, for the devil has sinned from the beginning. For this purpose the Son of God was manifested, that he might destroy the works of the devil. Whoever has been born of God does not sin [i.e., does not live a sinful life and fall into mortal and deliberate sins], for His seed remains in him; and he cannot sin because he has been born of God. In this the children of God and the children of the devil are manifest."[16]

The children of God lead a life according to the commandments of the Gospel, and they offer repentance for their slips and falls. If a servant of God for some unfortunate reason happens to fall into a mortal sin, he is healed of the wound of sin by repentance and confession, and therefore he does not cease to be a child of God. Those who lead a sinful life out of love for it, who readily fall into any sin that comes their way, and who admit that they enjoy or find pleasure in a life of immorality in its various forms and in every other breach of the commandments of the Gospel, are children of the devil, even though they may take part in church services and ceremonies, even though they partake of the sacraments which they profane to their own condemnation.

Such is the spirit of repentance for every Christian. Still more does it constitute the essence of the monastic life. Entry into the life of a monastery is a confession of one's sinfulness, and the life itself is an unbroken course of repentance. A candidate for monasticism who wishes to take his monastic vows before God expresses his heart's pledge of repentance in the following manner at the beginning of the sacred rite of profession: "Hasten to open to me Thy fatherly arms. I have wasted my life like a prodigal [wrongly using the love of my heart and squandering it on my passions]. In view of the inexhaustible wealth of Thy compassion, O Savior, disregard not my now-destitute heart; for to Thee, O Lord, in compunction I cry: I have sinned, Father, against heaven and before Thee."

The greatest of the holy Fathers admitted that repentance was their sole occupation. Having given themselves up to this activity, they more and more widened its scope for themselves, since repentance not only cleanses a person from sins but also sharpens his sight so that he sees himself more clearly. When some spots of sin are removed by repentance from the garment of the soul, then suddenly the existence of other spots is discovered, less coarse but no less important, which have remained unnoticed till now on account of the dullness of our sight. Finally repentance leads a person who practices it to the most profound spiritual visions; there is disclosed to him his own fall and the fall of all mankind, his suffering and the suffering of mankind under the yoke of the prince of this world,[17] the wonderful work of redemption and the other mysteries, with which the reader must become acquainted by experience, for human speech is quite inadequate to tell of them.

St Arsenius the Great had repentance as his constant occupation, and it was so much a part of him that it expressed itself in the gift of tears; a handkerchief was always on his lap, and while his hands were busy with his handwork and his mind was occupied in penitential prayer, tears fell continually on his handkerchief.[18] St Sisoes the Great asked the angels who came to take his soul from his body and carry it to heaven to leave him in his body and give him time for repentance. And to his disciples, who were sure he had reached perfection, he said that he did not know whether he had really begun to repent, so high a conception had he of repentance! Evidently St Sisoes called the whole monastic life repentance; and by saying he had not yet begun his repentance, he expressed the humble opinion he had of his monastic life.

Those who have acquired a true, spiritual understanding of repentance include in it all their labors, prayer, and fasting, and consider it a day lost on which they have not wept over themselves, whatever other good works they may have done on that day.[19] There is no doubt that St Sisoes was immersed in the work of repentance and weeping. One of the properties of this work is that the penitent can never be satisfied, but the more it fills him, the more he longs for it, since it procures a purity most pleasing to God and at the same time produces a thirst for a still more perfect purity. Those who are purified by weeping see how impure they are and continue to acknowledge their impurity.

We have already mentioned the advice given by St Sisoes to a brother who asked him how to please God and be saved. "If you want to please God," said the great soul, "quit the world, relinquish the earth, leave creatures, and come to the Creator. Unite yourself with God by prayer and weeping, and you will find rest in this and the future life."[20] To another brother he said, "Stay in your cell with vigilance, practice the presence of God with many tears and with heartfelt contrition, and you will find rest." Evidently the Saint gave each brother advice from his own experience. The first he advised to leave everything worldly and everything earthly, that is, all attachments; while he advised the second to stay constantly in his cell. That was because when there are attachments to creatures and when the cell is frequently left for no good reason, true repentance and prayerful weeping is impossible. The heart must be detached from everything and free from distractions; only then can it weep before God and immerse itself in mourning[21] as in an abyss, as an immersion in life.

When a brother asked Poemen the Great how he ought to stay in his cell in (mental) silence, the Saint replied, "Like a man who has sunk in stinking mud up to his neck, with a load on his back, and who cries to God, 'Have mercy on me.'" In these words the whole monastic life is included in weeping and penitential prayer. To another brother who asked what his activity should be, the same Saint said, "When the time comes for us to stand before God, then what shall we be anxious about?" The brother replied, "Our sins." Said Poemen, "And so, let us go into our huts, and there in solitude let us recall our sins [with repentance], and the Lord will hear us." Another brother asked Poemen what he should do. Said the elder, "When Abraham went up into the promised land, he bought himself a tomb, and with the tomb he began to take possession of the land." The brother asked, "What is the significance of the tomb?" Poemen replied, "It is a place of weeping and lamentation."

Another brother asked the same Saint, "What am I to do about my sins?" Poemen the Great answered, "He who wants to be delivered from sins is delivered from them by weeping, and he who wants to keep himself from acquiring them can keep himself free by weeping. This is the way of repentance handed down to us by Scripture and the Fathers who said, 'Weep, because there is no other way (to salvation) except weeping.'" Poemen the Great used to say, "Weeping has a double effect—it works and it keeps."

Once, Poemen was walking with Abba Anuva in the outskirts of Diolkos. There they saw a woman on a tomb, beating herself and weeping bitterly. They stopped and listened to her. Then when they had gone a little further, they met one of the local inhabitants and Abba Poemen asked him, "What has happened to that woman? Why is she weeping so bitterly?" The man said, "Her husband, son, and brother have died." Then Abba Poemen turned to Abba Anuva and said to him, "I tell you, unless a man mortifies all carnal desires and acquires weeping like that woman, he cannot be a monk, for the whole life of a monk consists in weeping."

News was brought to Poemen the Great of the death of Arsenius the Great. He wept and said, "Blessed Abba Arsenius! You wept over yourself in this life. He who does not bewail himself here will weep eternally. It is impossible not to weep—either willingly here, or unwillingly there in torments."[22]

Some who do not concern themselves with the interior life and activity of the soul—or do so very little, exercising themselves only in bodily activity with admixture of pharisaism, since mere bodily activity cannot get on without pharisaism—do not feel the sting of conscience convicting them of sin in the least. Therefore they think their state of peace commendable. They are upheld and confirmed in this opinion by their many good works and by human praise. On this foundation, they regard their state of peace as a direct result of activity pleasing to God and a blameless and virtuous life. From time to time, their peace turns into unaccountable joy. They never stop thinking this joy is a gift of grace. What woeful self-deception! What soul-destroying blindness! Self-deception is here due to self-opinion or conceit, and conceit is an injury to the eye of the soul that is born of wrong activity and in turn gives birth to activity that is even more misguided.

Beloved brother, the peace which makes you think your way is right is simply insensitivity and unawareness of your sinfulness due to your negligent life, while the joy you feel from time to time as a result of outward success and human praise is not holy and spiritual joy at all; it is the fruit of self-opinion, self-satisfaction, complacency, and vainglory. Such a state of false peace the holy Fathers call insensibility—the deadening of the soul and death of the mind before the death of the body.[23] Insensibility or deadening of the soul consists in the deprival and loss of a sense of repentance and mourning from our spirit, and a loss of that salutary pain called contrition from our heart. Painlessness of heart or illusory peace is a true sign of a wrong outlook, wrong struggle, self-deception. "However great may be the life we lead," says St John of the Ladder, "if we have not acquired a suffering and painful heart, we may count it stale and spurious."[24] Painlessness comes from an inattentive life, from untimely exits from one's cell, from untimely conversations, jokes, laughter, idle talk, gossiping, from glutting and overeating, from attachments, from accepting and appropriating vainglorious thoughts, from presumption and pride.²⁵ "If you are without compunction," say the Fathers, "know that you have vainglory; for it does not allow the soul to come to compunction."²⁶

The way to attain compunction is an attentive life. "The beginning of repentance comes from the fear of God and attention," as the holy martyr Boniface says. "The fear of God is the father of attention, and attention is the mother of inner peace, which gives birth to a conscience which enables the soul to see its deformity as in a kind of clear and still water, and so are born the beginnings and roots of repentance."²⁷ An attentive and regular life according to the commandments of the Gospel, even though it is the first cause of repentance, so long as it is not overshadowed by divine grace and is without fruit, it will not produce heartfelt contrition, compunction, mourning, and tears—all of which constitute true monastic repentance. In confirmation of this most important teaching of experience, we will summon the evidence of the holy Fathers. St John of the Ladder says, "The man who has withdrawn from the world in order to shake off his own burden of sins, should imitate those who sit outside the city among the tombs and should not discontinue his hot and fiery streams of tears and voiceless heartfelt groanings till he, too, sees that Jesus has come to him and rolled away the stone of hardness from his heart, and loosed Lazarus, that is to say, our mind, from the grave-clothes of sin, and ordered His attendant angels: 'Loose him' from passions, 'and let him go'²⁸ to blessed dispassion. Otherwise, he will have gained nothing [from his withdrawal from the world]."²⁹

St Isaac the Syrian: "*Question:* What are the true marks and the indubitable signs whereby an ascetic may know that the hidden fruits of his labor are beginning to appear in his soul? *Answer:* When he is granted the gift of tears, flowing abundantly and without any effort. Tears are to the mind the sure distinction between the bodily and the spiritual state, between the state of passion and that of purity. As long as one has not yet received this gift, the labor of his service is still in the outward man, and this to such an extent that he does not perceive anything of the hidden activity of the spiritual man. But where he begins to leave the bodily life of this world and passes into that inner realm which lies beyond this visible nature, then at once he attains the grace of tears. These tears begin in the first mansion of that hidden life and they will lead him to the perfection of the love of God. When he has reached this point, tears will be so copious that he will imbibe them with his food and drink, so abundant and constant are they. This is a true sign that the mind has left this world and perceives the spiritual world. But the more the mind approaches this [material] world, the more these tears diminish. And when the mind is completely immersed in worldly things, it will be also completely without tears. This is a sign that a person is sunk in the passions."[30]

St Symeon the New Theologian: "Before obtaining mourning and tears, let no one deceive us with vain words, and let us not deceive ourselves: there is no repentance in us, no true self-reproach, no fear of God in our hearts. We have not blamed ourselves; our soul has not reached any perception of the future judgment and eternal torments. If we had blamed ourselves, we should have acquired and attained this perception; tears would also at once have procured it. Without them it will never be possible to soften the hardness of our heart, nor will our soul acquire a spirit of humility; we cannot be humble. Without becoming humble, it is impossible to be united with the Holy Spirit; without being united to Him, it is impossible to come to the vision and knowledge of God, and our heart is secretly not fit to learn the virtue of humility."[31]

An attentive life leads to compunction; compunction, then, especially when accompanied by tears, procures an increased attention that is the gift of grace. Mourning and tears are the gift of God. Therefore, with an attentive life, ask for this gift with earnest prayer. "Ask, and it will be given to you; seek, and you will find; knock, and it will be opened to you.... much more will your Father who is in heaven give good [spiritual] things"—mourning and tears.[32]

"When I consider the actual nature of compunction," says St John of the Ladder, "I am amazed at how that which is called mourning and grief contains joy and gladness interwoven within it like honey in the comb. What are we to learn from this? That such compunction is in a special sense a gift of the Lord."[33]

St Symeon the New Theologian has very soundly said that the first cause of mourning and tears is our free will. It depends upon us to renounce distraction, to give up roaming from cell to cell to visit the brethren and going out of the monastery to call on acquaintances, to give up joking, idle talk, and chatter. A simple resolve of the will is all that is needed to begin an attentive life of prayer and reading the word of God, while restraining the stomach from excess and dainties. Such an attentive life cannot fail to produce compunction and mourning, especially when we ask God to give us this salutary gift with fervent prayer. And when we receive the gift, we must guard it as a priceless treasure. That is just what it is! It is priceless spiritual treasure and wealth. Even when obtained, it is easily lost if we give ourselves up to distraction, dissipation, indulgence of our passions and fancies, men-pleasing or currying favor, worldliness, greed, gossip, slander, even much talking.

Without noticing it, we can pass from a state of tender compunction to a state of insensibility. So important is a state of insensibility for our invisible enemy that he does all in his power to hold us in it and harden it, without disturbing us either with other passions or with temptations from outside. That is because self-opinion and self-satisfaction—which usually accompany insensibility—and self-deception and pride—which are the usual consequences of insensibility—are sufficient to cause the loss of all spiritual gifts, and even one's soul. Insensibility is all the more terrible because its victim does not realize his fatal condition. He is deluded and blinded by his self-opinion and self-satisfaction.

"Compunction," says St Symeon the New Theologian, "is a fruit of obeying the commandments and a cause of all spiritual fruits. It is the creator and cause of all the virtues, as the whole of inspired Scripture testifies. Therefore, whoever wishes to cut out the passions and acquire the virtues should, before all virtues and with all virtues, earnestly seek compunction. Without it he will never see his soul pure; and unless he acquires a pure soul he will never acquire 'a pure body.' A dirty garment cannot be washed without water; and without tears, it is impossible for the soul to be washed and cleansed of its defilements and impurities. Let us not offer pernicious and idle or rather quite false excuses which only serve as a cause of our perdition, but let us seek with all our might the queen of virtues. Whoever seeks her with all his soul finds her; or rather, she comes and finds him who is seeking her with anguish. And even if he has a heart harder than brass or iron or stone, by her coming she makes it softer than any wax. She is the divine fire that destroys mountains and rocks, leveling and changing everything, transforming into gardens those souls that receive her. In the heart of these souls, she makes a fountain flow with the water of life. This water, as from some cistern, unceasingly descends on near and distant [parts of the garden], and fills to overflowing souls that receive the Word with faith.[34] First it washes its partakers of all uncleanness; then it rinses out the passions, rubs and removes them like scabs covering wounds, and discards them. I say it discards and repudiates double-dealing, envy, jealousy, vainglory, and all the others that follow these. It not only does this, but like some flame scouring everywhere, it gradually destroys them, burning and consuming them hourly like thorns. At first, it arouses in us a desire for perfect freedom and purification from the passions, then a longing for God Who saves and prepares His blessings for those who love Him.[35] All this the divine fire of compunction does with the cooperation of tears, or rather by means of tears. Without tears, as we have said, not one of these blessings ever has been or will be, either in us or in anyone else. It is impossible to find in Divine Scripture a case of anyone at any time without tears and constant compunction being purified and becoming holy, or receiving the Holy Spirit, or seeing God, or feeling Him coming within, or receiving Him as the dweller in his heart. Nothing of this could happen until it has been preceded by repentance and compunction, until tears pouring as from a fountain and constantly flooding the eyes have washed out the temple of the soul and the soul itself, bedewing and refreshing the whole personality, enveloping and inflaming it with the unapproachable fire.[36] Those who say that it is impossible to shed tears and weep every night, every day, confess that they are deficient in every virtue. If our holy Fathers have said, 'He who wants to cut out the passions will cut them out by mourning,' it is clear that he who does not weep daily will neither cut out the passions nor accomplish the virtues, even though deceived by self-opinion he thinks he will accomplish them. Tell me, what is the use of the tools of some craft when there is no craftsman who knows how to use either the tools or the material? What is the use of a gardener if he cultivates a whole garden, plants and sows in it every kind of herb or plant, but no rain from above falls on the garden and no one waters it? Certainly no use whatever. Just so, he who practices other virtues and labors at them will get no benefit whatever without this holy and blessed lady and accomplisher of all the virtues. Just as a king without his troops is powerless and easily defeated by all, and is even not called a king but an ordinary man, so on the other hand a large army without its king and leader is easily scattered and destroyed by enemies. Such is the relation between weeping and other virtues. Under the figure of an army, understand a gathering of all the virtues of a novice; under the figure of a king and leader, understand blessed lamentation and weeping by which the whole army is set in order, is animated, encouraged, strengthened, and begins to act with a weapon corresponding to the time, circumstances, enemies.... Weeping arranges all this. Without it a multitude of people (other virtues) are easily defeated. And so, brethren, before all other activities and with all our actions, let repentance be the work of us all, combining mourning with repentance, and accompanying mourning with tears. There is no mourning without repentance; there are no tears without mourning. These three are united and bound one to another, and it is impossible for one of them to appear without the other two."[37]

The spiritual way of repentance and mourning has such power that it is immune to demonic deception, or so-called diabolic delusion. The fallen spirit, in order to dupe the ascetic, first tries to convince him of his worth or merits, as may be seen from the examples cited in our previous counsels. But how can he dupe a person who seeks with all his power to discover his sinfulness, who bewails what has been revealed to him and is roused by it to seek further insights, whose sole endeavor is to see in himself the one and only plea of a sinner, so that both by his outer and inner activity he may offer to God the realization and confession of his sinfulness. "When the devil," says St Gregory of Sinai, "sees someone living a life of mourning, he does not stay near him, being repelled by his humility born of weeping."[38] Though the devil does also tempt those who mourn, yet he is easily recognized by them and repulsed. A self-opinionated person, who thinks he has some worth or merit, cannot repulse the devil's seduction from without, because he is possessed and chained by him within.

Ignorant and quack ascetics think they have reached their goal when they see themselves as saints, when the world thinks and proclaims them such. They rejoice at the self-deception and self-opinion that has got into them, not understanding how fatal self-opinion is, not realizing that human praise is the sign of a false prophet. This sign is extremely important. It is given by the God-Man Himself. "Woe," said the Lord, "Woe to you when all men speak well of you, for so did their fathers to the false prophets."[39] Woe, spiritual woe and disaster, eternal misery!

A true monk rejoices when he begins to see his sin, when in his own opinion of himself he becomes lower and more sinful than all his neighbors, when he begins to shake with fear at the thought of God's judgment and the eternal torments, when he feels like a criminal and convict, when during his prayers torrents of tears begin to flow and sighs and groans burst from his breast, when his mind purified by tears stands before God face to face, and he sees the Invisible by means of a vivid sense of the presence of God. O blessed vision! In this light the criminal or delinquent can offer true repentance for the crimes or offenses committed by him, he can move the All-Merciful to mercy by his abundant tears, by humble words and by laying bare his woeful condition, he can ask the compassionate God for forgiveness, and therewith also for a multitude of priceless, eternal, spiritual gifts. A monk's greatest success is to see and acknowledge that he is a sinner. It is a great success when a monk proves by all his actions that he sincerely and really admits that he is a sinner. "When the mind begins to see its sins like the sand of the sea for multitude, it serves as a setting and starting point for the soul's enlightenment and is a sign of its health," says the hieromartyr St Peter of Damascus.[40]

The mind can see its sins when the grace of God touches it. Darkened by the fall, of itself it is incapable of seeing them. The sight of our sins and our sinfulness is a gift of God. The Holy Orthodox Church teaches her children to ask God for this gift with fasting and prostrations, especially during the days of holy Lent.[41] The gift of seeing our sins, our fallen state, the fellowship or intercourse of fallen man with the fallen angels, was inconceivably abundant in the great holy Fathers; and in spite of the abundance of their spiritual gifts which clearly bore evidence to their holiness, it urged them to unceasing repentance and mourning, to a continual washing of themselves with their tears. The sayings of the Fathers from this state or level are incomprehensible to carnal minds. Thus, Poemen the Great used to say to the brethren who lived with him: "Brothers! Believe me, where Satan will be thrown, I shall be thrown, too."[42] "Everyone who exalts himself will be humbled, and he who humbles himself will be exalted,"[43] said the Lord.

CONCLUSION

Adaptations of the Rules for Present-Day Monasticism

An attentive reader of the works of the holy Fathers on monasticism will easily notice that the Fathers composed their instructions to suit the circumstances of the time and the condition of those monks for whom they were writing. That is why nearly all the works of the holy Fathers on monasticism have their own special aim, their own one-sided slant. That is also why it was impossible even in the flourishing times of monasticism for each monk to apply to himself wholesale all that the Fathers wrote. Still more is it impossible in our times, and many who have tried to do so have labored much but have gained very little.

We will cite the book of St John of the Ladder as an example. This servant of God wrote his books for cenobitic monks whose chief virtue should be obedience. That is why he speaks with caution, briefly and as if reluctantly, concerning silence or hesychasm, warning us of the danger of undertaking it prematurely or wrongly. On the other hand, he speaks of obedience in great detail, and commends and extols that way of life. The Saint does that not because silence or hesychasm, under certain conditions, is not a way of salvation, but so as not to dampen the zeal of cenobitic monks, and in order to brace and encourage them in the life of obedience which they have taken upon themselves and not give them a pretext for duplicity and for aspiring to undertake a way of life for which they are not fitted or ready, and so fall into self-deception and diabolic delusion, always such an imminent danger for the young and for those who are not young but are self-willed and self-opinionated.

It is evident that a monk not living in a community might be confused and upset from reading St John of the Ladder. He would surely imagine that apart from obedience in a community there can be no success or progress in the monastic life. This inspired book proved to have just that effect in actual experience. St Anthony the New, who was living as a solitary deep in the

210

wilds, read *The Ladder of Divine Ascent*. As a result of this reading, he left the wilds and entered a cenobitic monastery.¹

Not everyone can change his outward situation. But what of that?² A monk who stays in his place out of necessity when he has lost confidence in his place or state as a way of salvation falls into despondency, loses his enthusiasm for the monastic vocation, and begins to lead a negligent life. In our time, when we are separated by many centuries from the ways and circumstances in the heart of which the Fathers lived and produced their teaching, the application of their doctrine to the contemporary situation of monasticism in our country would appear to be especially urgent and promises to bring great profit.

Such was our aim in writing the present book. We hope it may serve as a guide for the monks of our time in the particular situation in which they find themselves by the providence of God. We hope that our poor work may be found useful both in the ordinary cenobitic communities and in the state-subsidized monasteries, and for a monk serving as a priest in a convent or at a shrine or chapel, or acting as a ship's chaplain by the rules and requirements of the government, or serving a long obedience in the world, or for a monk professed in a theological seminary and serving there on the teaching staff or in some administrative capacity. We hope that even lay people who wish to make their calling and salvation sure by living with special care and diligence in the midst of the world may also find our book helpful.³

The fulfillment of the commandments of the Gospel has always been the core and essence of the monastic life and activity, and the same is true today. Every place and situation offers many conveniences for this vocation and labor of love. Brethren, accept this spiritual offering, and do not criticize it for its inadequacy! The inadequacy of the offering is eloquent of the inadequacy of the writer. By your faith and zeal, supply the deficiencies of this inadequacy, and repay by your prayers and blessing him who has labored a little for your salvation as well as his own.

The rich landlord gave a sumptuous dinner to His friends and acquaintances and to a large number of people whom He invited to the dinner so as to enlarge His circle of friends and acquaintances. An infinite quantity of spiritual foods of unimaginable and unthinkable quality was provided for the guests on the spiritual table. At the end of the dinner, the guests were generously given spiritual gifts.

When the invited guests of honor had left, the Landlord looked outside the wedding hall and saw at the doors a crowd of hungry beggars⁴ who would have been glad to enjoy the scraps that remained after the wonderful dinner. The most merciful Lord told the servants to stop clearing the table. He invited the beggars to come in, notwithstanding their filth and rags which were quite out of keeping with the magnificence of the wedding hall, and He set before them the remains of the banquet.

Timidly and wonderingly the beggars entered the spacious hall, went up to the table and stood by it just where they happened to be, and each beggar began to take and eat whatever he found lying before him. They picked up all the scraps. Naturally none of them tasted a single whole dish, or saw the orderly attendance of the servants, or the precious plate and cutlery which were used by the guests, or heard the vast choir of singers or the music which resounded throughout the universe and rose to heaven. That is why none of the beggars, even though there were some among them with natural intelligence, could form a clear and exact idea for himself of the banquet. Having satisfied themselves with the scraps, they had to be content with a conjectural and approximate idea of the splendid and delicious dinner that the honored guests had enjoyed.

Having cleaned up everything edible on the table, the beggars fell at the feet of the Landlord, thanking Him for food such as they had never eaten or seen before. He said to them, "Brothers, in making my arrangements for the banquet, I did not have you in view. So I have not given you a proper dinner, and I am not giving you the gifts which have all been given away according to a previously made calculation which only I can understand."

With one voice the beggars exclaimed, "Lord, who are we to have gifts or a grand dinner! We are unspeakably grateful that you have not disdained us. You have admitted us, who are racked with every kind of defect, to your wedding hall and have saved us from starving to death."

The beggars dispersed, thanking and blessing the kind-hearted Landlord. Then, turning to the servants, He said: "Now clear the table and lock up my hall. There will be no more guests, and what could have been offered in the way of food has been offered. Everything is finished."

Oh, the depth of the riches both of the wisdom and knowledge of God! How unsearchable are His judgments and His ways past finding out! "For who has known the mind of the Lord? Or who has become His counselor?" "Or who has first given to Him and it shall be repaid to him?" For of Him and through Him and to Him are all things, to whom be glory forever. Amen.[5]

PART II

RULES OF OUTWARD CONDUCT
FOR NOVICES

Rules of Outward Conduct for Novices

INTRODUCTION: ON THE NEED FOR RULES

The Church Typikon says that, according to the teaching of the holy Fathers, measure and rule should be observed in everything. After mentioning the holy Fathers in general, the Typikon quotes this remarkable saying of St Ephrem the Syrian: "Great misery exists where life is not guided by lawful rules." On this foundation, we offer our beloved brethren who are beginners in the monastic life the following rules for their outward conduct.

The Meaning of a Monastery

I

The holy Fathers call a monastery a hospital. Exactly! A monastery is a moral hospital. We come out of the world into a monastery in order to abandon the sinful habits acquired in our worldly life and, outside the influence of the temptations of which the world is full, to acquire habits and conduct that are truly Christian. In return for a truly Christian life on earth, we hope to obtain eternal beatitude in heaven. And so we must make every effort to attain the end for which we enter a monastery, so that our life in the monastery may serve as a means of our salvation, and may not be a cause of greater condemnation for us in the judgment of Christ.

On Obedience and Obediences

2

Those who come to a hospital in order to benefit by it are obliged to be guided in everything by the direction of the physician, without allowing themselves to use food, clothing, movement, or medicine at their own discretion; otherwise, instead of getting benefit, they will do themselves harm.

So, too, everyone who comes to a monastery is obliged to exercise himself not in those penances and labors that seem to him necessary and beneficial, but in those that will be shown to him and appointed by the superior personally or through the mediation of other monastic authorities.[1]

3

All monastic exercises and duties in general are called obediences. Obediences should be carried out with all care, with strict guarding of the conscience, believing that such fulfillment of obediences is essential for our salvation. Monastic occupations are called obediences because they imply the renunciation of one's own will and of one's own reasoning. For this reason, when fulfilling obediences, the conscience is subjected to constant tests. The fruits of exercise in obediences are true humility and spiritual understanding. Voluntary labors performed out of self-opinion or at one's own whim or fancy, especially with the refusal of obedience, however great they may be, not only bring no spiritual fruit whatever, but on the contrary, being themselves the result of self-opinion and pride, greatly increase these passions in the monk and completely estrange him from the supernatural Christian way of thought, that is, from evangelical humility. St John Cassian says, "The care and principal education [of the novice-master], through which the novice may be able in due course to mount to the greatest heights of perfection, will be to teach him first to conquer his own will [or wishes]. While carefully and diligently exercising him in this, he will deliberately contrive to give him such orders as he knows to be contrary to his will or liking. For, taught by experience, the great Egyptian Fathers say that a monk—and especially a younger one—cannot control the desire of concupiscence unless he has first learned by obedience to mortify his will. They declare that a man who has not first learned to overcome his will or desires cannot possibly extinguish anger or sulkiness or the spirit of fornication, nor can he maintain true humility of heart or lasting unity with the brethren, nor even remain for long in the monastery. And so, by those practices, they hasten to impress and instruct those whom they are training for perfection with the alphabet, as it were, and first syllables, as they can clearly see by these whether they are grounded in false and imaginary or in true humility."[2]

On the Treatment of Sins

4

The sins into which we fall on account of the weakness and infirmity we share with all men must be confessed to our spiritual father, and sometimes, according to the nature of the sin, to our superior; then, without falling into despondency and inertia, we must resume our obedience with renewed zeal. If we do not at once understand earthly arts and sciences, and while learning them are subject over a long period of time to various doubts and errors, how much more natural is it to fall into errors while learning the art of arts and science of sciences—the monastic life?

On Prayer and Conduct in Church

5

Prayer is the mother of virtues. For this reason, the greater part of the time in a monastery is consecrated to prayer. For a novice, it is unprofitable to pray alone. Therefore, the Church Typikon forbids self-willed prayer and orders that all living in a monastery should offer the prayers to God together, in the church of God, with the exception of the sick who are kept in their cell by illness, and elders who have become spiritually mature for prayer in the solitude of the cell.

6

Prayer is the mother of virtues. And so all the brethren are invited to the diligent and unremitting[3] performance of the appointed prayers, and therefore to diligent and unremitting[3] attendance in the church of God.

7

When going from your cell to church to stand before the face of God, you should walk reverently, and on no account run; you should not look to the side, but have your eyes cast down to the ground, and should not wave your hands but have them hanging down at your sides.

8

Every brother, when going to church, should make the sign of the cross before the doors and make a bow to the waist, thereby giving honor to God's dwelling, which is the church.

9

After entering the church, every brother is obliged to stand in the middle before the royal gates and make the sign of the cross with a bow to the waist three times, but during the Great Fast, make the sign of the cross with prostrations. Then, having bowed on both sides to the people present, he should go to his place.

10

If a brother belongs to the right choir, then when he comes to his choir he should reverently make a bow to the waist before the icon of the Savior, bow to the brethren standing in the choirs, turning first to the left choir, then to the right, and modestly take his place. But if a brother belongs to the left choir, he should make a bow to the waist before the icon of the Mother of God, and, having bowed to the choirs, first to the right, then to the left, he should go to his place.

11

The church is heaven on earth. Those standing in it should stand with reverence, in an orderly manner, like the holy angels; they should have their eyes cast down to the ground, should not lean against the walls, should hold their hands straight down at their sides, should not fold their arms, and should not rest one leg but stand on both legs equally.

12

The church is the tribunal of God. One may go out of it either justified or condemned, according to the testimony of the Holy Gospel. [4] And therefore the reading and singing should be performed with all possible attention and reverence; on no account can talking be allowed, still less laughter and joking. Otherwise, we shall go out of the church condemned, having angered the King of heaven by standing before Him irreverently.

13

We must not look back at the people present during divine service. We must do all in our power to guard our sight as a kind of window into the soul through which the most infectious passions can enter.

14

In the choirs, each person must occupy the place appointed to him. In the absence of anyone, the next in order will take the vacant place, but on no account should the younger supplant the older because of self-will, self-opinion, or boldness. Exceptions are to be made when those in authority in the choirs find it necessary to group singers according to their voices.

15

Into the sanctuary, which is the holy of holies, on no account may any unconsecrated person enter, with the exception of sacristans and those on duty, according to the Nineteenth Canon of the Council of Laodicea, and according to the custom received in well-ordered Orthodox monasteries. God hears the commemoration of relatives equally from the church, from the place where you are standing, as from the sanctuary. Your prayer will be more acceptable to God from the church when, out of reverence for Him, you do not enter the sanctuary, than from the sanctuary when you enter it without due reverence and break the rule given to you.

16

A brother who is obliged to enter the sanctuary or to go through it, must do so with the greatest reverence and fear of God. On entering the sanctuary, make the sign of the cross with three prostrations toward the holy altar, but on Sundays, Saturdays, and Feast Days, with three bows to the waist; then turning toward the icon in the high place, make the sign of the cross with one bow to the waist; after this, bow to the superior, and take his blessing; if the superior is not in the sanctuary, take the blessing from the priest who is serving.

17

Unconsecrated people should not go around the holy altar. But if out of extreme need you have to pass the altar, then this should be done with great fear of God and care. You should walk slowly and quietly, and in going round the throne of God you should keep as far away from it as possible.

18

Never stand in the sanctuary unnecessarily, but when you have done what you have to do, go out immediately. Moreover, whoever has entered the sanctuary even out of extreme necessity or has been sent by those in authority should reproach himself, saying, "Woe is me, sinful and unclean, who have dared to enter the holy of holies and so condemn myself!" Even the sacred ministers whose vocation it is to serve and stand before God in the sanctuary make themselves worthy of this ministry by acknowledging their unworthiness and by endeavoring to wash themselves before the service with abundant tears of penitence and humility, and by performing the actual service with the greatest reverence, attention, and fear of God.

On the Duties of Readers

19

Those who read the psalms and the Daily Office—that is, Vespers, Matins, and the Hours—should prepare in good time and find the troparions and kontakions of the day beforehand, so as not to make mistakes during the reading in church and not have to stop to look for troparions and kontakions and thereby spoil the spirit of prayer. The reader should stand straight, with his hands at his side; he should read without hurrying and without dragging, and he should pronounce the words clearly and distinctly. He should read simply and reverently in a monotone without expressing his feelings by modulations and changes of voice. Let us leave the holy prayers to act on the listeners by their own spiritual power. The desire to convey to the bystanders one's own feelings is a sign of vanity and pride.

20

The Daily Office begins with Vespers. The reader who is to begin the Office should stand near the one who is finishing the Ninth Hour. When the latter finishes, they both bow together toward the sanctuary, and then bow to one another. The new reader stands before the lectern, and the one who has finished goes and stands in his place.

21

The reader of the Apostle,[5] when going to and from the choir, should hold the book in his left hand, slightly leaning its upper part towards his breast. When going to read, the reader of the Apostle stands first before the icon of the Savior or the Mother of God, according to which choir he belongs, and makes a bow to the waist before the icon; then he bows to his own choir, and after that he goes and stands in the middle of the church before the royal gates. Here he makes a bow toward the sanctuary, and when the priest says "Peace to all," he bows to him and begins to say the prokeimenon. After announcing the title of the Apostle, when the officiating priest or deacon says "Let us attend," the reader again bows to the priest and begins the reading of the Apostle. After finishing the reading, when the priest says "Peace to thee," the reader bows to him before the royal gates; then he goes and stands beside his choir before the icon, and bows before it; then he bows first to the opposite choir and then to his own choir, and goes to his place.

22

In reading the Apostle, one should on no account shout excessively or indecorously, out of vainglory. On the contrary, one should read in a natural voice—reverently, distinctly, majestically—without that exertion which is offensive both to the ear and the conscience, so that our sacrifice of praise may be acceptable to God, lest we offer to God only "the fruit of our lips"[6] and offer the fruit of our mind and heart to vanity, while even the fruit of our lips is rejected by God as a polluted sacrifice. This should be remembered by singers, too, because for all the choir brothers there is in general vainglory an extremely dangerous passion, through which other vices enter the soul, especially pride, and then the protecting grace of God leaves the man.

On Movement in Church

23

In going to and from the middle of the church, the singing should be begun and ended all together; moreover, the hands should not be waved, the eyes should be on the ground, and on no account should there be any looking about. The brothers should go in order, quietly, one after the other, without pushing or hurrying one another. On reaching the middle of the church, they should level themselves so that one does not stand in front of another. In returning to the choir, the same order and rules should be observed as have been given above for going from the choir to the middle of the church. While standing in the middle of the church, the arms should be held straight down, and on no account folded, prostrations should on no account be made voluntarily, and when they are appointed they should not be made separately but all together, so that the brothers who are in the middle of the church should be like one body, according to the expression of the Church Typikon. In order that the worship may be uniform and reverent, all the brothers should adjust themselves to the precentor who must see that the prostrations are made at the proper times and that his own prostrations are not hurried or too early, and that the brothers can conform themselves with him.

On Bows and Prostrations

24

The following bows and prostrations are appointed during divine service, and in the following order: when the officiating priest goes out of the sanctuary and stands before the royal gates to bless the reading of the Ninth Hour or Nocturns, or is about to bless the reading of the Hours in the sanctuary, before the exclamation "Blessed is our God," he makes *three* bows to the waist; the brethren should also do this. The same rule is observed before the beginning of the Divine Liturgy. At the beginning of the All-Night Vigil, *three* bows to the waist are appointed when the precentor exclaims "Come let us worship." In fact, in all the services, at every Trisagion and every "Come let us worship," *three* bows to the waist are appointed, except at the very beginning of

Matins when it is the custom only to make the sign of the cross three times, as also at the beginning of the Six Psalms when "Glory to God in the heights" is read three times, and also in the middle of the Six Psalms when "Alleluia, alleluia, alleluia, glory to Thee, O God" is read thrice. Usually the sign of the cross is made *once* at the beginning of the Symbol of Faith (or Creed) in the Divine Liturgy. During the singing of the Verses (*stikhiri*) and versicles (*stikhi*) only *one* bow to the waist each time is appointed whenever the words of a verse incite to worship. But neither in the middle of the church nor in the choirs should we bow in a disorderly and self-willed manner, but should always follow the precentor. When during and after the kathismas, and after the Six Psalms, "Alleluia, alleluia, alleluia, glory to Thee, O God" is said thrice, *three* bows to the waist are appointed, except on Sundays, Saturdays, and Feast Days when these bows are omitted.

When the brethren go to the middle of the church and before leaving it again, they all make together *one* bow to the waist, and then all together at the same time, bow to one another. At the first petition of each litany, and at the exclamation with which the officiating priest concludes the litany, *one* bow to the waist is appointed. Before and after the reading of the Holy Gospel, *one* bow to the waist is appointed. At the ninth song of the canon, during the singing of "More honorable than the Cherubim," at each repetition of these words, *one* bow to the waist is made. During the Divine Liturgy, after "Come let us worship and fall down before Christ," *one* bow to the waist is appointed. After finishing the whole "Song of the Cherubim," that is, after "alleluia," *three* bows to the waist. At the Great Entry, honor is given to the unconsecrated Gifts by *one* bow to the waist, and, after that, by bowing the head. After finishing "We praise Thee," *three* profound bows to the waist are appointed, but for those not in the choir *one* prostration. During the singing of this holy song, the consecration of the Holy Gifts takes place. After "It is meet and right," *one* bow to the waist. Before the Lord's Prayer, those not in the choir make one prostration, while those in the choir only make the sign of the cross because they have to sing immediately. After the Lord's Prayer, when the officiating priest says "For Thine is the Kingdom" and the rest of the exclamation, *one* bow to the waist is appointed. At the exclamation "The Holy Things for the Holy," *three* bows to the waist are appointed. When the Holy Mysteries are carried out with the words "With the fear of God, with faith and love draw near," *one* profound bow to the waist is made by those in the choirs with great reverence as to Christ Himself invisibly present in the Holy Mysteries, but those not in the choirs make *one* prostration. Exactly the same should be done when the holy chalice is carried out the second time with the words "Always, now and ever, and to the ages of ages." At the end of the Divine Liturgy, *three* bows to the waist are appointed, and the juniors of both choirs turn to the seniors, and all greet one another with a bow. On Sundays, Saturdays, and Festivals, prostrations are not made in church.

On Uncovering the Head

25

Kalimavkions[7] are taken off and rested on the shoulder so that the cross formed by the klobuk should not leave your shoulders at the following times during the services:

- In the Liturgy: at the Entry with the Gospel, at the reading of the Gospel, at the Great Entry, at Christ's words "Take, eat" till "It is meet" inclusive, during the singing of "Our Father," and at the appearance of the Holy Mysteries.
- At Vespers, during the Entry.
- At Matins, during the reading of the Gospel and during the singing of "More honorable."

To read the Apostle in the Liturgy and for the readings in Great Vespers the reader takes off his kalimavkion. The brethren take off their kalimavkions during the singing of "Our Father" before meals and "It is meet" after meals. The brethren should take off and put on their kalimavkions all together, and not one after another.

On Maintaining Strict Reverence in Church

26

In general, the greatest possible reverence and order should be maintained in the church of God, both for the glory of God and for one's own spiritual profit, and for the spiritual profit of the people present who are edified by the reverence of monks but are confused, scandalized, and harmed by their irreverence. One should not go out of church before the time; one should not allow oneself the least infringement of the rules of orderliness and reverence. From carelessness in small and insignificant things, we soon pass to carelessness in what is most important and in everything. In order to be attentive to one's important duties, one must constantly keep watch over oneself and be attentive in everything, even in one's smallest actions.

27

In case of necessity, superfluous phlegm should be carefully gathered in a handkerchief and not spat on the floor with an indecent noise. One should not cough or blow one's nose loudly. These and other similar natural needs should be done quietly and decently. Snuff should not be used in church. If food, which is a natural necessity for man, is not allowed to be used in church, how much more impermissible is snuff which is not at all a requirement of nature, but just a bad habit, a mere fad and fancy. In fact, those entering the monastic order should give up the use of tobacco entirely. Our worldly brethren are greatly scandalized when they see monks using tobacco. The unfailing duty of love requires that we should not give cause for scandal to our worldly brethren who, if scandalized by something trifling, will not trust us in what is important either. Those who cannot overcome their habits should acknowledge their weakness and make amends for their lack of self-denial by self-reproach,[8] but they should not display their habit before the brethren, because harm caused to one is not so grave as harm caused to many. Such is the opinion of the Fathers about our defeat by our weaknesses.

On Behavior in Refectory and Use of Food

28

The strictest order and reverence is appointed to be observed in church. This applies equally to the refectory. The time spent in the refectory for fortification with food should be, as it were, a continuation of divine service. While nourishing the body with prudent sufficiency with the foods set before them, the brethren should at the same time nourish their soul with the word of God which is read during meals. For this reason, profound silence is observed in the refectory. If it is necessary to say anything, it is said extremely quietly and briefly, so as not to interrupt the reading.

29

All the brethren should take food in the common refectory and not in their cells, with the exception of the sick who are allowed to have food brought to their cell, but only with the knowledge and permission of the superior. Try to partake of the common table and not to miss it for any slight cause that has a mask of truth. In due time you will see special spiritual profit from constant participation in the common refectory.

30

The use of food both in the refectory and in the cells should be regulated by prudence in regard to quantity. Novices should take food almost to fullness, but not to satiety. Fasting, which is so useful for a monk later, in the case of a novice should be moderate. If a novice does not eat outside the refectory, such a fast will be fully sufficient for him. The partaking of food in the refectory almost to fullness is necessary for a novice because he is obliged to do his obediences which are sometimes difficult, and so as not to weaken his bodily strength excessively. For the due weakening of the body, the quality and quantity of the monastic food in the refectory is sufficient. The passions diminish in novices not through violent fasting, but through the confession of sinful thoughts, through labors, and through shunning free intercourse with others.

On the Use of Wine

31

Although the use of wine in the refectory is permitted by the Church Typikon, it is allowed only for those old monks who are doing hard work, for whom it is necessary and beneficial. For the young, wine is harmful. Therefore, in spite of the fact that it is put on the table in certain monasteries, it is extremely profitable for the young to abstain from wine completely. "Praise for a monk is abstinence from wine," says St Symeon the Great Wonderworker; "and even if on account of bodily infirmity a monk is compelled to take it, let him take little." St Poemen the Great says, "Monks should on no account drink wine." "Young people should not even smell wine," says St Mark the Ascetic.

On Conduct in One's Cell and Reception of Visitors

32

In the cells, you should be occupied in spiritual reading and such handwork as does not excite attachment to it. Otherwise, all your attention will be drawn to the handwork to which you are attached. God and your salvation will become distant for you. Worldly books, and still more those that are harmful for morality, should on no account be read, or even kept in your cell.

33

Novices should not bring into their cells trinkets, that is, various fancy objects and luxuries. Such things attract a novice's mind and heart to themselves, and so distract them from God. Besides that, they excite reverie that is opposed to spiritual progress and proficiency. The best adornment for a monastic cell is a select library, which should consist of Holy Scripture and the writings of the Fathers on the monastic life. "It is essential to have Christian books," says St Epiphanius of Cyprus. "One glance at these books turns one away from sin and encourages one to virtue." Sacred books should be kept respectfully, rendering honor to the Holy Spirit Who lives in them. Elders known for their special piety and spiritual progress keep the New Testament by the holy icons.

34

It is prohibited for novices to receive women[9] in their cells, even their nearest relatives. As regards the reception of relatives and acquaintances of the male[10] sex, novices are obliged to ask the superior's permission.

35

Novices should not only refrain from receiving worldly people in their cells, but also from unduly visiting one another. Undue visiting from cell to cell is a cause of gossiping, joking, and impudence, whereby the fear of God and delight in the ascetic life are destroyed, and the most violent action of the passions is stirred up, especially despondency, anger, and lust. For this reason, the great Elder Symeon the Reverent ordered his disciple, St Symeon the New Theologian, on his entry into the monastery, to renounce all acquaintanceship inside and outside the monastery. By carefully carrying out the Elder's order, the disciple soon reached high spiritual proficiency.

36

Novice! Often visit the cell of your confessor or elder for your spiritual edification and confession of your sins and your sinful thoughts. Happy are you if you have found a confessor with knowledge, experience, and good intention. A satisfactory director in our times is the greatest rarity. Honor as a shrine that cell in which you hear the life-giving word of God. And if there is not a satisfactory director in the monastery, then go more often to your spiritual father for confession, but be guided by the Gospel, and the ascetical books written by the holy Fathers. Your cell will become for you a haven and refuge from emotional upheavals and thought-storms, disturbances of mind and heart.

37

There should be no food of any kind in your cell, no dainties, and especially no drinks. We do not come to a monastery to enjoy ourselves by fulfilling the desires of the flesh, for earthly joys and amusements. We enter a monastery in order that, by means of true repentance uninterrupted by distractions and enjoyments, we may be reconciled with God and receive from Him the priceless gift of salvation.

On Clothing

38

Clothing should be as simple as possible, but as decent and tidy as is required by the custom and position of the monastery and its relations with visiting worldly people who may be offended both by luxurious and untidy clothing. Do not have colored cassocks (*podriasniks*) and colored linings for gowns (*riassas*). Such clothing is unsuitable for those who are weeping over their dead soul. They should have black clothing, which people wear as a sign of deep sorrow. It is essential for a novice to observe this rule; because the state of his soul conforms to the state of his body, and he cannot maintain a sense of penitence when his body is adorned with showy and elegant clothing. Vainglory and hardness of heart come from a novice's wearing luxurious clothing, and his flesh revives for lustful feelings and movements. It is unfitting for a sinner to have beautiful clothes; otherwise, he will be like a white-washed and gilded coffin: bright and rich outside, but inside a stinking corpse.

On Relations with Brethren of the Monastery

39

Respect should be shown to elders, and priests should be approached for their blessing with faith and reverence. This respect should stem from a sense of duty and love, and not from a desire to please men or from any other motive of this world, foreign to the monastic outlook and alien to the spirit of the Church.

40

The brethren should bow affably and courteously to one another when they meet, honoring the image of God in their neighbor, honoring Christ Himself.[11]

41

The young must try to love all equally and must avoid, as a snare of the devil, exclusive love for any companion or worldly acquaintance. Such love in the young is nothing but a passion that they do not understand, and which violently drags them away from their duties to God.

42

In mutual meetings, extreme care should be taken to guard the sense of touch, and it should be guarded to such a degree that on no account should a brother[12] be held by the hand. Similarly, other greetings unsuitable for a holy monastic community should be avoided. This precaution was strictly observed in the ancient monasteries. Breakers of this rule were subjected to public monastic punishment in the Egyptian communities that were the best in the Christian world. St John Cassian tells us this.[13]

43

One ought to avoid, as the greatest danger, association with a brother who leads a slack life, not in order to condemn him, but for another reason: nothing is so catching, so infectious as a brother's weakness. The Apostle ordered, "We command you, brethren, in the name of our Lord Jesus Christ, that you withdraw from every brother who walks disorderly and not according to the tradition which he received from us."[14] "[Do] not keep company with anyone named a brother, who is sexually immoral, or covetous, or an idolator, or a reviler, or a drunkard, or an extortioner—not even to eat with such a person."[15] Why? Because, the same Apostle says, "Evil company corrupts good habits."[16] Are you on friendly terms with a drunkard? Be sure of this: in his company you, too, will learn to drink. Do you often talk to an adulterer? Be sure of this: he will infect you with his lustful feelings. Your friends and intimate acquaintances should be those whose sole aim is to please God. That is how the holy Prophet David acted. He says of himself, "I have walked in the innocency of my heart in the midst of my house." But in spite of such innocence, "I have hated the workers of iniquity" with a hatred pleasing to God which consists in keeping away from them.

> Whoso privily slandereth his neighbor, him did I drive out;
> whoso hath a proud look and a greedy stomach,
> with such I did not eat.
> Mine eyes look upon such as are faithful in the land,
> that they may dwell with me;
> whoso leadeth a godly life, he shall be my servant.
> The proud doer hath not dwelt in the midst of my house;
> he that speaketh unjustly
> shall have no place in my sight.[17]
> But Thy friends have been very dear to me, O God.[18]

St Poemen the Great has said, "The sum [end, crown] of all instruction for a novice is: avoid bad company [companionship, friendship], and keep good company."

On Leaving the Monastery

44

You should not go about with an uncovered head in the monastery; this is a breach of modesty and reverence. Also one should not allow oneself to shout or to make disorderly, overly free movements of the body. Such things disturb the interior peace of a novice, disturb the order of the monastery, destroy the quiet of the brethren, and are a cause of temptation for worldly visitors to the monastery.

45

One must never go outside the monastery enclosure without previously asking permission to do so from those in authority.

46

It is never allowed to go for walks alone, but always in twos or threes. This regulation existed in the ancient as well as in the newest of the well-ordered holy communities. In this way, many temptations, and even falls, have been prevented. "Woe to him who is alone!" [19] When some temptation begins to assail him, there is no one to restrain him. On the other hand, a brother who is helped by another brother, divine Scripture likens to a secure and elevated city. [20]

47

Do not love going to town, do not love visiting worldly places. How can the soul of a young monk or novice who wishes to take upon himself the vows of monasticism not be harmed by the frequent sight of temptations and by mixing with temptations to which his heart is still alive, which he enjoys and to which he is attracted? Unless he enjoyed the glamour and delusions of the world, he would not be attracted by them. A monk who feels an impulse to go frequently out of the monastery into the world is wounded with the devil's arrow. A monk who follows the morbid impulse of his heart frequently to leave the monastery and wander among the temptations of the world has voluntarily received into himself the deadly, poisonous arrow shot at him by the devil, and has allowed its poison to flood his soul and poison it. A novice given to roaming about must be regarded as unfit for the monastic life, and should be put out of the monastery in good time. A monk given to roaming about must be regarded as having betrayed and been false to God, to his conscience, and to his monastic vows. For such a monk, nothing is holy; all the most dastardly deeds, every sin and crime he considers permissible for himself, being drawn and darkened by the passion of love for the world which includes the service of all the passions. Be particularly vigilant with regard to such a monk, because he will not scruple to do as much harm as possible to the community. Using the help of his corrupt connections in the world, he will justify his behavior and foil every attempt to check his misconduct.

48

Everything depends on habit. If we are slack, we shall get into a bad habit that will rule over us like a cruel master over his slaves. If we force ourselves, we shall acquire a good habit that will act in us like a beneficial natural property. Choose what is good for you, and practice it; habit will make what is good pleasant. Force yourself to acquire the good habit of patiently staying in the monastery, of going out of it only in extreme necessity, of remaining out of it as short a time as possible, of returning to it as soon as possible. The father of monasticism, St Anthony the Great, has said, "Just as fish die if they stay long on dry land, so monks who remain with worldly people outside their cell lose the disposition for silence. Just as a fish rushes to the sea, so we should rush to our cells, lest by delaying outside we forget the inner watch." From the habit of staying in the monastery we easily pass to another still better habit, the habit of staying in one's cell. Then the merciful Lord will lead us to the holy habit of remaining within oneself. [21]

49

He who observes prudent silence, who guards the senses of sight and touch, who avoids special love for any of the brethren, or worldly people, who avoids attachment to earthly things, who shuns familiarity and all that infringes upon modesty and reverence, will soon feel within himself that deadness from which life radiates. [22] On the other hand, he who gives way to distraction and dissipation, who does not watch over himself, who allows himself to be attached to people and familiar with them, will never attain anything spiritual even though he were to spend a hundred years in a monastery.

On Venerating the Miraculous Icons and Holy Relics

50

Each of the brethren is obliged every day to kiss the wonder-working icon or holy relics that are in the monastery. You should kiss them with three reverent prostrations and with heartfelt prayer that the saints may help you to accomplish the course of monasticism for the glory of God and for the salvation of your soul. Two of the three prostrations are made before kissing the icon or relics, and one after kissing. That is what reverent monks do in all monasteries where they have wonder-working icons and holy relics. The monks kiss the icons and relics usually after Matins or after Vespers, or else after the Evening Prayers.[23]

CONCLUSION

The keeping of the above rules can bring the outward conduct of a monk into good order, and can teach him constant reverence and constant watchfulness over himself. He who has brought his outward conduct into order is like a well-made vessel without cracks. Into such a vessel, precious myrrh can be poured with the certainty that the myrrh will be preserved intact. And a monk who has reduced his habits to order becomes capable of spiritual action, which is preserved intact by good bodily habits, while it cannot possibly be retained in a monk whose outward conduct is disorderly. St Isaac the Syrian says, "Bodily activity precedes that of the soul, just as the creation of the body preceded the breathing of the soul into Adam. He who does not perform bodily labor, cannot perform spiritual labor either. For the latter is born of the former, as an ear from a grain of corn. And he who is without spiritual activity, is also devoid of spiritual gifts." The same Saint says in another place, "Many great and admirable fathers I have found who cared for the ordering of their senses and their bodily habits more than for other labors, because thence is born the ordering of the thoughts. Many causes, independent of his will, meet a man and make him leave the domain of his freedom. And if his senses were not guarded through the regularity of his previously acquired habits, they would for long prevent him from entering within himself and from finding his former quiet." In another place: "Behave reverently in the presence of your friend. By so doing, you will be of profit to yourself and to them. For usually under the pretext of friendship the soul casts off the reins of watchfulness. Beware of meeting people; it is not always profitable. In gatherings, prefer silence; for it prevents much harm. Guard your sight more than your stomach; for inner war is undoubtedly easier than outer. Do not believe, brother, that inner thoughts can be controlled without the control of the body. Fear bad habits more than devils."

When Basil the Great arrived in Antioch, the philosopher Libanius, director of the school of Antioch and a comrade of Basil's in the school of Athens, asked him to deliver a lecture to his youthful listeners. St Basil did this. Telling them that they should guard purity of soul and body, he gave them detailed rules for their outward conduct. He ordered them to have a modest gait, not to talk loudly, to observe propriety in conversation, to take food and drink reverently, to keep silent in the presence of their elders, to be attentive to the wise, obedient to their superiors, to have a sincere love for equals and juniors, to avoid the wicked and those who are infected with passions and who love to please the flesh, to speak little, carefully to gather knowledge, not to speak without thinking beforehand what you are going to say, not to talk much, not to be quick to laugh, to make modesty and other virtues their outward adornment. Wise Basil gave the youths an instruction mostly relating to their outward conduct, knowing that good order passes at once from the body to the soul, and that bodily order soon brings the soul into order.

Special attention should be paid to getting out of the habit of being familiar with people, a practice that is so approved and so loved in worldly society. In our times, many who have become accustomed to familiarity in worldly life retain it in the monastery. Others who have already entered the monastery try to acquire it, finding in it something especially attractive. The harmful consequences of familiarity are not noticed owing to distraction, to inattention to oneself, and to the constant multiform action of countless temptations; but for a monk they are fatal. The holy Fathers speak in vigorous terms against familiarity, which they call impudence.

Once, a brother came to St Agatho who was distinguished among the fathers of the Egyptian Scetis at that time for a special gift of discernment and said, "I intend to live with brethren. Tell me, how should I live with them?" The elder replied, "Spend the whole of your stay with them like the first day of your arrival. Throughout your life maintain a state of pilgrimage [i.e., behave in the monastery like a stranger and pilgrim, and not like an inhabitant and member of the community], and do not allow yourself to feel at home or become familiar." Abba Macarius, who happened to be there, asked, "What significance has familiarity?" The elder replied, "Familiarity is like a great heat wave, before the face of which all run as it approaches and the fruits are spoilt on the trees." To this, Abba Macarius replied, "Is familiarity so harmful?" Abba Agatho answered, "There is no passion more terrible than familiarity. It is the parent of all the passions. An ascetic should refrain from all familiarity in his relations with others." Saints Barsanuphius the Great and his disciple St John the Prophet said, "Acquire firmness and it will banish from you familiarity in your relations with your neighbors, the cause of all evils in man. If you want to be delivered from shameful passions, do not be familiar with anyone, especially with those whom your heart is inclined to love inordinately. [24] In this way, you will be freed from vainglory, too. For vainglory is connected with man-pleasing, man-pleasing is connected with familiarity, and familiarity is the mother of all the passions." And St Isaac the Syrian says, "Shun familiarity like death." [25]

It is evident and understandable for everyone that familiarity, which so very easily and frequently becomes the greatest impertinence and insolence, is a cause of quarrels, anger, and spite; but it is not evident and understandable for everyone that from familiarity is kindled the most violent passion of fornication. Let my beloved brethren who have started on the invisible course of martyrdom[26] and have undertaken to fight the passions of the flesh and spirit realize this, so that by the grace of God, which overshadows the efforts of ascetics, they may master them and receive from Christ's hand for their victory the crown of salvation. In general it must be said that the monk is subjected to quite different laws from the layman, and needs to exercise the strictest watchfulness over himself, constant carefulness, and continual distrust of his mind, heart, and body. The monk can be compared to a hothouse flower and the layman to a field flower. In the fields, it is impossible to find such beautiful and precious flowers as may be seen in a hothouse, but, on the other hand, hothouse flowers need special care; they cannot bear changes of weather and a slight fall in temperature may damage them, whereas the field flowers need neither care nor attention; they grow wild, and easily bear changes of temperature. All the holy Fathers order monks to exercise the strictest watchfulness over themselves, and to be always on their guard. An apparently insignificant circumstance may be for a monk an occasion of the greatest temptation, and even a fall. A careless touch, a casual glance, have suddenly changed *the* whole state of a monk's soul, all his innermost feelings, even his way of thinking, as has been proved by unfortunate experiences. One must be constantly on the watch. The previously mentioned St Agatho used to say, "Without the greatest watchfulness over oneself, it is impossible to make progress in one single virtue."

From their very entry into the monastery, novices should direct all their attention to protecting themselves with reverent habits and customs, and they should make every effort to acquire them, even at the cost of much hard work. A good habit that is acquired with difficulty in youth becomes your natural property and accompanies you everywhere. Protected by good bodily habits, you can hopefully gather spiritual riches; and they will be kept intact through being guarded on all sides by good bodily habits. On the other hand, a bad habit can, in a very short time, cause the loss of all the spiritual riches that have been gathered over a long period, so that a fresh gathering of riches becomes extremely laborious. The reason for such spiritual disasters is an inclination to familiarity and to frequent absences from the monastery and from one's cell. These absences are directly connected with the tendency to familiarity and breed it.

Brethren! Let us implore the Lord, combining prayer with special effort, that He may instruct us in the reverence that He has enjoined, [27] and that He may set a watch over our mouth[28] and our other members, as well as our senses, that, if left unguarded, become open doors to sin that enters the soul through them and kills it. Amen.

GLOSSARY

Akathist: A stylized form of prayer consisting of thirteen kontakia, each
followed by a refrain, and the first twelve followed also by an ekos
and a fixed number of lines beginning with the word "Rejoice!"
The word *akathist* means literally "not sitting" as it is customary to
remain standing throughout the reading or singing of an akathist
(compare *kathisma* below).

Archimandrite: In Greek the word means literally the head or ruler of a
mandra or fold. In this sense, it was used originally as equivalent
to the Greek *hegoumenos* (Russian *igumen*), the leader or abbot of
a monastery. Sometimes an archimandrite was charged with the
supervision of a number of monasteries. Now an archimandrite
ranks above an hegoumenos or abbot, and corresponds to a mitered
abbot, since he has the right to wear a miter like a bishop. In modern
times, archimandrite is sometimes simply a title of honor given to
monastic priests, and there may be several in one monastery.

Bows: First, the worshipper makes the sign of the cross, then bows—either
slightly, or by a bow to the waist when he touches his hand to the
floor, or by a prostration when he touches the ground with his fore-
head. On Sundays the joy of the resurrection overwhelms even the
sense of penitence, so bows replace prostrations. On great feasts also
bows to the waist are made instead of prostrations, for example,
upon entering and leaving the church and at certain points in the
services, as when the consecrated chalice is brought out to the people
through the royal doors and the priest says, "With the fear of God,
with faith and love, draw near."

Canon: (1) A rule or regulation; (2) a form of prayer, often in poetic verse in
Greek (but not in Slavonic), made up of nine odes (in practice, usually eight, except during Lent) with the themes of the nine songs or

canticles of the Old Testament saints from Moses to Zachariah, each ode being followed by a number of troparia preceded by a refrain. The choir sings the odes, and the refrain and troparia are read by a reader.

Cell Rule: In addition to the sequence of services in church, a monk is normally expected to fulfill a further rule of prayer privately in his own cell. This cell rule varies from one monastery to another, and may be adapted and modified according to the needs of the individual.

Ekos: Ekos/oikos is a short stanza following the kontakion sung after the Sixth Ode of a canon that reiterates the teaching of the former text in summarizing the meaning of the feast being celebrated. Its ending phrase is normally identical to that of the kontakion.

Gift of Tears: Spiritual weeping is a special gift from God, by no means merely of emotional or nervous origin.

Great Fast: Another term for Lent. This fast, which is followed by Lazarus Saturday, Palm Sunday and Passion Week, is in preparation for Easter.

Great Schema/Habit: The highest degree of the monastic life in the Orthodox Church, conferred only on a small minority of monks or nuns. A monk or nun of the Great Schema is expected to follow a stricter life of fasting, silence, and prayer. He or she is often a hermit, and if within a community, he or she remains in strict seclusion. If they speak with others, it is in order to impart spiritual direction or assistance. Russian practice differs somewhat from Greek practice. Thus in Greek practice, only those who have the Great Schema are considered full monks or nuns.

Hermitage: A monastic house or settlement stressing solitude and contemplation. Sometimes a center to which people come in considerable numbers for confession, advice, direction, guidance, and counseling.

Hesychasm: The silent life of contemplative prayer.

Hesychast: A recluse or a hermit.

Hierodeacon: A monk in deacon's orders.

Hieromartyr: A bishop or priest who died as a martyr and is canonized.

Hieromonk: A monk in priest's orders.

High Place: The bishop's throne in the sanctuary behind the altar.

Holy: A word often having a technical meaning. *Holy community* means a monastic community; *holy Fathers* (with a capital letter) is used in this book to mean the Church Fathers; *holy fathers* (no capital) is used to mean monks, either of ancient times or now living.

Kathisma: (1) A troparion that is sung after the reading of the Psalms appointed for the day and during which one may sit; (2) one of the twenty divisions of the Psalter. During the reading of a kathisma of the Psalter, it is customary to sit. The word comes from the Greek verb *to sit* (in Slavonic, *sedalyen* or *kafisma*).

Kontakion: A form of prayer in prose or verse, similar to a troparion, which is read or sung at various fixed points in the services. There is a kontakion for every day, every feast, and for almost every saint. After the Sixth Ode (Song) of the canon at Matins, the kontakion of the day is usually sung. After the Entrance in the Divine Liturgy, the choir sings the troparia and kontakia appointed for the day. It roughly corresponds to a collect, summarizing the theme of the feast.

Liturgy: In the Latin Church, Liturgy refers to the entire Divine Office or church services as a whole, whereas in the Orthodox Church it usually means the Divine Liturgy or Holy Eucharist, the main service of the Church.

Passion: A passion is an emotion so subtle and intense that the spirit, mind, or body is as if unconsciously influenced by it.

Royal Gates or Royal Doors: The two central doors in the iconostasis (icon screen) that separates the sanctuary from the body of the church where the faithful stand. Only priests and deacons may go through the royal (holy) doors, and only at specified points in the services.

Sanctuary: The eastern part of a church containing the altar or holy table or throne. It is separated from the nave or catholicon or main body of the church by the iconostasis (icon screen). In Greek and Russian, the whole sanctuary is usually called the altar.

Schemamonk: A monk of the Schema or Great Habit (see above).

Six Psalms: Psalms 3, 37, 62, 87, 102, and 142 in the Greek–Latin numbering of the Psalter (in Hebrew numbering, 3, 38, 63, 88, 103, 143). These Psalms are read at the beginning of Matins by a reader who stands in the middle of the church.

Staretz (plural *startsy*): A Slavonic word meaning an elder or old man. In its technical sense it is applied to a person who by the grace of God has received spiritual gifts such as spiritual insight and discernment, enabling him to act in a special way as a spiritual guide or director.

Troparion: A short prayer in prose or verse, whether forming part of a canon or occurring elsewhere in the services. There is a vast number of these short hymns which may be read or sung according to their position in the service, and they are classified according to use. Examples include *anastasimon, anatolikon, apolytikion, aposticha, automelon, despotikon, dogmatikon, eisodikon, exaposteilarion, eulogetarion, theotokion, idiomelon, kathisma, katabasis, katanyktion, martyrikon, megalynarion, nekrosimon, proeortion, prosomoion, stavrotheotokion, hypakoe, photogogikon* (the corresponding Slavonic names are considerably different). There is a special troparion for each saint or feast appointed for every day of the year, known as the troparion of the day. This is read at each of the Hours, and is sung at the Liturgy.

Typikon: A large book of rules and regulations and calendar for the ordering of the church services, explaining and amplifying the rubrics, and providing for every possible predicament or conjunction of feasts. Without this book it is impossible to know the order of the daily services.

Unconsecrated Persons: Those who are not authorized to enter the sanctuary or to handle the sacred vessels or vestments.

A Short Biography of St Ignatius (Brianchaninov)

The future St Ignatius was born on April 15/28, 1807, in the village of Pokrovskoye in the Vologda region of Russia. His given name at birth was Dimitry Alexandrovitch Brianchaninov. Of noble birth, his father was a wealthy provincial land-owner. In due course, the young Dimitry was sent to study at the Pioneer Military Academy in St Petersburg to be educated as a military officer.

Even before entering the academy, Dimitry had aspired to the monastic life, but his family did not support these plans. Nevertheless, as a student he was able to find some time to devote to prayer and the inner life, and to find other students with similar aspirations. Remaining obedient to his parents, he remained diligent in his studies, winning the praise of his teachers and coming to the attention of the Grand Duke Nicholas Pavlovich, the future Tsar Nicholas I.

After graduating from the academy, he took up his first commission in the army but soon became seriously ill. This made it possible for him to request an honorable discharge and, having made a full recovery, to at last embrace the monastic life. He was tonsured as a monk in 1831 and given the name Ignatius. His spiritual father was the revered elder, Leonid of Optina. Shortly after his tonsure he was ordained as a priest.

Meanwhile, his absence from the army had come to the attention of Tsar Nicholas. As soon as he was able to locate Father Ignatius in his small monastery near Vologda, he ordered him back to the capital. So, at the age of only twenty-six, Father Ignatius was made an archimandrite and appointed as head of the St Sergius Monastery in St Petersburg. He served faithfully in that capacity for the next twenty-four years.

In 1857 he was ordained to the episcopacy, serving as bishop of Stavropol and the Caucasus. This period of his life lasted for only four years, after which he withdrew into seclusion at the Nicolo-Babaevsky Monastery in the Kostroma region of Russia. Here he was able to devote the remaining six years of his life to spiritual writing and correspondence with his numerous spiritual children. He composed five volumes of *Ascetical Works*, the fifth of which, *The Arena*, has been translated into English.

Bishop Ignatius reposed on April 30/May 13, 1867. The Russian Orthodox Church canonized him at its local council in 1988 and his relics now reside at the Tolga Monastery in the Yaroslavl region of Russia.

NOTES

A ll references to source material in the original text were to the clas-
sic Russian language editions. The author and translator followed a
Russian cultural practice where one is not necessarily expected to provide all
background detail and source material.

Foreword
   1. Introduction, xxii.
   2. For the meaning of this and other technical terms used in the
Orthodox Church, see the Glossary.
   3. Conclusion to Part I, 211.
   4. Chapter 3, 10.
   5. Chapter 50, 197.
   6. First Letter, 7:1.
   7. 1 Cor 15:32
   8. Acts 19
   9. Bishop Ignatius mentions *Staretz* Leonid in Chapter 11, 32.
   10. Edited by Cardinal Newman, London, 1882.
   11. Bishop Ignatius (Brianchaninov), *On the Prayer of Jesus*, translated
by Archimandrite Lazarus, London, 1952.
   12. In the original Russian text, the "Rules of Outward Conduct
for Novices" came first, and then the "Counsels for the Spiritual Life of
Monks." But in an edition intended for an English-speaking public, it was
thought better to reverse the order.—Trans.
   13. Chapter 11, 32.
   14. Chapter 1, 3.
   15. Chapter 6, 15.
   16. Introduction, xxi.

17. Both are available in English translation: St John of the Ladder, *The Ladder of Divine Ascent*, translated by Archimandrite Lazarus, London, 1959; St Isaac the Syrian (Isaac of Nineveh), *Mystic Treatises*, translated by A. J. Wensinck, Amsterdam, 1923.

18. There is as yet no full translation of this in English; extracts are included in *Early Fathers from the Philokalia*, translated by E. Kadloubovsky and G. E. H. Palmer, London, 1954.

19. Large parts of this may be found, translated into English, in H. Waddell, *The Desert Fathers*, London, 1936, and in Thomas Merton, *Sayings of the Desert Fathers*, 1960.

20. He does not mention the most important of the fourteenth-century hesychasts, St Gregory Palamas (1296–1359), probably because the works of Palamas were not available to him.

21. Introduction, xxii.

22. Conclusion to Part I, 210.

23. Matt 22:37–40; Chapter 15, 52.

24. Chapter 16, 57; Chapter 17, 59.

25. Tito Colliander, *The Way of the Ascetics*, London: Hodder & Stoughton, 1961, 73.

26. For a fuller discussion of the Jesus Prayer, see the introduction to Igumen Charriton's anthology, *The Art of Prayer*, translated by E. Kadloubovsky and E. M. Palmer, London, 1966.

27. See Chapter 24.

28. See Chapters 25–26.

29. Chapter 8, 19.

30. Eph 6:12.

31. See Chapters 43–46, and 48.

32. Introduction, xxi.

33. Chapter 29, 86.

34. Chapter 37, 128.

35. Chapter 44, 178.

36. Chapter 50, 208.

37. See Chapters 15 and 45.

38. See Chapter 11.

39. Chapter 12, 42.

40. St John of the Ladder, *The Ladder of Divine Ascent*, 7:49. quoted in Chapter 50, (p. 205) at note 33.

41. St Macarius the Great, Homilies 15, 26, 36 (Migne, *Patrologia Graeca*, XXXIV, 593B, 600D).

42. Luke 18:14.

43. Rom 11:33.

Introduction

1. Rev 6:14.

2. Ps 119:6.

3. Ps 68:3, 4.

4. Ps 142:3.

5. Ps 21:15, 16.

6. Ps 17:5, 6.

7. Ps 142:4.

8. St John of the Ladder, *The Ladder of Divine Ascent*, 26:14.

9. Prov 4:25–28 OSB.

Chapter 1

1. Matt 28:19–20.

2. John 14:21.

3. John 14:23.

4. John 15:5–6, 9–10.

5. Matt 7:21–23.

6. Matt 5:19.

7. See the commentary of Blessed Theophylact the Bulgarian.

8. John 6:63.

9. 1 Cor 2:14.

10. 1 Cor 15:49.

11. 1 Cor 15:50.

12. Ps 72:27. The soul is God's bride. To forsake Him is adultery (Hos 2:2; Isa 54:5; Exod 20:5; Deut 5:9).

13. Ps 72:28.

Chapter 2

1. Matt 25:31–46; John 5:22–27.

2. John 12:48–50.

Chapter 3

1. St John of the Ladder, *The Ladder of Divine Ascent* 1:4. Bishop Ignatius' quotation is not a very accurate rendering of the Greek, but it conveys the meaning.—Trans.

2. Ps 1:1–3.
3. Ps 77:1.

Chapter 4
1. In other words, he is always in the arena, there is always scope for his enterprise, and he makes capital out of everything.
2. Matt 7:24–25.
3. Matt 7:26–27.
4. 1 Cor 1:24.
5. John 14:23.
6. Ps 36:29.
7. The mouth of the soul is the eyes. Just as food enters the body through the mouth, so knowledge enters the soul through the eyes.
8. Ps 36:30–31.

Chapter 5
1. *Alphabetical Patrology.*
2. St Isaac the Syrian, *Mystic Treatises*, ch. V of English translation.
3. "Scetis" is the Wadi El Natrun, a 22-mile-long, below sea level depression to the west of the Nile Delta in Egypt. It was a major center of early monastic life, and the word scetis is derived from the Greek for "ascetic."
4. St John Cassian, *The Cenobitic Institutes and Conferences*, "First Conference on Discretion."
5. *Alphabetical Patrology.*
6. 2 Samuel 11.

Chapter 6
1. Monasteries in the nineteenth and early twentieth centuries of Russia were divided into state-funded and unfunded monasteries. See Scot Kenworthy, *The Heart of Russia: Trinity Sergius, Monasticism, and Society after 1825* (Washington, D.C.: Woodrow Wilson Center Press, 2010).
2. St Nil Sorsky. [Nil is pronounced "Neel"—Trans.] See English translation in G. P. Fedotov, *A Treasury of Russian Spirituality*, London, 1950: 130–132.
3. St Barsanuphius the Great and St John the Prophet, *Directions for the Spiritual Life*, Answer 108.
4. Ps 118:96.

Chapter 7

1. John 12:25. [Or, "The man who loves himself is lost, but he who hates himself in this world will be kept safe throughout eternal life." —Trans.]
2. Mark 8:34–35.
3. Luke 14:26.
4. Matt 19:27.
5. Matt 19:28–30.
6. Ps 140:5.
7. Sir 32:19 OSB.
8. St Barsanuphius the Great and St John the Prophet, *Directions for the Spiritual Life*, Answer 59.
9. 1 John 2:23.
10. Matt 15:8.
11. Matt 6:1–18.

Chapter 8

1. St Isaac the Syrian, *Mystic Treatises,* ch. 61 (ch. VIII of English translation).
2. Ps 91:12.
3. St Peter of Damascus, "On the Eight Mental Visions," *The Philokalia*, bk. I; St John of the Ladder, *The Ladder of Divine Ascent*, 27:26.
4. 1 Pet 5:8; 2 Tim 4:17; Ps 21:22; Wis 2:24.

Chapter 9

1. In all well-ordered cenobitic monasteries, the explanation of the Gospel for the day given in *The Herald* is read daily at Matins. (1 Cor 11:2; 2 Thess 2:15.)
2. The author stresses the priority and primacy of the Gospel.
3. St John of the Ladder, *The Ladder of Divine Ascent*, 27:28. [Russian translation differs widely from the Greek.—Trans.]
4. St Symeon the New Theologian, "On the Three Ways of Prayer"; St Gregory of Sinai, "On Reading," ch. 11.

Chapter 10

1. St John of the Ladder, *The Ladder of Divine Ascent*, 27:1.
2. Ibid., Step 4 in 118.
3. Acts 27:21–44.

Chapter 11

1. "Life of St Anthony the Great," *Menologion* for January 17. Cp. Vitae Patrium Patrologiae cursus compl., T. LXXIII.

2. *Alphabetical Patrology.*

3. *Alphabetical Patrology* and *Notable Sayings.*

4. "Life of St Mary of Egypt," *Menologion* for April 1.

5. St John of the Ladder, *The Ladder of Divine Ascent*, 4:119 (Russian translation).

6. Ibid., 27:55.

7. The *angelic image* or *angelic likeness* is a common term for the monastic habit. The monastic life follows as closely as possible the angelic life.

8. Acts 8:9–24.

9. *The Prologue* for January 9.

10. *Petchersk Patrology* and *Menologion* for February 14.

11. *Petchersk Patrology* and *Menologion* for January 31.

12. Five of the tiny loaves are used for every Eucharist in the Russian Church (Greeks use one prosphoron).

12. "The Palestine recluse" is most probably a reference to St Sabbas the Sanctified who reposed in A.D. 532.

13. See note 24 of this chapter.

14. Ps 9:30.

15. *The Philokalia.* This is a free rendering of the Greek by the author; we have translated Bishop Ignatius' Russian fairly literally.—Trans.

16. St Pachomius the Great, *Menologion* for May 15.

17. St Mark the Ascetic, "On the Spiritual Law," *The Philokalia,* ch. 34.

18. Eph 5:16–17.

19. See the Lives of Anthony the Great, Onuphrius the Great, and other hermits and solitaries.

20. St Barsanuphius the Great and St John the Prophet, *Directions for the Spiritual Life*, Answers 312 and 313.

21. *The Ladder*, 8:10, 18, 21, 25; 27:13, 36.

22. St Symeon the New Theologian, *The Philokalia*, chs. 1–88.

23. St Gregory of Sinai, *The Philokalia*, chs. 128, 131, and 132.

24. *Life of Francis of Assisi.* The greatest saint is only a brand snatched from the fire. Apart from Christ, God sees nothing good in him (1 Cor 1:30).

25. Hab 2:5.

26. Emperor Jovian, Julian's successor, died six months later in 364.

Chapter 12

1. St John Cassian, *The Cenobitic Institutes and Conferences*, "On the Rule of Cenobites," bk. 2, ch. 3.

2. Matt 15:14; St Symeon the New Theologian, *The Philokalia*, chs. 32 and 34.

3. *Alphabetical Patrology* and *Memorable Sayings.*

4. St John of the Ladder, *The Ladder of Divine Ascent*, 4:110.

5. St Isaac the Syrian, *Mystic Treatises,* ch. 1.

6. 2 Thess 2:10–12.

7. Matt 9:29.

8. *Alphabetical Patrology*, letter F.

9. "Life of St Theodore," *Menologion* for July 9.

10. 2 Thess 3:6.

11. *Alphabetical Patrology.*

Chapter 13

1. "Life of St Anthony," *Menologion* for January 17.

2. Ps 11:2–3.

3. St Symeon the New Theologian, *The Philokalia,* ch. 33.

4. St Symeon died in 1022.

5. John 5:39.

6. Rom 15:4; St Nil Sorsky, "Foreword" to *The Monastic Rule or Tradition*.

7. St Nil Sorsky, *Tradition*. It will not be superfluous to remark here that, although St Nil had the grace of God, he did not dare to explain Scripture arbitrarily, but followed the exposition made by the Fathers. The way of humility is the only true way to salvation.

8. Matt 12:36.

9. Ps 11:4–5.

10. 1 Pet 4:10–11.

11. 1 Cor 7:23.

12. It is not outward monastic obedience that is referred to here—not monastic tasks and occupations appointed by the monastic authorities—but moral, hidden obedience, performed in the soul.

13. This is the opinion of St Peter Damascene and other Fathers.

14. 2 Tim 4:2.

15. *Alphabetical Patrology* and *Memorable Sayings*, ch. 2, concerning Abba Macarius of Alexandria.

Chapter 14

1. Ps 29:6.

2. 1 Cor 2:11.

3. Ps 142:10.

4. Ps 118:18–19.

5. *The Law of God* is a Russian term signifying Holy Scripture and Holy Tradition as taught by the Church.—Trans.

6. John 6:38–40.

7. John 12:49–50.

8. Gal 5:24; Col 3:9–10.

9. Rom 12:2.

10. John 1:18. The Slavonic might also be rendered as "the One Who narrates, expounds, interprets, or confesses God."

11. John 17:6, 26.

12. Eph 6:16.

13. Saints Kallistus and Ignatius, *The Philokalia*, ch. 16.

14. Heb 11:33–34.

15. 1 Pet 5:6–7. If we do not humble ourselves under God's grace, He will humble us under His judgments.

16. Dan 3:24–45. In some Bibles, this prayer and the song of the three children is relegated to the so-called Apocrypha.—Trans.

17. Matt 18:7. The word rendered *temptation* may mean: trap, snare, hindrance, obstacle, stumbling-block, occasion of sin, scandal.

18. Matt 24:6.

19. Luke 21:16–17.

20. John 16:2, 33.

21. Luke 21:18.

22. Luke 21:19.

23. Acts 21:14.

24. Matt 16:21–23. Peter was capable of being a rock of faith and a rock of offense or stumbling.

25. Ps 118:6–7.

26. Ps 24:5.

27. St John of the Ladder, *The Ladder of Divine Ascent*, 26: 1. See Isa 6:5–7; Matt 5:8; Heb 10:22.

Chapter 15

1. Matt 22:37–40.

2. 1 John 2:23.

3. 2 John 1:6.

4. *Alphabetical Patrology* and *Memorable Sayings*, chs. 9 and 37.

5. St Mark the Ascetic, "On the Spiritual Law," *The Philokalia*, ch. 6.

6. Matt 5:21–48.

7. Matt 7:11.

8. Matt 7:12.

9. Matt 18:23–35.

10. St Isaac the Syrian, *Mystic Treatises,* ch. 8 (Russian translation).

Chapter 16

1. Matt 25:40.

2. The carnal and human point of view has no authority or power here. *Perfect love* casts out fear and restores spiritual vision. We must make our vision of Christ so clear that nothing is left of the self or the "old man."

3. *In mind:* literally "in memory."

4. Gen 18.

5. Gen 19.

6. Ps 67: 32.

7. Mark 2:19; St John Cassian, *The Cenobitic Institutes and Conferences,* "On Gluttony," bk. 5, ch. 24.

8. 1 Tim 1: 15.

9. St Isaac the Syrian, *Mystic Treatises,* ch. 89 (Russian translation). Actually St Isaac calls it "sowing in the sea."

10. St John of the Ladder, *The Ladder of Divine Ascent*, 28:33.

Chapter 17

1. Matt 22:37–40.

2. St John of the Ladder, *The Ladder of Divine Ascent*, 28:45.

3. Ibid., 28:34.

4. Ps 40:12–13.

5. 1 Cor 6:17.

6. There are only two words in the original and both are ambiguous. The first may mean *regularity* or *correctness*, and the second means *progress, success,* or *proficiency.* We have given a double translation to the second word only.—Trans.

Chapter 18

1. Sir 18:22 OSB.

2. St John of the Ladder, *The Ladder of Divine Ascent*, 28:3.

3. Mark 11:25–26.

4. Ps 50:18–19.

5. Ps 142:2.

6. Ps 50:6.

7. Ps 142:2.

8. *The Ladder*, 28:1.

9. Col 4: 2; see Phil. 4:6.

10. 1 Thess 5:17–18.

11. Col 2:6–7.

12. Phil 4:4–6.

Chapter 19

1. Gen 3:17; Heb 6:8. Thorns and thistles represent conceit and hypocrisy, self-delusion and formality (2 Tim 3:2–4).

2. St John of the Ladder, *The Ladder of Divine Ascent*, 28:17.

3. Eph 6:17.

4. *The Ladder*, 28:1, quoted freely with omissions.

5. *Alphabetical Patrology* and *Memorable Sayings* of Abba Agatho, ch. 9.

6. "Those who are Christ's have crucified the flesh [the fallen self-life] with its passions and desires" (Gal 5:24).

Chapter 20

1. *Ascetics* here means anyone who wishes to live the spiritual life.

Chapter 21

1. Literally "ground-bows and belt-bows."

2. Ps 24:18.

Chapter 22

1. Matt 13:25.

2. This intercession is usually called "Commemoration of the Living and the Departed" in Russian prayer books, and generally comes immediately after the "Prayers on Rising from Sleep."

3. St Symeon the New Theologian, "On the Three Ways of Prayer," *The Philokalia*.

Chapter 23

1. *Silent contemplatives*: or, "those who practice silence."

2. St John of the Ladder, *The Ladder of Divine Ascent*, 27:33 (Russian translation).

3. Ibid., 27:77.

4. Joel 2:32.

5. Rom 10:13.

6. Rom 10:9.

7. Acts 4:8–12.

8. John 13, 14, 15, 16.

9. John 14:13–14.

10. John 16:23–24.

11. John 14:26.

12. Saints Kallistus and Ignatius, "Directions to Hesychasts," *The Philokalia*, ch. 12.

Chapter 24

1. St John of the Ladder, *The Ladder of Divine Ascent*, 28:46.

Chapter 25

1. Matt 7:7.

2. Luke 18:7–8.

3. 1 Thess 5:17.

4. 1 Tim 2:8.

5. St Isaac the Syrian, *Mystic Treatises,* ch. 69 (Russian translation).

6. Ps 85:3–4.

Chapter 26

1. St Philotheus of Sinai, "Sobriety: or Vigilance," *The Philokalia*, vol. 2 (Russian translation).

2. Gal 6:14; 2 Tim 2:11; 2 Cor 4:10–16; Rom 8:13.

3. *Ardor:* or, devotion, aspiration, craving, yearning, longing, elan.

4. On the powers of the soul, see St Philotheus of Sinai in *The Philokalia*.

5. *Knowledge:* see note 8 below.

6. John 4:24.

7. 2 Cor 6:16.

8. *Knowledge:* the word also means on occasion *understanding, reason* (2 Cor 4:6).

9. *Constant and increased:* or, forcible, energetic, strenuous, painstaking. Literally "forced, exerted." We must force and exert ourselves to obey. "If you love Me, keep My commandments" (John 14:15). "The kingdom of heaven suffers violence, and the violent take it by force" (Matt 11:12).

10. Ps 118:32.

11. Optina editions, 1847.

Chapter 27

1. *Penance:* or, *repentance.*

2. St John of the Ladder, *The Ladder of Divine Ascent*, 27:10–11. We translate from the Greek, not Bishop Ignatius' loose rendering.—Trans. *Hesychast:* solitary.

3. *Hesychasm:* the silent life of contemplative prayer.

4. *The Ladder*, 25:11 (Greek translation).

Chapter 28

1. Eph 2:1–6; Col 3:1; Rom 8:11, Rom 8:36; Heb 11:13–16; 2 Cor 4:10.

2. Job 15:15.

3. Literally "self-opinion"; it includes conceit and confidence in one's own efforts.

4. Rev 20:1–3.

5. Vita sancti Pachomii, abbatis Tabennensis. Patrologia, Tom. LXXIII.

Chapter 29

1. *Skorb* (in Greek: *thlinsis*) means trouble, tribulation, distress, affliction, hardship, sorrow, adversity, or suffering. No single English word is quite equivalent to it, so we vary our translation.—Trans. Compare with "Then they will deliver you up to *tribulation*, and kill you" (Matt 24:9); "For then there will be great *tribulation*" (Matt 24:21); "For out of much *affliction* and anguish of heart I wrote to you" (2 Cor 2:4).

2. Matt 7:14.

3 John 16:33, 15:18, 16:2–3

4. Matt 10:16.

5. Sir 2:1–5, OSB.

6. Wis 1:12–16 OSB.

7. Luke 6:21, 25.

8. Matt 9:13.

9. St Tikhon of Voronezh, Cell Letter 99, Vol. XV.

10. Luke 23:40–43.

11. Heb 11:37, 13.

12. Heb 13:12–13.

13. Heb 12:8.

14. Heb 12:6.

15. Rev 3:19.

16. Mark 10:21.
17. Acts 20:24.
18. Jas 1:2.
19. Matt 5:11–12.
20. 1 Pet 2:21.
21. Luke 14:27.
22. 1 Pet 4:19.
23. Ps 33:19.
24. That is, through a sudden rush of feelings or passion.
25. Ps 33:21 (Slavonic).
26. Ps 36:7, 1.
27. Ps 72:3–4.
28. Ps 72:5.
29. Ps 72:6.
30. Heb 12:5.
31. Rev 3:19.
32. 2 Cor 1:8–10.
33. 2 Cor 12:10; Gal 6:14.
34. The soul is compared with a house (see Matt 7:25).
35. John 15:1–2.
36. John 15:4.
37. John 15:6.
38. "Let not your foot step into trouble" seems to be the sense of the Slavonic.
39. Ps 120:3.
40. Deut 6:16; Matt 4:7.
41. Sir 2:7–18 OSB.
42. John 19:10–11.
43. Luke 21:19; Matt 24:13; Heb 10:38.

Chapter 30
1. St John of the Ladder, *The Ladder of Divine Ascent*, 4:44.
2. Ibid., 4:36.
3. Ps 93:19.
4. *The Ladder*, 4:43; Ps 70:20–21.
5. Ibid., 4:44.
6. Ibid., 4:88.
7. Ibid., 4:103. *Gall:* or, *bile*. Honey easily causes biliousness, unless taken in small quantities.

8. Ibid., 4:27.

9. St Isaac the Syrian, *Mystic Treatises,* ch. 75.

10. Phil 1:29.

11. 1 Pet 3:14.

12. 1 Pet 4:13.

13. Rom 3:19.

14. Ps 90:5; St Isaac the Syrian, *Mystic Treatises,* ch. 31 (Russian translation).

15. 1 Cor 10:13.

16. St Macarius the Great, Word 7, ch. 18.

17. 1 Pet 2:21.

18. Phil 2:7–8.

19. Isa 53:7–8.

20. Matt 5:39–44.

21. Acts 14:22.

22. Mark 8:34.

23. Matt 5:12.

24. Rom 16:27.

Chapter 31

1. 1 Pet 5:6–7.

2. "If you endure chastening, God deals with you as with sons; for son is there whom a father does not chasten?" (Heb 12:7).

3. "In the last days perilous times will come. For men will be lovers of themselves, lovers of money, boasters, proud, blasphemers, disobedient to parents, unthankful, unholy, unloving, unforgiving, slanderers, without self-control, despisers of good, traitors, headstrong, haughty, lovers of pleasure rather than lovers of God, having a form of godliness but denying its power. And from such people turn away!" (2 Tim 3:1–5).

4. Jas 3: 5.

5. Ps 11:1–3.

6. Dan 3:37–38 OSB.

7. Eph 6:2.

8. Matt 18:7.

9. Matt 24:12.

10. Luke 18:8.

11. Ezek 38:18.

12. Dan 3:26–32, 34, 39, 42–43 OSB.

13. That is, (1) have as little to do with people as possible, and (2) when you do speak with people, avoid all levity and familiarity.

14. "Whatever you do, do it heartily, as to the Lord and not to men . . . for you serve the Lord Christ" (Col 3:23–24).

15. "Do not be conformed to this world, but be transformed by the renewing of your mind, that you may prove what is that good and acceptable and perfect will of God" (Rom 12:2).

Chapter 32

1. Jas 1:14.
2. Compare with the expression, "The end justifies the means."
3. St Macarius the Great, Word 4, ch. 6.
4. Rom 8:28.
5. "Be doers of the Word, and not hearers only" (Jas 1:22). "For not the hearers of the law are just in the sight of God, but the doers of the law will be justified" (Rom 2:13).
6. That is, tollgates in the regions of the air where those with spiritual debts have to pay for their sins. The toll money is spiritual suffering (see Matt 5:26; 1 Cor 3:13–15). "Forgive us our debts, as we forgive our debtors" (Matt 6:12).
7. St Macarius the Great, Word 7, ch. 14.
8. Luke 23:39.
9. Acts 3: 8; 1 Pet 2:21.

Chapter 33

1. Ps 50:5.
2. *Oshchushchenia* (Russian) may also be translated *sensations, sentiments, feelings.*
3. "The law of Christ" (Gal 6:2) and "the helmet of salvation and the sword of the Spirit" (Eph 6:17).
4. Ps 9:30
5. Jas 5:16.

Chapter 34

1. Matt 26:41.
2. Mark 13:37.
3. St Hesychius of Jerusalem, *The Philokalia*, ch. 3.
4. Ibid., ch. 1.
5. Ibid., ch. 5.
6. Ibid., ch. 6.
7. Deut 15:9.

8. *Attraction* (in Greek: *prosvole*): or, application, kiss, proposal, suggestion, impact, assault, attack.

9. St Hesychius of Jerusalem, *The Philokalia*, ch. 2.

10. *Dispassion:* freedom from passion.

11. 1 Pet 5:8–9.

12. "Life of St Euthymius the Great," *Menologion* for January 20.

13. St Barsanuphius the Great and St John the Prophet, *Directions for the Spiritual Life*, Answers 260, 261, and 583.

14. Luke 21:34–36.

15. Luke 12:37.

16. Ps 118:105.

17. 2 Pet 1: 9.

18. 1 Cor 15:50.

19. Isa 8:6.

20. St Isaac the Syrian, *Mystic Treatises*, chs. 46 and 45.

Chapter 35

1. Gen 3:17–19.

2. St Mark the Ascetic, Homily 7, "On Sweat and Humility"; St Isaac the Syrian, *Mystic Treatises,* ch. 19; St Macarius the Great, Homily 26:21.

3. Matt 22:12.

4. The Slavonic translation here is *mortify.* There is not a trace of death or mortification in the Greek word, which means rather to "beat black and blue," "pester," or "discipline" (see 1 Cor 9:27; Luke 18:5). For "mortification," see Rom 8:13; Col 3:5 ("put to death"); 2 Cor 4:10 ("carrying about in the body the dying of the Lord Jesus").

5. St Isaac the Syrian, *Mystic Treatises*, ch. 50 (English translation). "If the senses are lax, the heart also is lax," says St Isaac.

Chapter 36

1. 1 Cor 2:14–16; Jas 3:15. *Animal* (Latin *anima* means soul) here means that which pertains to the sentient, sensual, or natural life, which we share with animals.

2. Matt 7:3–5.

3. Rom 8:6.

4. St Dorotheus, Homily 9.

5. *Alphabetical Patrology.*

6. Here, by "true faith" is meant active faith, not dogmatic faith. For the difference, see Saints Kallistus and Ignatius, *The Philokalia*, ch. 16.

7. Rom 15:1.

8. Gal 6:1.

9. Gal 5:22.

10. St Isaac the Syrian, *Mystic Treatises*, ch. 50.

11. Conversation of St Maximus Kapsokalivitis with St Gregory of Sinai.

Chapter 37

1. St Symeon the New Theologian, "Practical and Theological Principles," *The Philokalia*, ch. 16.

2. Matt 19:21; also Mark 10:21.

3. Luke 14:33.

4. St John of the Ladder, *The Ladder of Divine Ascent*, "Word to the Shepherd."

5. Rom 14:4; St Barsanuphius the Great and St John the Prophet, *Directions for the Spiritual Life*, Answers 249, 250, and 251.

Chapter 38

1. Matt 6:19–21

2. Eph 5:5.

3. Luke 12:15–34.

4. Ps 51:9 (52:7).

5. Luke 12:19–20.

6. *Alphabetical Patrology* and *Vies des pères des deserts d'Orient*, Vol. IX, ch. 16.

7. Luke 16:9.

8. 1 Tim 6:10.

Chapter 39

1. John 5:44.

2. John 12:42–43.

3. John 9:22.

4. Matt 25:23.

5. John 12:26.

6. John 5:41.

7. John 18:36.

8. John 6:15.

9. John 16:30–32.

10. Luke 24:26, 46.

11. John 1:18; John 3:13; John 17:5.

12. Phil 2: 7–11.

13. 1 Cor 2:9.

14. St Isaac the Syrian, *Mystic Treatises,* ch. 1.

15. For example, see the story about Eulogius the Stonecutter in the *Alphabetical Patrology.*

16. "Life of Eustace Placidus," *Menologion* for September 20.

17. See St Isaac the Syrian, *Mystic Treatises,* ch. 47.

18. St Isaiah the Solitary, "Attend to Yourself," *The Philokalia*, ch. 28.

19. Luke 16:14; Mark 4:19.

20. St Symeon the New Theologian, "Practical and Theological Principles," 105.

21. Luke 14:27.

22. St Isaac the Syrian, *Mystic Treatises,* ch. 75.

23. James 2:1–9.

24. Luke 6:26, 22–23.

25. Matt 18:10–11; cf. Luke 19:10, 1 Cor 6:20, 2 Cor 5:14.

Chapter 40

1. 1 John 4:8, 16.

2. Matt 7:7.

3. *Menologion* for February 9.

4. *Menologion* for February 27.

5. St Mark the Ascetic, "On the Spiritual Law," *The Philokalia*, ch. 170.

6. Ibid., ch. 94.

7. Matt 5:39. *Injury:* the Greek may also mean *the evil one.* And so St Chrysostom says, "Must we not resist the devil? We must, but not like this; rather as the Savior has told us: in other words, by readiness to endure injury. In this way you really do conquer the evil one."

8. "On the Spiritual Law," *The Philokalia,* ch. 45.

9. Eph 6:16.

Chapter 41

1. John 3:16–17.

2. John 1:29.

3. John 15:18–19.

4. 1 John 2:15–17.

5. God longs for man's friendship. The fall interrupted it. The soul espoused to God is guilty of spiritual infidelity or adultery when it loves creatures instead of its Creator.

6. Jas 4:4.

7. Blessed Theophylact the Bulgarian, "Explanation of the Gospel of St Matthew," 18:7.

8. John 1:9–11.

9. John 3:19.

10. Luke 6:22, 26.

11. Matt 7:13–14; cf. Luke 13:23–24.

12. Matt 11:19. The New King James Version has not been used in this instance as its rendering of the verse "wisdom is justified by her children" does not have the same connotation of fewness.

13. Ps 11:1–3.

14. Gal 6:14.

15. Abba Dorotheus, Homily 1.

16. Col 2:8.

17. St Isaac the Syrian, *Mystic Treatises,* ch. 2.

18. Ibid., ch. 227.

19. Jas 4:4. See the translation of J. B. Phillips in *The New Testament in Modern English* (London, 1958): "You are like unfaithful wives, flirting with the glamour of this world, and never realizing that to be the world's lover means becoming the enemy of God."

20. Ps 30:24.

21. Ps 72:27.

22. John 3:2.

23. Matt 27:42.

24. Matt 2:3.

25. Matt 2:5–6.

26. Matt 23:35.

27. Matt 23:32.

28. John 5:43.

29. 2 Thess 2:7–9.

30. *Menologion* for December 18.

31. 1 Tim 6:6–9.

Chapter 42

1. Jas 1:22–27.

2. 1 Cor 15:33.

3. *Menologion* for February 4.

4. St Seraphim of Sarov, Instruction 9.

5. "The stomach will take any food, yet some foods are better than others. . . . Any woman is a mate for any man, yet some women are better than others" (Sir 36:18, 21 OSB).

6. St Jerome, Letter 22 to Eustochium.

7. Deut 1:35.

8. In this way, did then-Archbishop of Alexandria Theophilus explain the words and conduct of the saint of Roman fame. On hearing Arsenius' explanation, the Roman lady was satisfied and set at rest (*Alphabetical Patrology*).

9. St Macarius the Great, extract from a letter to monks.

10. St Macarius the Great, VIIIth Instruction to Monks, Tome 1.

11. Delilah is sometimes also spelled Dalida or Dalila.

12. Judg 16:4–21.

13. Gal 3:28; Gal 6:15.

14. Gen 3:12.

Chapter 43

1. Eph 6:12.

2. 1 Pet 5:8.

3. Rom 8:38–39.

4. Ezek 28:16.

5. Isa 14:13–14.

6. Isa 14:12–20; Eph 6:12.

7. Rev 12:4.

8. St Macarius the Great, Homily 4:7.

9. St Anthony the Great, "Conversation on Spirits," *Menologion* for January 17.

10. Gen 3: 4.

11. Holy martyrs Timothy and Maurus, *Menologion* for May 3.

12. *Dogmatic Theology of the Orthodox Catholic Eastern Church*, sec. 106. See also St John Chrysostom, *Homilies on Acts* (Acts 12:15), and "Life of St Basil the New," *Menologion* for March 26.

13. *Alphabetical Patrology*.

14. Ps 118:25.

15. St John Chrysostom, Homily 8 on the Epistle to the Romans.

16. "Life of St Macarius the Great," *Menologion* Jan 19.

17. *Alphabetical Patrology*.

18. St Barsanuphius the Great and St John the Prophet, *Directions for the Spiritual Life*, Answer 69.

19. Matt 12:43–45.

20. St John of the Ladder, *The Ladder of Divine Ascent*, "Step 18."

21. St John Cassian, *The Cenobitic Institutes and Conferences*, Conf. 24, ch. 4.

22. *Athos Patrology*, ch. 1, 187 (Russian ed., 1860).

23. *Alphabetical Patrology.*

24. The holy Fathers mentioned above remained in unceasing prayer, and therefore they did their handwork with prayer—for example, the recitation by heart of psalms or meditation (i.e., the repetition of some short prayer, principally the Jesus Prayer), outside the regular prayer times or rule of prayer. When they stood for prayer, they left their handwork, as St John of the Ladder says, "No one at the time of prayer should engage in any side action, or rather distraction. For the angel who attended Anthony the Great taught him this clearly" (*The Ladder*, 19:7).

25. Luke 17:26–30.

26. *Menologion* "Life of St Macarius the Great," Jan 19. Also *Alphabetical Patrology.*

27. St John Cassian says that this was the custom in all the cenobitic monasteries of Egypt. Institutes, 2:12.

28. "Life of St Macarius the Great," *Menologion* for January 19.

29. St John Karpathios, "Encouraging Chapters," *The Philokalia*, ch. 87.

30. Caloric was the term given in the nineteenth century to what was understood to be a type of matter responsible for the phenomena of heat and combustion.

31. St Macarius the Great, Word 2:31.

32. Ibid.

33. Matt 7:15.

34. Rom 16:18.

35. *Directions for the Spiritual Life*, Answer 59.

36. This can be seen from the teaching on spirits that St Anthony the Great gave his disciples. Precious teaching! St Anthony speaks with extraordinary clarity from his own experience and inspired knowledge of fallen spirits. See "Life of Anthony the Great" by St Athanasius in the *Menologion* for January 17, in which the teaching is abbreviated.

37. Luke 24:39.

38. St Macarius the Great, Word 4:6–7.

39. Ps 106:30; Ps 33:6.

Chapter 44

1. Gen 3.

2. John 8:44.

3. St Hesychius of Jerusalem, "On Sobriety and Vigilance," ch. 43.

4. St John Cassian, *The Cenobitic Institutes and Conferences*, bk. 4, ch. 37.

5. This life is included in the Homilies of St Dorotheus.

6. St John of the Ladder, *The Ladder of Divine Ascent*, 4:32 and 39.

7. Abba Dorotheus, Homily 5.

8. *Menologion* for April 1.

9. Eph 6:17.

10. *Alphabetical Patrology.*

11. St Isaac the Syrian, *Mystic Treatises,* ch. 30 (Russian translation). St Isaac lived in the seventh century A.D.

12. *The Ladder*, 15:24–26.

13. Ibid., ch. 80.

14. Ibid., ch. 81.

15. Ibid., ch. 53 and 54.

16. *Alphabetical Patrology.*

17. Luke 12:35–40.

18. In the life of St Anthony, the following is related: during a violent conflict with the devil, the saint was suddenly illumined by an ineffable light in which the demons and their temptation vanished. Realizing that the Lord had come to him, Anthony cried, "Lord, where were You all this time?" And he heard a Voice: "I was here, but I wanted to see your courage" (*Menologion* for January 17).

19. John 6:64.

20. Rev 21:7.

Chapter 45

1. Matt 5:22–24; Matt 18:21–35; Jas 1:20; Col 3:12–14; Eph 4:29–32, etc.

2. St Barsanuphius the Great and St John the Prophet, *Directions for the Spiritual Life*, Answer 177.

3. Matt 4:3–7.

4. Matt 26:41

Chapter 46

1. Luke 16:27–31. Were the unbelievers led to believe by the raising of Lazarus and the Resurrection of Christ? (See Matt 28:11–15; John 11:53; John 12:10.)

2. St John of the Ladder, *The Ladder of Divine Ascent*, 3:27–29.

3. St John Cassian, *The Cenobitic Institutes and Conferences*, "On Discernment."

4. Rom 8:9–16.

5. St Macarius the Great, Word 7:12; cf. Gal 2:20; Col 1:27.

6. John 15:4.

7. Matt 1:18–23.
8. Matt 2:13.
9. Matt 2:19–22.

Chapter 47

1. St Mark the Ascetic, *The Philokalia*, "Word on Repentance" and "Word on Baptism."
2. Ps 118:128, 101.
3. Jas 2:10.
4. Thus, in the Gospels *all* demons are called "unclean spirits."
5. 2 Cor 7:1.
6. St Macarius the Great, Word 7:4.

Chapter 48

1. Zech 3:1.
2. "Life of St Anthony," *Menologion* for January 17.
3. St Nil Sorsky, "On Prayer," ch. 47. See English translation in G. P. Fedotov, *A Treasury of Russian Spirituality*, London, 1950.
4. Heb 5:7.
5. St Macarius the Great, Word 2.
6. 1 Sam 17:25–36.
7. Saints Kallistus and Ignatius, ch. 29.
8. "But I tell you not to resist an injury"(Matt 5:39).
9. Matt 6:12–15.
10. John 5:41, 44.
11. Matt 6:5, 16.
12. Matt 6:1–13.
13. Matt 6:3, 18.
14. Matt 6:24.
15. Luke 14:33.
16. Matt 4:1–11 and Luke 4:1–13.
17. Sir 2:13 OSB.
18. St Gregory of Sinai, ch. 110.
19. Phil 2:5; 1 Cor 2:16.
20. St John of the Ladder, *The Ladder of Divine Ascent*, Step 25 (heading). See 2 Cor 1:22; 2 Cor 5:5; Eph 1:14; Eph 5:18 (pledge).
21. Jas 4:7; 1 Pet 5:9; Luke 21:15.
22. Jas 5:16; cf. Eph 6:18.
23. See Gal 5:16–26; Rom 7:23–25.

24. *Alphabetical Patrology*, letter J.

25. 1 Tim 6:12; 2 Tim 2:3–5.

Chapter 49

1. Adam was told to keep (guard) the garden of Eden. Evidently the earthly Paradise was exposed to invasion or loss. See Gen 2:15; Prov 4:23.

2. Matt 6:22.

3. 1 Thess 5:23.

4. St Macarius the Great, Homily 7:8, says, "The mind is the eye of the *soul*."

5. Luke 11:34-35.

6. 2 Tim 3:8.

7. 1 Cor 1:18.

8. John 8: 44.

9. St Hesychius of Jerusalem, "On Sobriety and Vigilance," ch. 77.

10. 1 Cor 3:16–17; 6:20.

11. See Chapter 41, note 5.

12. See Luke 16:22–23. The uncompassionate man was buried in hell.

13. Gal 6:7–9.

Chapter 50

1. Matt 5:4.

2. Luke 17:10.

3. St Mark the Ascetic, "On the Spiritual Law," *The Philokalia*, ch. 34.

4. Ps 50:7 (51:17).

5. Ps 50:19 (51:19).

6. *Menologion* for February 20.

7. Matt 4:17.

8. Luke 24:26, 45–47.

9. Acts 2:38.

10. Acts 20:21.

11. John 3:20.

12. 2 Cor 6:14–15.

13. Acts 14:22.

14. Prov 24:16.

15. 1 John 1:8–10.

16. 1 John 3:6–10.

17. See Eph 2:1–3; John 14:30.

18. *Alphabetical Patrology*.

19. St John of the Ladder, *The Ladder of Divine Ascent*, 5:33.

20. St. Sisoes, ch. 43, 102.
21. Matt 5:4. "Blessed [happy] are those who mourn."
22. *Alphabetical Patrology.*
23. *The Ladder*, Step 18 (heading).
24. Ibid., 7:64.
25. Ibid., Step 18.
26. Saints Kallistus and Ignatius, ch. 28.
27. John 11:44.
28. St Seraphim, "Fifteenth Spiritual Instruction."
29. *The Ladder*, 1:6.
30. St Isaac the Syrian, *Mystic Treatises,* ch. 35 (ch. 21 of Russian translation).
31. St Symeon the New Theologian, *The Philokalia*, part I, ch. 69 (Russian translation).
32. Matt 7:7, 11.
33. *The Ladder*, 7:49.
34. Jas 1:21.
35. 1 Cor 2:9.
36. Exod 3:2; 19:18; Heb 12:29; 1 Tim 6:16; 2 Thess 1:8.
37. St Symeon the New Theologian, Word 6.
38. St Gregory of Sinai, "Instructions to Hesychasts," ch. 7, *On Delusion.*
39. Luke 6:26.
40. St Peter of Damascus, Book 1, ch. 2.
41. The Great Fast of forty-eight days before Easter.
42. *Alphabetical Patrology*, see Rev 20:10.
43. Luke 18:14.

Conclusion, Part I
1. *Alphabetical Patrology*, letter A.
2. It is usually our outlook, not our outward situation, that needs changing. It is not the place that sanctifies us, but by a holy life we can sanctify both the place and ourselves. If the place were sufficient, angels would not have fallen from heaven, nor men from Paradise.—Trans.
3. See 2 Pet 1:10–12; Phil 2:12–15.
4. See Matt 22: 11.
5. Rom 11:33–36.

Rules
1. St John of the Ladder, *The Ladder of Divine Ascent*, 4:3–5.
2. St John Cassian, *The Cenobitic Institutes and Conferences*, bk. 4, ch. 8 and 9.

3. Literally, *unomitting* (i.e., without missing or omitting).

4. Luke 18:14.

5. The books of the New Testament excluding the Gospels and the Apocalypse are called "the Apostle."

6. Heb 13:15.

7. The kalimavkion is the monastic headwear. The klobuk is the kalimavkion plus the veil. (Kalimavkion in Russian is *kamilavka*.)

8. "By self-reproach, a novice can turn his failure into victory" (St Nil Sorsky, ch. 5, *On the Measure to be Observed in the Matter of Food*).

9. That is, people of the opposite sex. The principle applies equally to women novices.

10. That is, people of the same sex.

11. Matt 25:40.

12. The same rules apply in women's convents.

13. St Cassian of Rome, *The Cenobitic Institutes and Conferences*, bk. IV, ch. 10 and 11.

14. 2 Thess 3:6.

15. 1 Cor 5:11.

16. 1 Cor 15:33.

17. Ps 100:2–7.

18. Ps 138:17.

19. Eccl 4:10.

20. Prov 18:19.

21. Matt 6:6; Col 1:27; Luke 17:21; John 14:23.

22. See "Always carrying about in the body the dying [or mortification] of the Lord Jesus, that the [risen] life of Jesus also may be manifested in our body" (2 Cor 4:10).

23. The veneration and kissing of icons and relics is an expression of love for God Who sanctifies and dwells in them by His holy and life-giving Spirit (2 Kgs 13:20–21).

24. Literally, "to whom your heart is drawn in the passion of lust."

25. St Isaac the Syrian, *Mystic Treatises,* ch. 9 (Russian translation).

26. "Those vowed to chastity are pledged to undergo a sort of perpetual martyrdom" (St Methodius).

27. "Thus you shall separate the children of Israel from their uncleanness" (Lev 15:31).

28. Ps 140:3.

SUBJECT INDEX

Citations in parentheses following page numbers refer to note numbers; for example, 63(n5) refers to text associated with note 5 on page 63.

SCRIPTURE INDEX

Citations in parentheses following page numbers refer to note numbers; for example, p. 199(n9) refers to the text associated with note 9 on page 199.